200 ☑ **W9-CEW-330**

B 20555374

IN MODERN SOCIETY

SEXISM AND

THE GENDER SCIENCE OF JANET TAYLOR SPENCE

EDITED BY

WILLIAM B. SWANN, JR.
JUDITH H. LANGLOIS
LUCIA ALBINO GILBERT

AMERICAN PSYCHOLOGICAL ASSOCIATION

WASHINGTON, DC

Published by
American Psychological Association
750 First Street, NE
Washington, DC 20002

Copies may be ordered from
APA Order Department
P.O. Box 92984
Washington, DC 20090-2984

In the U.K., Europe, Africa, and the Middle East, copies may be ordered from
American Psychological Association
3 Henrietta Street
Covent Garden, London
WC2E 8LU England

Typeset in Minion by EPS Group Inc., Easton, MD
Printer: Data Reproductions Corp., Auburn, Hills, MI
Cover designer: Minker Design, Bethesda, MD
Technical/Production Editor: Amy J. Clarke

Library of Congress Cataloging-in-Publication Data
Sexism and stereotypes in modern society : the gender science of Janet Taylor Spence /
    edited by William B. Swann, Jr., Judith H. Langlois, Lucia Albino Gilbert.—1st ed.
        p.   cm.
    Includes bibliographical references and index.
    ISBN 1-55798-531-6 (hardcover : acid-free paper)
    1. Sex role.   2. Sexism.   3. Stereotype (Psychology)   4. Spence, Janet T.
    I. Swann, William B.   II. Langlois, Judith.   III. Gilbert, Lucia Albino.
HQ1075.S4948   1998
305.3—dc21
                                                                98-24925
                                                                CIP

British Library Cataloguing-in-Publication Data
A CIP record is available from the British Library.

Printed in the United States of America
First Edition

APA expects to publish volumes on the following conference topics:

which, collaboratively with the APA Board of Scientific Affairs, evaluates the proposals and selects several conferences for funding. This important effort has resulted in an exceptional series of meetings and scholarly volumes, each of which has contributed to the dissemination of research and dialogue in these topical areas.

The APA Science Directorate's conferences funding program has supported 47 conferences since its inception in 1988. To date, 41 volumes resulting from conferences have been published.

RICHARD C. McCARTY, PHD   VIRGINIA E. HOLT
Executive Director   Assistant Executive Director

Contents

Part Three: Modern Sexism and Its Consequences

Contributors

of Arizona

Leslie Barr, BA, School of Medicine, State University of New York at Buffalo

Monica Biernat, PhD, Department of Psychology, University of Kansas, Lawrence

Rebecca S. Bigler, PhD, Department of Psychology, University of Texas at Austin

Kay Deaux, PhD, Department of Psychology, Graduate Center, City University of New York

Jacquelynne S. Eccles, PhD, Departments of Psychology, Women's Studies, and Education, University of Michigan

Susan T. Fiske, PhD, Department of Psychology, University of Massachusetts, Amherst

Lucia Albino Gilbert, PhD, Departments of Educational Psychology and Women's Studies, University of Texas at Austin

Peter Glick, PhD, Department of Psychology, Lawrence University

Robert L. Helmreich, PhD, Department of Psychology, University of Texas at Austin

Debra Jozefowicz, MSW, Departments of Psychology and Social Work, University of Michigan

Diane Kobrynowicz, BA, Department of Psychology, University of Kansas, Lawrence

Judith H. Langlois, PhD, Department of Psychology, University of Texas at Austin

Brenda Major, PhD, Department of Psychology, University of
California at Santa Barbara

Carol Lynn Martin, PhD, Department of Family Resources and
Human Development, Arizona State University

Margaret L. Signorella, PhD, Departments of Psychology and
Women's Studies, Pennsylvania State University, McKeesport

Janet Taylor Spence, PhD, Department of Psychology, University
of Texas at Austin

William B. Swann, Jr., PhD, Department of Psychology, University
of Texas at Austin

Josephine Zubek, PhD, Department of Psychology, State University of
New York at Buffalo

Introduction

O nce the province of a small group of theorists and researchers operating on the periphery of psychological science, gender research has charged into the psychological mainstream during the last 2 decades. To a remarkable degree, Janet Taylor Spence has been responsible for the ascendance of this subarea, for she spawned many of the key ideas that captured the imaginations and shaped the thinking of contemporary researchers.

To honor Spence for her contributions to American psychology in general and gender research in particular, we organized a festschrift to highlight some of the work that she has inspired. Although the chapters in this volume represent the most recent developments in the field, the work that laid the groundwork for these developments goes back several decades. Beginning in the late 1960s, Spence and her colleagues challenged the validity of biologically based conceptions of gender that attributed gender differences to basic temperamental qualities and cognitive capacities. She and her colleagues turned their attention to phenomena such as prescriptive and descriptive gender stereotypes, attitudes about gender roles, the nature of achievement motives in the male and female populations, the relation of concrete instances of masculine and feminine characteristics, and the interrelations among these various phenomena. During the 1970s, she developed several psychological instruments that were to become standard instruments in the field, such as the Personal Attributes Questionnaire (PAQ) and the Attitudes Toward Women Scale.

As research and theory in the area developed further, Spence and others became increasingly aware of developmental changes in each of these phenomena, some reflecting maturational influences and others the product of socialization, public policies, and institutional practices. Such developmental and temporal changes add an additional layer of complexity to these phenomena, making the task of understanding gender and gender roles more challenging but not intractable. Indeed, Spence's followers have recently made considerable progress in their efforts to understand these developmental processes.

Perhaps Spence's greatest achievement has been in guiding (and sometimes goading) gender researchers to replace traditional thinking about gender and gender roles with increasingly sophisticated and nuanced theoretical models. This volume at once celebrates these new models and considers state-of-the-art developments that have forced researchers to look more broadly at theoretical models of gender. These recently developed models not only help set an agenda for future research but also have exciting implications for the development of techniques for overcoming stereotyped beliefs that constrain the behaviors of both sexes.

THE GENESIS OF THIS BOOK

Spence has been a valued colleague and mentor to each of the volume's editors. For nearly 2 decades, Spence was a comember of the Social Psychology Program at the University of Texas at Austin with Bill Swann. During that period, Swann was ceaselessly amazed at Spence's tireless enthusiasm for her work and the dedication to her students, her university, and her field. He also valued her as a role model, a woman who somehow never lost her sense of grace and dignity while overcoming formidable obstacles.

Judith Langlois, a developmental psychologist, was for many years the only other female professor in the Department of Psychology at the University of Texas at Austin. Judy learned a great deal from Spence about negotiating an academic career in a male-dominated department. She and Spence shared many interesting lunches and dinners, during which they would dissect departmental meetings. Most, although not all, of these meals ended in uproarious laughter as the two "anthro-pologists" studied, largely with great affection, their tribe.

Lucia Albino Gilbert first met Spence when she was a graduate

chology at the University of Texas at Austin, her research interests, and her family.

In these and countless other ways, Spence has enriched the personal and intellectual lives of the editors. For this—and for her invaluable assistance in commenting on the chapters that appear in this volume —the editors are extremely grateful.

THEMES AND ORGANIZATION

The contributors to this volume are social and developmental psychol-ogists who have at least two things in common. First, all have gained national recognition for their exciting, cutting-edge research in the area of gender research. Second, in one way or another, they all owe an intellectual debt to Spence's multidimensional model of gender. The chapters presented here grew out of a series of talks that these authors gave during a conference in April of 1997 at the University of Texas at Austin. The conference presentations were the first drafts of the chapters for this volume, subsequently shaped and refined by discussions among the attendees, the editors, and Spence herself.

The contributions to the volume are organized into three parts: The Genesis of Gender Research, the Complexity of Gender Stereotypes, and Modern Sexism and Its Consequences. The material in each part is multifaceted and interactive and reflects both the complexity of the field and the richness and excitement of new theoretical and empirical di-rections. Each contribution builds on Spence's work while going beyond it to examine unique themes and broaden the utility of her conceptual contributions. Also, whereas each chapter stands alone, each is integrally tied to the volume's larger themes.

The first part, the Genesis of Gender Research, presents two key chapters, each helping to set the stage for understanding the remaining chapters. Deaux (chapter 1) sets the context for the festschrift chapters with "Defining Themes in Gender Research." Helmreich (chapter 2) then chronicles some of the key events in Spence's career and explains how they led to her contributions to gender research.

Three chapters then address the Complexity of Gender Stereotypes and invite readers to consider innovative ways to understand their formation and their operation. Martin et al. (chapter 3) first discuss evidence for the importance of cognitive models in the formation of children's gender stereotypes. Biernat and Kobrynowicz (chapter 4) then describe research that suggests that sexist thinking can survive in relatively subtle ways, despite its apparent disappearance (the "shifting standard" perspective). Signorella (chapter 5) then examines the multidimensionality of gender schemas and how this influences their development.

The four chapters in section 3 focus on some of the nuances and complexities of Modern Forms of Sexism and Its Consequences. Bigler (chapter 6) first considers why most interventions designed to counter sexism have failed and then presents a theoretical analysis that suggests how more effective intervention strategies might be developed. Eccles et al. (chapter 7) use their research with adolescents, parents, teachers, and others in adolescents' social environment to understand how gender may shape expectancies and values, which may, in turn, determine important life outcomes. Fiske and Glick (chapter 8) suggest that contemporary society's efforts to shed itself of traditional biases and stereotypic beliefs have left a legacy of ambivalent attitudes toward women that may be largely untractable. Major et al. (chapter 9) then provide a review and meta-analysis of research on gender differences and self-esteem. The volume closes with Spence's (chapter 10) discussion of the major ideas and contributions of the other authors, together with a vibrant vision of the future of gender research.

We hope this book will serve a variety of readerships: students

seeking an up-to-date introduction to the study of gender, gender scholars hoping to add to their knowledge of this rapidly growing subarea,
established scholars in other areas wanting an overview of advances in

prepared the conference brochure and handled advertisements for the
conference. Dean Sheldon Ekland-Olson, dean of the College of Liberal
Arts, and Randy Diehl, chair of the Department of Psychology, both at
the University of Texas at Austin, provided extensive staff and financial
support. We are particularly indebted to the Science Directorate of the
American Psychological Association for underwriting this effort.

REFERENCE

Spence, J. T., & Helmreich, R. L. (1972). Who likes competent women? Competence, sex-role congruence of interest, and subjects' attitudes toward
women as determinants of interpersonal attraction. *Journal of Applied
Social Psychology, 2,* 197–213.

PART ONE

The Genesis of

An Overview of Research

An overview of research on gender,[1] much like a review of Janet Taylor Spence's contributions to psychology, is a daunting task. Although I have ventured into this territory on more than one occasion (Deaux, 1984, 1985; Deaux & LaFrance, 1998; Spence, Deaux, & Helmreich, 1985), the continual expansions and reformulations of data and theory make each trip a new challenge. In reviewing the field on this occasion, I begin roughly when and where Spence herself began, in 1972 with the publication of "Who Likes Competent Women?," an article coauthored with Robert Helmreich (Spence & Helmreich, 1972b). In the 25 years since that article was published, the field of gender research has grown astronomically; Spence's contributions have been a significant part of that growth.

Defining a time frame is the easy part. Trying to summarize, to make sense, to fairly represent the work of the past 2 or 3 decades is

---

[1]By way of definition for those not familiar with the field, gender can be considered "a dynamic construct that draws on and impinges upon processes at the individual, interactional, group, institutional, and cultural levels" (Deaux & LaFrance, 1998, p. 788). It is a concept that is both socially constructed and contextualized. In contrast, the term *sex differences* generally implies stability and focuses on the person as the causal agent.

far more difficult. Marianne LaFrance and I faced a similar challenge in preparing a chapter on gender for the fourth edition of the *Handbook of Social Psychology* (Deaux & LaFrance, 1998).[2] Although our task was delimited to the social psychological literature, that literature is, in and of itself, enormous. Furthermore, although we assumed that we would be speaking primarily to social psychologists, we also wanted to address the larger context in which gender is conceptualized now at the end of the 20th century. The difficulty of satisfying these demands is perhaps best indexed by two comments that LaFrance and I received on the prepublication version of our chapter: One friend told us that "male social psychologists are not going to like it," and another said that we had failed in not writing a feminist account.

To make the personal political, or at least systemic, I take these diverse reactions as an index of the turbulence that exists in the field today—a field that is both intellectually challenging and politically charged. Much of this turbulence is energizing and will, I think, contribute to the field's growth. At the same time, much as postpositivist stances are challenging the social sciences generally, the road of change can be a little bumpy. Whether and how to do empirical research, how to acknowledge and incorporate diverse standpoints, when and how to link research to action and social change, and what language to use in one's analysis are the questions that few psychologists foresaw 25 years ago when the questions seemed obvious and the answers easy to attain.

These meta-theoretical questions are important ones, and it is fortunate that a number of feminist scholars are addressing them. One in particular is Jill Morawski in her recent book, *Practicing Feminisms, Reconstructing Psychology* (1994) a kind of point–counterpoint with herself. Morawski focused on three key issues in research—objectivity, subjectivity, and validity—and carefully peeled off layers of assumptions to find the essential questions. How can objectivity be understood when one acknowledges that investigators are themselves situated in particular contexts? How is the traditional notion of "subjects" trans-

---

[2]Spence, with me and Robert Helmreich as her coauthors, wrote the chapter on sex roles for the previous (third) edition of the *Handbook of Social Psychology* (Spence et al., 1985).

formed by recognizing agency, social practice, and personal experience? Whose standards and what criteria are used to establish validity? These

decidedly

1. Women and men are different, aren't they?
2. People think women and men are different, don't they?
3. Maybe this is all more complicated than we thought.
4. Psychologists are not alone.

These four themes can be plotted chronologically as well. The first two were key questions in the early stages of gender research, although important research in both domains continues into the present. The latter two statements are somewhat more recent themes in feminist psychology, a recognition of complexity and a broadening of the conceptual net. Each of these questions is addressed in some form and often in more detail by other authors in this volume. In dealing with them here as general themes, I hope to provide a useful introduction for what is to come.

MEN AND WOMEN ARE DIFFERENT, AREN'T THEY?

In many respects, this question reflects the beginning of psychology's interest in gender. Work on sex differences, in part derived from and embedded in a tradition of individual difference research, dominated the century prior to the period I defined for this review. The initial and persistent concern with possible differences between women and men is apparent in debates over brain size and variability (Fausto-Sterling, 1985; Shields, 1975), intelligence, and developmental theories of gender socialization. An early marker in the continuing saga of sex differences was a chapter by Catherine Cox Miles (1935) in Murchison's *A Handbook of Social Psychology*. Consistent with the taxonomic approach that characterized much of that volume (including attention to various racial groups as well as nonhuman species), this chapter surveys a wide range of biological, behavioral, and cognitive differences between women and men. Maccoby and Jacklin's (1974) comprehensive review of the literature of sex differences coincides with the beginning of the period of gender research that I marked for this chapter. Although the authors ultimately concluded that areas of difference between women and men (or girls and boys) are few in number, the form of the question continues a comparative emphasis. Since the publication of that review, the topics of the debate about sex differences have altered somewhat. Nonetheless, the concern with differences is a continuing theme in the gender arena, as evidenced by recent coverage in the *American Psychologist* (1995) and in *Feminism & Psychology* (Kitzinger, 1994).

A variation of the sex difference approach that occupied much time and space in the early days of research on gender concerned masculinity and femininity and the highly popularized derivative, androgyny. The attempt was to shift from a biological basis to a psychological basis of difference, much as Terman and Miles (1936) had accomplished half a century before. Spence, of course, played a central role in this development, together with colleagues Helmreich and Stapp (Spence & Helmreich, 1978; Spence, Helmreich, & Stapp, 1974, 1975). Yet whereas others were eagerly trying to make *androgyny* a sovereign concept, capable of predicting all facets of gender-related behavior, Spence was cautiously and sagely considering its limitations (Helmreich, Spence, & Holahan, 1979; Spence, 1991; Spence & Helmreich, 1979, 1980). Her theoretical dissections of the concepts of masculinity and femininity are more appropriately considered in the third theme that deals with complexity and multidimensionality. At the moment, I simply note that the more delimited concepts of *agency* and *communion* that she promoted have, for the most part, a more successful track record in establishing connections between personality and behavior.

The postulation and investigation of differences between women

and men, never far from the surface, have been reenergized in recent
years for at least three reasons—one methodological, one theoretical,
~~~ theoretical issue. On the *methodological* side, the

(1967), and ,

Hyde and Marcia Linn (1986).

Meta-analysis allows a more solid quantitative base for conclusions
about differences and, in its more accomplished versions, useful information about the potential moderators and relevant parameters of differences. Nonetheless, conclusions about differences do not go unques-
tioned. The debates featured in the *American Psychologist* (1995) and
Feminism & Psychology (Kitzinger, 1994) give a sense of the terrain.
Among those who engage in meta-analytic studies, there is considerable
disagreement as to the significance of effect sizes. How big does a statistical difference have to be for it to be meaningful in practical terms?
How much do the distributions of women and men overlap, even if
there is a statistically significant difference in means? How large are sex
differences as compared with other psychological effects? At a more
conceptual level, some have raised issues as to the potential gains and
losses that result from adopting a sex difference strategy. Some have
argued that the questions themselves are problematic, implicitly assuming sex differences and turning the attention away from issues of construction and context. Like many questions in the field today, no con-
sensus has been reached, but the issues are quite clearly defined.

When done well, I think, meta-analysis serves a useful purpose in
sorting out existent findings, doing a kind of "wheat from chaff" sorting. At the same time, it must be recognized that meta-analysis is limited by its input. Thus, if paradigms are too limited or questions too
narrow, a meta-analysis cannot correct for the gaps. To perhaps overdo
a metaphor, I suggest that the meta-analysis can rearrange the garden,

making it more orderly or more aesthetic, but cannot in itself create new varieties of flowers.

In the *meta-theoretical* realm, questions about sex differences are raised in the context of standpoint perspectives. As standpoint theorists have argued, one's particular location in the world inevitably affects experience, perspective, and values. Thus, one cannot assume universal laws but instead must be aware of the different vantage points that any one person can bring to bear. For the study of gender, this perspective has led to a variety of investigations with women as the starting point— and in more disaggregated form, particular types of women, defined by ethnicity, age, geography, or class. For this investigative approach, the experimental notion of a control or comparison group is, by and large, considered irrelevant. Yet although the methodology does not test for differences, these investigations often invoke comparisons between women and men. Both Gilligan (1982) and Belenky, Clinchy, Goldberger, and Tarule (1986) used previous research on men as a reference point for interpreting their findings. Thus, the ubiquitous tendency to make two-group comparisons can persist, even when the rationale for those comparisons is questioned.

As a more specific theoretical formulation, evolutionary psychology has also brought sex differences to the foreground. Many proponents of this perspective, particularly those with training in social and personality psychology, seek to document sex differences that are consistent with postulates from evolutionary theory. The key assumption is that women and men have faced different adaptive problems over the course of evolutionary history. Evolutionary psychologists first assume that women and men have faced different adaptive challenges in the course of history; from that assumption, they predict sex differences in related behavior. At the same time, if adaptive challenges are assumed to be equivalent for women and men, evolutionary psychologists would posit no difference (Buss, 1995, 1996). The task thus becomes one of identifying areas of potential difference and developing convincing arguments to support those claims.

The case for differential adaptive problems is particularly strong, the evolutionary position suggests, in the areas of mate selection. Accordingly, sex differences are predicted in a variety of related attitudes and behaviors, such as jealousy, attitudes toward casual sex, and the

ʿ ˡ···ᵢ··ˡ ···ₙₑₐᵣₐₙcₑ Adherents of this position have

ₙₙₐᵢₑ ₐₙₐ ₐₐ

production and consequent differences in the certainty ot parenmouu, can explain sex differences in jealousy (Buunk, Angleitner, Oubaid, & Buss, 1996). On the other hand, investigators have argued that beliefs about love and sexual infidelity are constructed differently for women than for men, creating attitudinal differences that need no evolutionary forces to account for them (DeSteno & Salovey, 1996; Harris & Christenfeld, 1996).

Many of the findings related to mate selection and jealousy can be predicted equally well, I believe, by models of belief systems and socialization practices as by deep-rooted evolutionary forces. Is the distal cause, whose existence can only be hypothesized, preferable to more proximal causes that are amenable to observation and recording? Although some might argue that the belief systems are themselves the product of evolutionary pressures, that hypothesis is essentially untestable. Furthermore, many psychologists (myself included) remain uncomfortable with the underemphasis placed on plasticity and variability in behavior, which, although acknowledged, rarely figures into evolutionary accounts.[3]

Nonetheless, evolutionary accounts, like any explanation linking behavior to the biological, have become remarkably popular during the

---

[3]This critique of evolutionary psychology is directed primarily at what has been termed the *genecentric* view of evolutionary psychology (Caporael, 1997), a view that when translated into psychological terms tends to focus on inherited traits and dispositions. More dynamic and complicated evolutionary frameworks have not yet been brought to bear on issues of gendered social behavior.

past decade. Particularly in the media, these stable, and sometimes assumed unchangeable, causes attract far more attention than the more complex, more difficult to explain contextual accounts. Perhaps this trend should be expected in the "decade of the brain." Or perhaps, like the popularity of *The Rules* (Fein & Schneider, 1995), recourse to old "truths" is more comfortable in an era of rapid change.

Whatever the forces, there is little doubt that a sex difference tradition will continue within gender research. Assumptions of difference are embedded in the culture and transmitted regularly through media and conversation. Nor is there doubt that women and men do differ, on some dimensions, in some circumstances, and at least some of the time. I only hope that psychologists can continue to document the complexities and variations of gender, as it is constructed and interpreted, eventually forcing an increasing sophistication in the discourse and the representations that convey gender in the larger world.

PEOPLE THINK WOMEN AND MEN ARE DIFFERENT, DON'T THEY?

In her 1972 article with Helmreich, "Who Likes Competent Women?" Spence initiated a program of research that dealt with individual differences but in attitudes rather than in personality. The Attitude Toward Women Scale, published in both long and short versions (Spence & Helmreich, 1972a; Spence, Helmreich, & Stapp, 1973), has become one of the most widely used measures of gender-role attitudes. The primary concern of its authors was to assess how people think about the rights and roles of women and, in the case of the Spence and Helmreich (1972b) study, how people judge those who either conform to or deviate from the norms for women.

Work on attitudes toward women and men, both implicit and explicit, has continued to garner attention during the past 2 decades. Documentation of changing attitudes toward gender roles in the direction of liberalization (cf. Spence et al., 1985) gave some feminists grounds for pleasure and satisfaction, although most indications are that the pace of these changes has slowed or stopped. Other work, particularly the ambivalence model of Glick and Fiske (1996), has helped psychologists to understand some of the contradictions that are evident in judgments of women—how a belief that "women are won-

research on stereotypes into the courts, where the discriminatory treat-
ment of Hopkins by the accounting firm of Price Waterhouse could be documented and understood through reference to the research literature on gender stereotypes. This research was subsequently summarized in an amicus brief to the U.S. Supreme Court (Fiske, Bersoff, Borgida, Deaux, & Heilman, 1991), where eventually Hopkins was vindicated and later reinstated at Price Waterhouse.

Work on gender stereotypes has continued to develop (see Biernat, chapter 4; Fiske and Glick, chapter 8; Martin, chapter 3; and Signorella, chapter 5). Psychologists know a lot more about the development, content, processes, and consequences of gender stereotypes now than they did even 10 years ago (Deaux & Kite, 1993; Deaux & LaFrance, 1998; Fiske, 1998; Fiske & Stevens, 1993). They better understand the nonconscious operation of gender beliefs and how those beliefs influence seemingly unrelated judgments and memories. Furthermore, significant progress is being made in understanding how themes of gender and power interweave (Fiske, 1993)—even though much remains to be learned about how gender and power operate in the matrix of class and race.

To borrow a term by Sandra Bem (1994), I see the "lenses of gender" as pervasive. Beliefs about gender influence many domains of action. In the past 15–20 years, the understanding of these influences has expanded substantially. I already referred to the issue of sex discrimination in the workplace. Other research areas that have benefitted from this expanded understanding of gender belief systems include studies of achievement and occupational choice (Eccles, 1994) and of sexual harassment and hostile work environments (Borgida & Fiske, 1995; Gu- tek, 1985), to name only two. These are action domains for feminist psychologists—domains now being charted in important ways with the concepts and findings of the research enterprise.

MAYBE THIS IS ALL MORE COMPLICATED THAN WE THOUGHT

As a general category, the work I discussed in the previous section can be summarized as a case of "gender as cue" (Unger & Crawford, 1992). The power of gender to influence people's perceptions, interpretations, and behaviors was originally set in the language of experimentation, sometimes referred to as a *sex of stimulus* approach. In those early days, many psychologists (myself included) were prone to think that any phenomenon could be manipulated as a variable in a 2 × 2 experiment. Thus, gender became the sex of stimulus.

I would be the last to disparage that approach, as it yielded many important demonstrations and valuable lessons about the influence that gender has on judgments and behaviors. These studies can serve as dramatic arguments about the influence of gender—arguments that may be convincing to judges and juries, doubting students, and skep- tical colleagues. At the same time, as the understanding has evolved, it is clear that gender cannot be fully represented in a few cells of an analysis of variance design. Women and men can be assessed and com- pared; similarly, targets can be described in terms consistent or incon- sistent with gender expectations. But because gender is complexly con- structed by society, the assignments and manipulations of the laboratory are dependent on the larger cultural context. Borrowing a concept from Serge Moscovici (1988), I see the "social representations" of gender as a vast network of beliefs and attitudes, from which psy- chologists in any study may extract and perhaps be aware of only a few key elements.

In other words, maybe this is all more complicated than psychol- ogists thought. The term *gender*, as social scientists have come to realize, is a very large umbrella, encompassing a wide array of beliefs and actions. Although she would probably not be comfortable with the label of social constructionist, Spence certainly was among the first in line

1980). Beginning with the contention that most scales purporting to measure global masculinity and femininity are in fact more restricted measures of agency and communion, Spence went on to develop a general model of gender identity that assumes variability and multidimensionality. She argued that the various gendered domains of life, such as personality traits, physical attributes, recreational interests, and occupational preferences, have different developmental histories and complex interactions. As a consequence, all people do not share the same meanings of masculinity and femininity. Furthermore, people can selectively pick from their own experiential history, taking on those aspects of masculinity and femininity that they find compatible with other values and dismissing those attributes that may be viewed as central by others. In other words, the package label may say masculine or feminine, but a careful look at the contents may hold some surprises.

Other models of gender introduced in recent years also stress the complexity and variability associated with gender. Eccles' (1994) work on achievement behavior, for example, offers a wonderfully developed model that places the person in a context, considering both individual preferences and opportunity structures, to better understand educational attainment and occupational choice [see also Eccles (Parsons) et al., 1983, and chapter 7, this volume].

In the model that Brenda Major and I offered (Deaux & Major, 1987), we suggested that variability is the rule rather than the exception. Referring to sex differences as a "now you see them, now you don't" phenomenon, we developed a model that considered the influence of other persons, self systems, and circumstances on the role that gender plays in social interaction. To the hypothesized sequence of events involving self, other, and situation, we added a raft of modifying conditions that could minimize or maximize the role of gender. This model, although not directly testable in a classic sense, offers a framework for considering the action of gender that many have found useful.

Some of the issues that Major and I (Deaux & Major, 1987) discussed in this article refer to the multiple identities that people have— a theme that I have developed further in recent years (Deaux, 1991, 1993b). In beginning my exploration of identity, which was given impetus by the analysis of gender, I soon recognized that gender was one of the most complicated of identity realms, precisely because it is not unidimensional in any respect. *Gendered identities* seems to be a much more appropriate term to use. Not only are there numerous forms of identity explicitly related to gender, such as mother, feminist, or Barbie doll, but also gender infuses and influences many other identities, including those of ethnicity, class, and occupation.

Thus, from many perspectives, social scientists have arrived at a position of recognizing complexity in the formulation of gender. Concepts are multidimensional, influences are bidirectional, and events are multidetermined. Far from operating in a vacuum, gender is deeply contextualized, both by location and history. In some areas, psychologists are only beginning to recognize the complexity of the questions. Issues of race and class, for example, have in the past typically been ignored or found unsuitable for laboratory techniques. Psychologists have much to learn in this regard, as people such as Landrine (1995) and Wyche and Crosby (1996) have tried to tell us.

This complexity is at least in part responsible for an expansion of the methods by which psychologists study gender. Ethnographic studies, longitudinal designs, and discourse analysis are just a few of the techniques that are being introduced to the methodological tool box. Whereas qualitative techniques have been somewhat out of favor among psychologists for the past several decades, as the allure of laboratory control dominated the methodological scene, they are now reentering the field with force. Some of the methods of neuroscience may well find their way into the repertoire as well, as studies of brain and behavior (with appropriate concerns for directionality and modifiability)

PSYCHOLOGISTS ARE NOT ALONE

A recognition of complexity in gender analysis almost inevitably leads to a recognition of context. One of the reasons that the sex of stimulus approach was so limited is that gender is deeply embedded in contexts. For this reason, a strictly psychological approach is, in a sense, too psychological. Colleagues in sociology and anthropology have of course known this all along, and many of the psychological analyses include a recognition of context. Particularly for those of us trained in social psychology, a focus on situational variables comes naturally. Yet before patting ourselves on the back too quickly, it should also be noted that the situations social scientists study are often artificially constrained and of questionable external validity. Thus, we too need to stretch our conceptual boundaries.

Spence, in developing a plan for coverage in her *Handbook of Social Psychology* chapter (Spence et al., 1985), began with an analysis of the social and historical context, reporting trends in women's educational attainment and patterns of women's employment. She also pushed her coauthors for coverage of the household division of labor, dual-career couples, and women in management—each an area in which contributions have come from multiple disciplines. Each of those topics involves a broadened social science perspective, and the reference list for that chapter reflects those cross-disciplinary ventures.

Many other investigators of gender have ventured across disciplinary lines as well. Eagly's (1987) social role model, for example, brings sociological concepts to bear; Gutek's (1985) analysis of gender and harassment in the workplace bridges psychology and organizations; Fine's (1992) work links discourses of psychology and education; Franz and Stewart (1994) have shown how the humanities and psychology can forge common ground. Each of these initiatives illustrates a new way of thinking about gender.

Yet these disciplinary links have their stressors as well. Particularly at a time in history when conventional intellectual paradigms are being questioned, shaken up, and sometimes discarded, visits to the neighbor's house can be disconcerting—or more. Postmodern perspectives, pervasive in the humanities and some of the social sciences, raise challenges to "business as usual." Quantitative approaches to research are sometimes pitted against qualitative styles, with the erroneous suggestion that only one path can be the right choice. Very few assumptions go unchallenged.

Most faculty involved in women's studies programs have participated in some of these epistemological debates and have recognized the challenges that crossing disciplinary lines presents. Yet for the analysis of gender, most social scientists would agree that the lines must be crossed and that the theories and questions need to be embedded within, or at least cognizant of, the broader intellectual field. This task confronts most disciplines today, where the habits of looking only inward are being questioned and the stimulation of encountering other disciplinary perspectives is being experienced. Scholars of gender and participants in women's studies programs serve as a model for these kinds of efforts.

THE TERMS OF APPRAISAL

In taking stock of nearly 3 decades of work on gender, I pose two questions to myself—and pose them to the reader as well. First, has research on gender had an impact on psychology? Second, has the psychology of gender had an impact on the larger society? Phrased in the absolute, the answers to both questions is certainly *yes*; I suspect most students of gender would agree. If phrased alternatively as a matter of degree—How much impact—the debate might be more lively.

was in order.) Now courses on psychology of women are regularly taught in most departments. Several journals within psychology as well as sister journals in sociology and women's studies focus on gender.

Literally thousands of studies related to women and gender have been published over the past 20–25 years. Scores of areas have been opened up to research in this time period. Think of how much research existed prior to 1970 on topics such as gender stereotypes; sexual harassment; effects of pornography; women and achievement; work and family roles; gender and emotion; gender, language, and communication; and so on. The amount of work is truly staggering. Some of this work enters the central forums of the discipline of psychology as a whole. Both the 1985 and 1997 editions of the *Handbook of Social Psychology* (see Spence et al., 1985, and Deaux & LaFrance, 1998, e.g.) have chapters on gender, after a hiatus of some 30 years. Undergraduate textbooks commonly include chapters or major sections on gender.

Yet I think that the influence—or perhaps infiltration—is not as great as it might be. Although many psychologists now make reference to gender in their research, these inquiries are often limited to fairly cursory consideration of sex differences, without much follow through in theory. Such investigations may be described as gender research. Yet if the underlying assumptions are not examined more closely, these studies may no more than represent the "old wine" of sex differences in a newly labeled bottle.

Further grounds for some pessimism is the fact that the proliferation of articles in gender-specific journals, such as *Sex Roles* or *Psy-*

chology of Women Quarterly, does not always surface in the broader psychology domain. For example, Michelle Fine (Fine & Gordon, 1989) created what she and her coauthor termed a *penetration index* to assess how often articles in feminist journals were cited in *Developmental Psychology* and *Journal of Personality and Social Psychology*. The numbers were very low and showed no evidence of change over the 5-year period they had surveyed. Similarly, it is my impression that many universities still feel no obligation to have a gender specialist on their faculty. Adjuncts or graduate students are often called in to teach the psychology of women course, providing little stability or legitimacy to that portion of the curriculum. Thus, ghettoization remains a potential problem for scholars of gender. In contrast, other fields of inquiry, particularly in the humanities but including sociology and anthropology as well, appear to have given more recognition and status to gender inquiries. This could be a case of "grass looking greener"—but I do not think so.

My sense of this failure to penetrate the mainstream was sharpened several years ago when I was asked to provide a commentary for an article submitted to *Psychological Science*, suggesting a particular strategy for use of the terms *sex* and *gender* (Deaux, 1993a). Most amazing about this article (Gentile, 1995), apart from the utter implausibility of the suggested solution, is that the author was apparently oblivious to the extensive debate that had been carried on in the literature—that is, the feminist literature—and offered his solution as if in a vacuum. As a case study for what is undoubtedly a much larger problem, this incident gives little evidence for shared assumptions or common ground.

In answering the second question, as to the impact of research on gender for the larger society, I am in fact more encouraged. Research on stereotypes and evaluation, for example, has played a significant role in the legal arena on cases dealing with discrimination and sexual harassment. In *Price Waterhouse v. Hopkins* (Fiske et al., 1991), *Robinson v. Jacksonville Shipyards* (1989), *Jensvold v. Shalala* (1994), and dozens of other cases, the research base has informed both judge and jury. Other work on the conditions and climate of sexual harassment (Borgida & Fiske, 1995; Burgess & Borgida, 1997; Fitzgerald, 1993; Gutek, 1985) has similarly informed the court and helped the cases of victims of such harassment.

the decision-making process of women who consider abortion (Major et al., 1990; Mueller & Major, 1989) has been incorporated into the material provided at clinics for women who are considering this action.

Work by Eccles [1994; see also Eccles (Parsons) et al., 1983] on achievement and educational attainment has influenced school curriculum and practices. The recent growth of research on women and health has begun to have an impact on health policy and practice (Gallant, Keita, & Royak-Schaler, 1997). Many other examples could be cited of decisions made or programs developed that would not have taken the form they did without a psychological research base. The world has been changed by gender research.

CONCLUSION

I end on an upbeat note because I truly believe that those psychologists who study gender have made a difference. The past 3 decades have been an exciting intellectual time, and the area of gender studies has been at the center of many debates. Unquestionably, many issues remain unresolved. The current intellectual climate is active and sometimes turbulent. Yet the value of the study of gender is accepted almost without question. For me personally, the value of an empirical approach is also clear—empiricism that is catholic in conception and diverse in particular but, unabashedly, empirical.

On the trail staked out over the past 3 decades, Spence's markers are all over the place. Often she has pointed psychologists in new directions. Often, too, she has showed investigators (myself included) that they were going astray and has pulled them back on track. Future generations of scholars will need to make similar commitments as the psychology of gender continues to develop—sometimes in familiar forms, sometimes perhaps in less familiar forms—but always as a rich and important part of psychological knowledge.

REFERENCES

Adler, N. E., David, H. P., Major, B. N., Roth, S. H., Russo, N. F., & Wyatt, G. E. (1990). Psychological responses to abortion. *Science, 248,* 41–44.

American Psychologist. (1995). *Current issues, 50,* 145–171.

Belenky, M. F., Clinchy, B. M., Goldberger, N., & Tarule, J. M. (1986). *Women's ways of knowing.* New York: Basic Books.

Bem, S. L. (1994). *The lenses of gender.* New Haven, CT: Yale University Press.

Borgida, E., & Fiske, S. T. (Eds.). (1995). Gender stereotyping, sexual harassment, and the law. *Journal of Social Issues, 51*(1).

Burgess, D., & Borgida, E. (1997). Sexual harassment: An experimental test of sex-role spillover theory. *Personality and Social Psychology Bulletin, 23,* 63–75.

Buss, D. M. (1995). Psychological sex differences: Origins through sexual selection. *American Psychologist, 50,* 164–168.

Buss, D. M. (1996). The evolutionary psychology of human social strategies. In E. T. Higgins & A. W. Kruglanski (Eds.), *Social psychology: Handbook of basic principles* (pp. 3–38). New York: Guilford.

Buunk, B. P., Angleitner, A., Oubaid, V., & Buss, D. M. (1996). Sex differences in jealousy in evolutionary and cultural perspective: Tests from The Netherlands, Germany, and the United States. *Psychological Science, 7,* 359–363.

Campbell, D. T., & Fiske, D. (1959). Convergent and discriminant validation by the multitrait–multimethod matrix. *Psychological Bulletin, 56,* 81–105.

Caporael, L. R. (1997). The evolution of truly social cognition: The core configurations model. *Personality and Social Psychology Review, 1,* 276–298.

Cozzarelli, C., & Major, B. (1995). The effects of anti-abortion demonstrators and pro-choice escorts on women's psychological responses to abortion. *Journal of Social and Clinical Psychology, 13,* 404–427.

Deaux, K. (1984). From individual differences to social categories: Analysis of a decade's research on gender. *American Psychologist, 39,* 105–116.

Deaux, K. (1985). Sex and gender. *Annual Review of Psychology, 36,* 49–81.

Deaux, K. (1991). Social identities: Thoughts on structure and change. In R.

~~⎺ ⎻⎼⎽⎻⎺⎻ ⎽⎺⎰⎓⎽ Theoretical convergences in psychoanal-~~

~~ʀaɪuuɪ (ʟᴅᴜ./, --/ ᴡᴄ⸴~~
107–139). Westport, CT: Greenwood Press.

Deaux, K., & LaFrance, M. (1998). Gender. In D. Gilbert, S. T. Fiske, & G. Lindzey (Eds.), *Handbook of social psychology* (4th ed., pp. 788–827). New York: Random House.

Deaux, K., & Major, B. (1987). Putting gender into context: An interactive model of gender-related behavior. *Psychological Review, 94,* 369–389.

DeSteno, D. A., & Salovey, P. (1996). Evolutionary origins of sex differences in jealousy? Questioning the "fitness" of the model. *Psychological Science, 7,* 367–372.

Eagly, A. H. (1987). *Sex differences in social behavior: A social role interpretation.* Hillsdale, NJ: Erlbaum.

Eagly, A. H., & Mladinic, A. (1994). Are people prejudiced against women? Some answers from research on attitudes, gender stereotypes, and judgments of competence. In W. Stroebe & M. Hewstone (Eds.), *European review of social psychology* (Vol. 5, pp. 1–35). Chichester, England: Wiley.

Eccles, J. S. (1994). Understanding women's educational and occupational choices: Applying the Eccles et al. model of achievement-related choices. *Psychology of Women Quarterly, 18,* 585–609.

Eccles (Parsons), J., Adler, T. F., Futterman, R., Goff, S. B., Kaczala, C. M., Meece, J. L., & Midgley, C. (1983). Expectancies, values and academic behaviors. In J. T. Spence (Ed.), *Achievement and achievement motives: Psychological and sociological approaches* (pp. 75–146). San Francisco: Freeman.

Fausto-Sterling, A. (1985). *Myths of gender: Biological theories about women and men.* New York: Basic Books.

Fein, E., & Schneider, S. (1995). *The rules.* New York: Warner Books.

Fine, M. (1992). *Disruptive voices: The possibilities of feminist research.* Ann Arbor: University of Michigan Press.

Fine, M., & Gordon, S. M. (1989). Feminist transformations of/despite psychology. In M. Crawford & M. Gentry (Eds.), *Gender and thought* (pp. 146–174). New York: Springer-Verlag.

Fiske, S. T. (1993). Controlling other people: The impact of power on stereotyping. *American Psychologist, 48,* 621–628.

Fiske, S. T. (1998). Stereotyping, prejudice, and discrimination. In D. Gilbert, S. T. Fiske, & G. Lindzey (Eds.), *Handbook of social psychology* (4th ed., pp. 357–411). New York: Random House.

Fiske, S. T., Bersoff, D. N., Borgida, E., Deaux, K., & Heilman, M. E. (1991). Social science research on trial: Use of sex stereotyping research in *Price Waterhouse v. Hopkins. American Psychologist, 46,* 1049–1070.

Fiske, S. T., & Stevens, L. E. (1993). What's so special about sex? Gender stereotyping and discrimination. In S. Oskamp & M. Costanzo (Eds.), *Gender issues in contemporary society* (pp. 173–196). Newbury Park, CA: Sage.

Fitzgerald, L. (1993). Sexual harassment: Violence against women in the workplace. *American Psychologist, 48,* 1070–1076.

Franz, C. E., & Stewart, A. J. (Eds.). (1994). *Women creating lives: Identities, resilience, and resistance.* Boulder, CO: Westview Press.

Gallant, S., Keita, G., & Royak-Schaler, R. (Eds.). (1997). *Health care for women: Psychological, social, and behavioral influences.* Washington, DC: American Psychological Association.

Gentile, D. A. (1993). Just what are sex and gender, anyway? A call for a new terminological standard. *Psychological Science, 4,* 120–122.

Gilligan, C. (1982). *In a different voice.* Cambridge, MA: Harvard University Press.

Glick, P., & Fiske, S. T. (1996). The ambivalent sexism inventory: Differentiating hostile and benevolent sexism. *Journal of Personality and Social Psychology, 70,* 491–512.

Gutek, B. (1985). *Sex and the workplace.* San Francisco: Jossey-Bass.

Harris, C. R., & Christenfeld, N. (1996). Gender, jealousy, and reason. *Psychological Science, 7,* 364–366.

Helmreich, R. L., Spence, J. T., & Holahan, C. K. (1979). Psychological androgyny and sex-role flexibility: A test of two hypotheses. *Journal of Personality and Social Psychology, 37*, 1631–1644.

~~Huda, J. S., & Linn, M. C. (Eds.). (1986).~~ *The psychology of gender: Advances*

Maccoby, E. E., & Jacklin, C. N. (1974). *The psychology of sex differences.* Stanford, CA: Stanford University Press.

Major, B., Cozzarelli, C., Sciacchitano, A. M., Cooper, M. L., Testa, M., & Mueller, P. M. (1990). Perceived social support, self-efficacy, and adjustment to abortion. *Journal of Personality and Social Psychology, 59*, 452–463.

Miles, C. C. (1935). Sex in social psychology. In C. Murchison (Ed.), *A handbook of social psychology* (Vol. 2, pp. 683–797). New York: Russell & Russell.

Morawski, J. G. (1994). *Practicing feminisms, reconstructing psychology: Notes on a liminal science.* Ann Arbor: University of Michigan Press.

Moscovici, S. (1988). Notes towards a description of social representations. *European Journal of Social Psychology, 18*, 211–250.

Mueller, P., & Major, B. (1989). Self-blame, self-efficacy, and adjustment to abortion. *Journal of Personality and Social Psychology, 57*, 1059–1068.

Robinson v. Jacksonville Shipyards, Inc., 173 Banks III, 72–81 (1989).

Shields, S. (1975). Functionalism, Darwinism, and the psychology of women: A study in social myth. *American Psychologist, 30*, 739–754.

Spence, J. T. (1985). Gender identification and its implications for the concepts of masculinity and femininity. In R. A. Dienstbier (Series Ed.) & T. B. Sonderegger (Ed.), *Nebraska Symposium on Motivation and Achievement. Vol. 32: Psychology and gender* (pp. 59–95). Lincoln: University of Nebraska Press.

Spence, J. T. (1991). Do the BSRI and PAQ measure the same or different concepts? *Psychology of Women Quarterly, 15*, 141–166.

Spence, J. T. (1993). Gender-related traits and gender ideology: Evidence for a multifactorial theory. *Journal of Personality and Social Psychology, 64,* 624–635.

Spence, J. T., Deaux, K., & Helmreich, R. L. (1985). Sex roles in contemporary American society. In G. Lindzey & E. Aronson (Eds.), *Handbook of social psychology* (3rd ed., pp. 149–178). Reading, MA: Addison-Wesley.

Spence, J. T., & Hall, S. K. (1996). Children's gender-related self-perceptions, activity preferences, and occupational stereotypes: A test of three models of gender constructs. *Sex Roles, 35,* 659–692.

Spence, J. T., & Helmreich, R. (1972a). The Attitudes Toward Women Scale: An objective instrument to measure attitudes toward the rights and roles of women in contemporary society. *JSAS Catalog of Selected Documents in Psychology, 2,* 66–67 (Ms 153).

Spence, J. T., & Helmreich, R. L. (1972b). Who likes competent women? Competence, sex-role congruence of interest, and subjects' attitudes toward women as determinants of interpersonal attraction. *Journal of Applied Social Psychology, 2,* 197–213.

Spence, J. T., & Helmreich, R. L. (1978). *Masculinity and femininity: Their psychological dimensions, correlates, and antecedents.* Austin: University of Texas Press.

Spence, J. T., & Helmreich, R. L. (1979). On assessing "androgyny." *Sex Roles, 5,* 721–738.

Spence, J. T., & Helmreich, R. L. (1980). Masculine instrumentality and feminine expressiveness: Their relationships with sex role attitudes and behaviors. *Psychology of Women Quarterly, 5,* 147–163.

Spence, J. T., Helmreich, R. L., & Sawin, L. L. (1980). The Male–Female Relations Questionnaire: A self-report inventory of sex-role behaviors and preferences and their relationships to masculine and feminine personality traits, sex-role attitudes, and other measures. *JSAS Selected Documents in Psychology, 10,* 87 (Ms. 916).

Spence, J. T., Helmreich, R., & Stapp, J. (1973). A short version of the Attitudes Toward Women Scale (AWS). *Bulletin of the Psychonomic Society, 2,* 219–220.

Spence, J. T., Helmreich, R., & Stapp, J. (1974). The Personal Attributes Questionnaire: A measure of sex-role stereotypes and masculinity–femininity. *JSAS Catalog of Selected Documents in Psychology, 4,* 43–44 (Ms 617).

Spence, J. T., Helmreich, R. L., & Stapp, J. (1975). Ratings of self and peers on sex-role attributes and their relations to self-esteem and conceptions of masculinity and femininity. *Journal of Personality and Social Psychology,*

McNally.

Wood, W. (1987). Meta-analytic review of sex differences in group performance. *Psychological Bulletin, 102,* 53–71.

Wood, W., Rhodes, N., & Whelan, M. (1989). Sex differences in positive well-being: A consideration of emotional style and marital status. *Psychological Bulletin, 106,* 249–264.

Wyche, K. F., & Crosby, F. J. (1996). *Women's ethnicities: Journeys through psychology.* Boulder, CO: Westview Press.

2

The Many Faces of

Janet Taylor Spence has shown many faces and has filled many roles during her distinguished career—scientist, scholar, editor, textbook author, administrator, supportive colleague, and role model to generations of aspiring psychologists. I would consider her impact to be comparable with that of Helen of Troy, the face that launched a thousand ships. In Janet of Austin, we have the face that launched a thousand dissertations.

THE TEACHING AND LEADERSHIP FACES

After graduating from Oberlin College, Janet began her graduate education at Yale University. Leaving Yale at the end of her first year for a clinical internship, she entered the University of Iowa. There she began her lasting personal and intellectual collaboration with Kenneth Spence.

The following is adapted from the after dinner presentation at the opening ceremony of the festschrift in honor of Janet Taylor Spence. The tone of the talk was twofold—a tribute to an extraordinary scholar and mentor and a light-hearted roast recounting her many faceted contributions. The presentation was enhanced by the computer magic of Judy Langlois, who morphed pictures of Janet at various points in her career into humorous images of a serious scientist.

Her doctoral dissertation was completed at the University of Iowa in 1949 under Kenneth's supervision.

After receiving her PhD, she joined the faculty of Northwestern University in 1949. At Northwestern, she continued to investigate and extend the drive theory paradigm. That phase of her career ended when she married Kenneth Spence and returned to Iowa City to the position of research psychologist at the Iowa City Veterans Administration Hospital. As a result of the participant population available, her research turned from anxiety in college students to motivational processes in schizophrenia patients.

Several years later, there was another change in her life when Kenneth accepted a position in the expanding Department of Psychology at the University of Texas at Austin; she joined the staff of the Texas State School for the Mentally Retarded and initiated a program of research with children, normal and retarded. This line of research continued after she accepted a faculty position in the Department of Educational Psychology in the School of Education at the University of Texas at Austin. (See chapter 10 for Janet's discussion of women in academia and nepotism rules as vocational barriers.)

After Kenneth's tragic death in 1967, she accepted a joint appointment with the Department of Psychology at the University of Texas at Austin. Shortly after this, she moved fulltime to psychology as the department chair. She assumed the chair during a period of turmoil over issues ranging from the Vietnam conflict and civil rights to feminism. Academic psychology was also changing as the "cognitive revolution" was underway and learning theories were no longer ascendant. After 4 years of exceptional leadership during these tumultuous times, she stepped down as chair but was tapped for several important positions at the University of Texas at Austin and the national level. She served as a graduate advisor in psychology for 5 years and served on a number of advisory panels and commissions, including the Board of Directors of the American Psychological Association. Two of her most important functions were as president of the American Psychological Association in 1984 and founding president of the American Psychological Society in 1989.

Editorial work is also one of the ways that the public spirited keep
the profession at the cutting edge intellectually. Janet's efforts here have
‸‸ ᶜʰ‸ ‸‸rᵛᵉᵈ ᵃₛ both associate editor and editor

aɴᵈ ᵗʰᵉ Uₙᵢᵥₑᵣₛᵢₜᵧ
from Hollins College.

Always devoted to teaching, Janet was a personal or symbolic mentor for graduate students in their writing of thousands of dissertations.
She has also influenced the undergraduate experience of two generations of students by coauthoring *Elementary Statistics* (Spence, Cotton,
Underwood, & Duncan, 1990), a widely used introductory textbook
now in its fifth edition. Despite these achievements and many others,
it is in the arena of scholarship and research that Janet has made contributions that will survive far past the millennium.

THE RESEARCH FACES

The First 20 Years

In her doctoral dissertation, Janet investigated the influence of manifest
anxiety on eyelid conditioning. This seminal study laid the foundations
for what came to be called "drive theory" (Taylor, 1956). Drive theory,
an extension of the Hull–Spence behavior theory so influential at the
time, focuses on the energizing or drive component of motivational
processes and its interaction with task and other situational variables
in determining performance (Taylor, 1953). One of the goals of this
line of research was to investigate the influence of anxiety as a dispositional trait. Not finding a suitable instrument in the literature, she
developed her own self-report instrument, the Taylor Manifest Anxiety
Scale (Taylor, 1953, 1955), which continues to be widely used and use-

ful. She rapidly became one of the most widely cited psychologists—a position she has maintained through her subsequent contributions.

In the 1950s and early 1960s, she published studies on reactions of schizophrenia patients and began an extensive program of research with children. In this area, she published an influential series of studies on the influence of various types of reinforcers on learning in children (e.g., Spence, 1970a, 1970b). At the other end of the phylogenetic scale, Janet published studies with Brendan Maher on the effects of handling and noxious stimulation on the albino rat (Spence & Maher, 1962a, 1962b).

In the pregender phase of her career, Janet edited two volumes on learning and motivation with Kenneth Spence (Spence & Spence, 1967, 1968). She also edited two other volumes and wrote chapters in the field of learning and behaviorism (Bower & Spence, 1969; Kendler & Spence, 1971; Spence, 1963). As an interesting precursor of the subsequent direction of her career, the first study that includes gender as a topic of investigation is also the last empirical study Janet published with Kenneth (Spence & Spence, 1966). In this article, they reported sex and anxiety differences in eyelid conditioning.

The Shift to Gender

As Janet has candidly admitted, by the early 1970s psychology had moved away from its focus on drive and learning theories; at the same time, as she also candidly admits, she was running out of research ideas that engaged her. Like many events in science, her shift of focus can be traced to serendipity. Her gender-related research and the beginnings of our long and happy collaboration began with a conversation at a cocktail party. We are both inveterate readers of The New Yorker, sometimes articles as well as cartoons. On this evening, we had both spotted one of The New Yorker's continuing contributions to the "War Between the Sexes." In this cartoon, a man and a woman are seated in an elegant restaurant, with requisite candlelight and champagne. The caption read as follows: "You are really stupid. I like that in a woman." The implications of this statement were portentous. Adding fuel to our discussion was a recent study I had conducted with Elliott Aronson and James

LeFan (Helmreich, Aronson, & LeFan, 1970). One of its major findings was that a competent male stimulus person was liked better than one ⁻ ⁻ ⁻⁻⁻⁻⁻ ⁺ʰᵉ ᶜᵒᵐᵖᵉᵗᵉⁿᵗ individual was even

ᵤₗₐᵤₒᵢᵢ:

The idea remained viable even when we realized that we had not only to create stimulus material for the experimental part of the study but also to develop a measure of sex-role attitudes to classify our participants. The first fruits of our collaboration were the Attitudes Toward Women Scale (Spence & Helmreich, 1972a) and the article "Who Likes Competent Women?" (Spence & Helmreich, 1972b). The rest, as they say, is history.

Janet's many subsequent contributions to the study of sex roles and other gender-related issues are well documented in this volume. However, it would be remiss of me not to point to later work that extends far beyond the War Between the Sexes. Whereas the Personal Attributes Questionnaire (Spence & Helmreich, 1978; Spence, Helmreich, & Holohan, 1979) is most often viewed as a measure of masculinity and femininity and referenced in connection with gender studies, it is, as Spence and I have often argued, a very traditional personality assessment instrument, demonstrating considerable validity in predicting the behavior of normal people in the real world. Extending this interest in performance, we developed a new, multifactorial measure of achievement motivation, the Work and Family Orientation Questionnaire (WOFO; Helmreich & Spence, 1978) that has proven to be an excellent predictor of attainment in populations as diverse as research scientists, pilots, astronauts, and students (e.g., Helmreich, Spence, Beane, Lucker, & Matthews, 1980).

A related line of research explores the nature of the Type A personality constellation (Friedman & Rosenman, 1974). Deriving two scales from the usual measure of Type A, Spence and I found that one, Achievement Striving, predicted academic and scientific attainment whereas the second was associated with physical symptoms, such as sleep disorders and other ailments (Helmreich, Spence, & Pred, 1989; Spence, Helmreich, & Pred, 1987; Spence, Pred, & Helmreich, 1989). The findings indicated that Type A, as formulated, had two components, with only one related to adverse health.

In the late 1980s, Janet began a series of investigations into the dimensions of workaholism (Spence & Robbins, 1992), an appropriate venue for one imbued with the joy of work (also not surprisingly one of the dimensions isolated by her measure). Once again, she opened a line of investigation that may launch another series of dissertations and provide important insights into the human condition.

Retirement is a word that seems utterly out of place when applied to Janet. Although she has returned to her beloved Cape Cod (MA), all of her days will not be passed idling on the beach. She continues as an editor and consulting editor, and she and I are in the midst of a large study of the multiple components of identity. The faces of Janet Taylor Spence will continue to serve as a role model and a source of wisdom and of ideas for many years to come.

REFERENCES

Bower, G., & Spence, J. T. (Eds). (1969). *The psychology of learning and motivation* (Vol. 3). New York: Academic Press.

Friedman, M., & Rosenman, R. H. (1974). *Type A behavior and your heart.* Greenwich, CT: Fawcett.

Helmreich, R., Aronson, E., & LeFan, J. (1970). To err is humanizing—Effects of self-esteem, competence, and a pratfall on interpersonal attraction. *Journal of Personality and Social Psychology, 16,* 259–264.

Helmreich, R. L., & Spence, J. T. (1978). The Work and Family Orientation Questionnaire: An objective instrument to assess components of achievement motivation and attitudes toward family and career. *JSAS Catalog of Selected Documents in Psychology, 8,* 35 (Ms. 1677).

Helmreich, R. L., Spence, J. T., Beane, W. E., Lucker, G. W., & Matthews, K. A. (1980). Making it in academic psychology: Demographic and personality correlates of attainment. *Journal of Personality and Social Psychology, 39,* 896–908.

. Making it without losing

431–450.

Spence, J. T. (1970a). The distracting effects of material reinforcers in the discrimination learning of lower- and middle-class children. *Child Development, 41,* 103–111.

Spence, J. T. (1970b). Verbal reinforcement combinations and concept-identification learning: The role of nonreinforcement. *Journal of Experimental Psychology, 85,* 321–329.

Spence, J. T., Cotton, J. W., Underwood, B. J., & Duncan, C. P. (1990). *Elementary statistics* (5th ed.). Englewood Cliffs, NJ: Prentice-Hall.

Spence, J. T., & Helmreich, R. (1972a). The Attitudes Toward Women Scale: An objective instrument to measure attitudes toward the rights and roles of women in contemporary society. *JSAS Catalog of Selected Documents in Psychology, 2,* 66–67 (Ms. 153).

Spence, J. T., & Helmreich, R. (1972b). Who likes competent women? Competence, sex-role congruence of interest, and subjects' attitudes toward women as determinants of interpersonal attraction. *Journal of Applied Social Psychology, 2,* 197–213.

Spence, J. T., & Helmreich, R. L. (1978). *Masculinity and femininity: Their psychological dimensions, correlates, and antecedents.* Austin: University of Texas Press.

Spence, J. T., Helmreich, R. L., & Holahan, C. K. (1979). Negative and positive components of psychological masculinity and femininity and their relationships to self-reports of neurotic and acting out behaviors. *Journal of Personality and Social Psychology, 37,* 1673–1644.

Spence, J. T., Helmreich, R. L., & Pred, R. S. (1987). Impatience versus achievement strivings in the Type A pattern: Differential effects on students' health and academic achievement. *Journal of Applied Psychology, 72,* 522–528.

Spence, J. T., & Maher, B. A. (1962a). Handling and noxious stimulation of the albino rat. I. Effects on subsequent emotionality. *Journal of Comparative and Physiological Psychology, 55,* 247–251.

Spence, J. T., & Maher, B. A. (1962b). Handling and noxious stimulation of the albino rat. II. Effects on subsequent performance in a learning situation. *Journal of Comparative and Physiological Psychology, 55,* 252–255.

Spence, J. T., Pred, R. S., & Helmreich, R. L. (1989). Achievement strivings, scholastic aptitude, and academic performance: A follow-up to "Impatience versus achievement strings in the Type A pattern." *Journal of Applied Psychology, 74,* 176–178.

Spence, J. T., & Robbins, A. S. (1992). Workaholism: Definition, measurement, and preliminary results. *Journal of Personality Assessment, 58,* 160–178.

Spence, K. W., & Spence, J. T. (1966). Sex and anxiety differences in eyelid conditioning. *Psychological Bulletin, 65,* 137–142.

Spence, K. W., & Spence, J. T. (Eds). (1967). *The psychology of learning and motivation* (Vol. 1). New York: Academic Press.

Spence, K. W., & Spence, J. T. (Eds). (1968). *The psychology of learning and motivation* (Vol. 2). New York: Academic Press.

Taylor, J. A. (1953). A personality scale of manifest anxiety. *Journal of Abnormal and Social Psychology, 48,* 285–290.

Taylor, J. A. (1955). The Taylor Manifest Anxiety Scale and intelligence. *Journal of Abnormal and Social Psychology, 51,* 347.

Taylor, J. A. (1956). Drive theory and manifest anxiety. *Psychological Bulletin, 53,* 303–320.

PART TWO

The Complexity of

3

A Developmental Perspective

The puzzle of gender development has many pieces: People carry a biological message about gender in their chromosomes, develop gender identities, develop friendships and interests based on gender, and use gender stereotypes. Janet Taylor Spence and her colleagues (e.g., Spence, 1993; Spence & Helmreich, 1978), Aletha Huston (1983), and Anne Constantinople (1973) have all suggested that aspects of gender are multidimensional and that psychologists need to examine the relations among the various aspects rather than assuming unity among them.[1] Furthermore, once the multifactorial nature of gender is accepted, the obvious next step is to consider the notion of different etiologies for the different factors. The entire picture of gender has been changed by these views: No longer is there a monolithic idea of gender

---

[1]The terms *sex* and *gender* have been the source of a continuing debate. The sex versus gender debate often involves assumptions of causality, with *gender* being used for socially based characteristics and *sex* being used for biologically based characteristics. I would prefer not to adopt such a system that is based on presupposing the origin of a characteristic because causality is more complex than that system implies. Instead, I have loosely adopted Deaux's (1993) use of these terms, in which *sex* is used to refer to classifications of people based on the demographic categories of female and male and *gender* refers to judgments or inferences about the sexes, such as stereotypes, roles, and masculinity and femininity, or any other cases in which sex might be construed inaccurately (see also Ruble & Martin, 1998).

that rests on the unipolar concepts of *masculinity* and *femininity*; now, gender is considered a complex, multifaceted, and dynamic system.

Many social and developmental psychologists have followed the advice to consider the multidimensional and multifactorial nature of gender. The meaning of these ideas varies across areas, however, because of a focus on different theoretical concerns. On the basis of S. L. Bem's (1981) version of gender schema theory and Spence's (1985; Spence & Hall, 1996) multifactorial theory, social psychologists have focused attention on assessing the predictive value of personality characteristics, especially expressive and instrumental qualities. From this research, multidimensionality is clearly evident: Expressive and instrumental qualities seldom predict other aspects of gender in adults, and recent evidence suggests that they do not predict such aspects of gender in older children either (Spence & Hall, 1996). In contrast to research focusing on gender-related instrumental and expressive traits, on the basis of developmental schema theories (Martin & Halverson, 1981) and Kohlberg's (1966) cognitive developmental theory, developmental researchers have focused on examining the predictive value of gender constancy, gender identity and labeling, and gender stereotyping (e.g., Downs & Langlois, 1988).

After conducting an extensive review of the developmental literature for our chapter on gender development in the *Handbook of Child Psychology*, Diane Ruble and I concluded that the multidimensional approach is useful in understanding gender development (Ruble & Martin, 1998). We cautioned researchers, however, not to assume that there is no unity among gender constructs, especially for young children.

There are a number of reasons for such a stance. First, our review (Ruble & Martin, 1998) suggests that some areas of unity are seldom considered. For instance, many children show consistency in important aspects of gender: They develop gender identities congruent with their biological sex, develop gender-typed interests, prefer same-sex playmates, develop gender stereotypes and apply these when making judgments of others, and later develop a sexual interest in the other sex. Second, gender effects are pervasive and powerful in young children, suggesting some sort of organizing role for gender. Third, certain gender concepts show better predictive value than others. For instance, gender identity, that is, children's understanding of their own sex, seems

areas in which powerful gender effects are found in children. Although biological and social influences are mentioned, this chapter emphasizes cognitive aspects of gender development. Many of the studies I reviewed were designed to test the developmental gender schema perspective of Martin and Halverson (1981, 1987; Martin, 1991), in which the child is assumed to be actively involved in learning about gender. The second section of this chapter is a discussion of some of the issues that arise in considering the multidimensional view in the developmental literature. In the last section, I outline some new directions for investigating gender concepts and development in children.

A SELECTED REVIEW OF GENDER EFFECTS

To better understand gender development in children, researchers need to consider some of the areas in which gender effects are especially strong. In this section, three areas are briefly reviewed: toy play, sex segregation, and gender-based inferences.

Toy Play

Most children like gender-typed toys. Many boys like trucks, cars, airplanes, and blocks; many girls like dolls, jewelry, makeup, dress-up clothes, art materials, and kitchen sets. The earliest indications of gender-typed patterns of toy play are around 2 years of age (Fagot, Leinbach, & Hagan, 1986; O'Brien & Huston, 1985), but some studies suggest that this may occur at even younger ages (Roopnarine, 1986; cf. Caldera, Huston, & O'Brien, 1989). The consequences of gender-typed toy play may be long lasting, in that the experiences children acquire when playing with toys may account for some later sex differences, such as in spatial abilities (Liss, 1983; Miller, 1987).

Why do children like gender-typed toys? Social factors are important, in that parents buy these toys for their children (Pomerleau, Bolduc, Malcuit, & Cossette, 1990; Rheingold & Cook, 1975), children are encouraged in sex-appropriate activities and punished or not encouraged for sex-inappropriate play (Fagot & Hagan, 1991; Langlois & Downs, 1980; Lytton & Romney, 1991; Roopnarine, 1986; but cf. Caldera et al., 1989), and they see other children of their own sex playing with these toys (Shell & Eisenberg, 1990). It is interesting that many of these social pressures seem concentrated on infants and toddlers (Ruble & Martin, 1998).

Biological factors may also play a role. If boys' higher activity level predisposes them to want to be active with toys, they may be more drawn to toys that require action, such as cars, trucks, and airplanes. Findings on girls with exposure to high levels of prenatal androgen suggests the importance of hormones: These girls often prefer playing with boys' toys more than other girls do (e.g., Berenbaum & Hines, 1992; Berenbaum & Snyder, 1995).

Cognitive factors also play a role in children's toy preferences. We would expect that children's knowledge of how to play with same-sex toys would increase their likelihood of playing with these toys, which then would further increase their knowledge of these toys. Similarly, children's beliefs about who likes to play with particular toys should also be influential. Using developmental gender schema theory, we would expect children to avoid toys that the other-sex likes and to play with toys that the same-sex likes because they know the gender labels associated with these toys (Martin & Halverson, 1981). Investigating the roles of labels has been challenging because children have already learned the labels associated with most toys and have had differential exposure to gender-typed toys by an early age. The investigation of the role of labels when all else is held constant requires the use of unfamiliar toys presented to children with gender labels, such as "boys really like to play with this toy."

In several studies, researchers have used novel objects to test the

have been labeled for the other sex (Bradbard et al., 1986). This finding suggests that children may have selective attention or memory for information that is same-sex relevant (see Signorella, Bigler, & Liben, 1997), thereby increasing their knowledge of how to play with gender-typed toys.

What happens if children are shown very attractive toys that are not initially gender typed and then are supplied with information about boys' and girls' preferences for these toys? If it were the case that toys purely have an inherent quality of attractiveness, then boys who are told that girls like a toy they have found interesting should not change their own behavior with the toy. However, if it were the case that toys are played with partly because of children's gender-typed beliefs about toys, then we would expect boys to lose interest in toys that are labeled for girls. At the meeting of the Society for Research in Child Development in 1987, Bruce Carter (personal communications, April 30) told a story relevant to this issue. A boy in their laboratory school had been playing with a racecar and its driver when the driver's helmet fell off revealing long blond hair. The driver was a woman. The boy dropped the racecar like it was a hot potato.

Martin, Eisenbud, and Rose (1995) designed a labeling study to test the "hot potato" effect. We were interested in whether children would show a hot potato effect if we gave them unfamiliar toys, half of which were really interesting toys and half of which were less interesting. Children were shown six toys: Two were labeled as toys that girls really like, two as toys that boys really like, and two were unlabeled. Children rated how much they liked each toy and how much other girls and boys would like each toy. The results generally showed that children liked the toys, but for both their own liking of toys and even more so when they predicted how much other children would like the toys, children showed the hot potato effect: They liked toys labeled for their own sex and expected others to like the toys labeled for their sex better than the other toys labeled for the other sex.

Labels are not the only cues that children use to select toys. Sandra L. Bem (1981) argued that knowing about gender means that people have a broad range of metaphorical information about gender, including information that masculine things are hard, rough, and sharp whereas feminine things are soft and smooth. In an interesting set of studies, Leinbach, Hort, and Fagot (1997) evaluated children's use of these gender metaphors. Children were asked to say whether usually non-gender-typed objects were associated with one sex more than the other sex. They found, for example, that children believed that fir trees are "for boys" but rounded maple trees are "for girls." Taking this idea to the extreme, in a different study they took typically gender-typed toys and gave them many of these metaphorical gender cues. They painted a teaset brown and put spikes on the teapot. They cut the mane of a long-haired pastel pony ("My Little Pony"), painted it black, and gave it spiked teeth. With these strong cues, all of the children said these were boys' toys and several of the boys said they wanted them for Christmas presents (Hort & Leinbach, 1993).

Children's interest in particular toys is guided by some cognitive factors, such as their knowledge of who likes different kinds of toys, as well as social and biological factors. Only future research will determine how these factors initially drive interests, how they relate to individual differences in interests later in childhood, and how they relate to each other.

Play Partners

One of the strongest and most pervasive developmental phenomena is sex segregation in play partners (Maccoby, 1988). By the age of 2–3 years of age, children begin to play more with same-sex peers, and these

tendencies increase with age (Fagot, 1995; Jacklin & Maccoby, 1978; La
F~~niere~ Straver, & Gauthier, 1984; Serbin, Moller, Gulko, Powlishta, &
¹·¹¹⁴~~n~~ ᵒf both sexes play with

& Edwards, 1988), ana wiiˑˑ ˑˑˑˑ
(Thorne, 1986). In contrast, when children have choices and are iii iˑˑˑ
structured settings, sex segregation is strong. Also some children show
less of a tendency to segregate by sex than others, although there is a
fairly strong tendency in most children to prefer same-sex peers.

The consequences of sex segregation are pervasive. Because play in
boys' groups is marked by concerns with dominance and constriction
of interaction whereas play in girls' groups is marked by cooperation
and facilitating interaction, girls and boys potentially learn very different styles of interaction in their peer groups, which may lead to many
later sex differences in behavior (see Leaper, 1994; and Maccoby, 1988,
1990, for reviews). There is some speculation that early play partner
preferences may even relate to the type of sexual orientation expressed
by adults (D. J. Bem, 1996).

In a recent study, Martin and Fabes (1997) illustrated the strength
of sex segregation. In a university lab setting where teachers are probably more aware of gender issues than in other child-care centers, high
rates of sex segregation were found. Observations were conducted every
day for several months of 110 boys and 113 girls from 4 to 6 years of
age. The observations involved noting who children played with and
what they were doing. Overall, both sexes showed high levels of sex
segregation: Of the time spent interacting with others, about 60% of
the time children spent with same-sex children versus about 18% with
other-sex children and the remainder of the time in mixed-sex groups
or interacting with teachers or adults. As illustrated in Figures 1 and 2,
sex segregation is powerful; the distributions of play patterns were quite

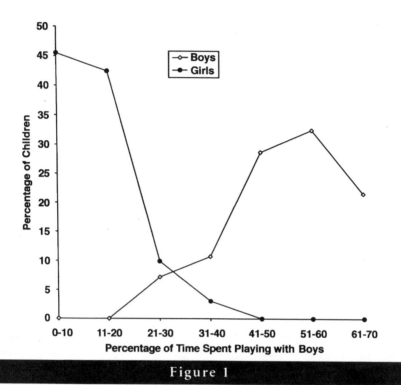

Figure 1

Percentage of children who played with boys as a function of sex of child and percentage of time in social interaction with boys.

distinct for girls and boys. Overall, as illustrated in Figure 1, many boys spent over 50% or more of their time in social interactions playing with boys, whereas no girls spent that much time with boys. Many girls spent less than 10% of their time playing with boys. In Figure 2, the reverse pattern is illustrated. Many girls spent over 50% of their social interaction time playing with girls, but fewer than 5% of boys spent that much time with girls. Many boys spent less than 20% of their time with girls. The origins and factors that maintain sex segregation are of interest to developmental researchers. The original explanation of sex segregation was that children of the same sex share common interests. However, toy and activity preferences are not the only driving factors in same-sex peer preferences because even when playing in sex-

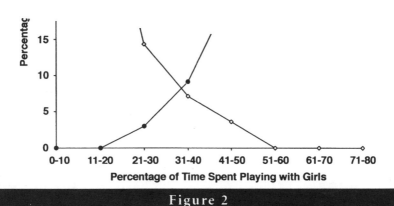

Figure 2

Percentage of children who played with girls as a function of sex of child and percentage of time in social interaction with girls.

segregated groups, children often play with neutral toys and in neutral settings (Maccoby & Jacklin, 1987). Biological factors, especially levels of arousal and inhibition, may lead some children to seek out others like themselves, which may then promote sex segregation. For instance, young boys and even male monkeys are more likely to engage in rough-and-tumble play than young girls and female monkeys (Carter, 1987; Di Pietro, 1981). Each sex may find their own level of arousal matches the same sex better than that of the other sex and leads to more fun and interesting play, as proposed by Fabes (1994). Similarly, in other mammals, young females withdraw from rough-and-tumble play with males (Meaney, Stewart, & Beatty, 1985). Hormone levels have also been implicated in play partner preferences. Girls exposed more to androgens than is typical during prenatal development had a slightly higher preference for playing with boys than did the control girls (Hines & Kaufman, 1994).

From a cognitive perspective, the major question is whether children's ability to label the sexes initiates sex segregation. Thus far, psychologists do not have enough relevant data to decide. In two studies, children's ability to label the sexes related to their same-sex playmate preferences (Fagot, 1985; Fagot et al., 1986). However, a new study by Moller and Serbin (1996) suggests that the children who first began sex segregating were those with different activity and play styles but virtually all of the children had already distinguished males and females from one another. Additional studies and more sophisticated testing of children's understanding and recognition of their sex are needed to answer this question about the early origins of a powerful gender-related behavior.

Cognitive factors may play a role in the maintenance and increase in sex segregation with age. Sex segregation may become more exaggerated as children learn to associate particular forms of play with each gender group as they grow older. For instance, girls may develop the belief that playing with boys will be more active or rough than they would like, so they avoid boys. Similarly, boys may develop the belief that playing with girls is too slow and boring for them, so they may chose to avoid girls. If these sorts of cognitions influence their play partner choices, girls may avoid playing with boys, regardless of their level of activity, simply because the girls believe that the boys might play rough. The expected social consequences of different play partners also may influence children's playmate selections. For instance, children may develop ideas about whether they will be teased because of their playmate choices. A boy who holds the belief that he will be teased about being romantically involved with a girl if he plays with girls is more likely than another boy to avoid other-sex play.

Gender-related cognitions about children's ability to influence others also may influence sex segregation. Between 3 and 5 years of age, boys and girls begin to adopt different strategies of influence: Girls use polite suggestion, and boys use direct commands. However, girls' methods are not effective with boys (Serbin, Sprafkin, Elman, & Doyle, 1984).

˙˙˙˙ ˙˙˙ may develop a belief that they are unlikely to have

˙˙˙˙ even though

ull, ˙˙˙˙˙, ˙

and develop more extensive beliefs ˙˙˙˙˙ ˙˙˙

creasingly motivated to avoid the other sex. In addition, children who develop more extensive beliefs may be more likely to have same-sex playmate preferences than children who do not develop similar beliefs.

Some empirical evidence supports these ideas. Martin et al. (1997) found that preschool children who held strongly gender-typed beliefs tended to play in sex-segregated groups more than children with less gender-typed beliefs; this pattern was found across several different types of beliefs. For instance, children who held beliefs about sex segregation—that is, they thought that other girls liked to play with girls and other boys liked to play with boys—were more likely to spend their time with same-sex children and less likely to spend time with other-sex children. Similar patterns were found when we examined children's gender-typed beliefs about whether they thought other people would approve of their playing with same-sex and other-sex children. The more children had gender-typed beliefs about others' approval, the more sex segregated they were in their play. More interesting, children's beliefs about others' play patterns but not their beliefs about approval mediated the relation between age and sex segregation. This finding suggests that at least some of the age-related increases in sex segregation are accounted for by children's development of more extensive and gender-typed beliefs about others' play.

Gender-Based Inferences

People often are faced with the situation of having to make a decision about someone based on very limited information. How are these judgments made? One powerful source of information that is readily used is the person's sex (S. L. Bem, 1974). In the last 10 years or so, a number of researchers have become interested in how adults and children use information about a person's sex and about their gender-related interests to make inferences (e.g., Beauvois & Spence, 1987; Cowan & Hoffman, 1986; Gelman, Collman, & Maccoby, 1986). One issue of interest is whether children and adults make social judgments in the same way.

The research suggests that developmental changes occur in the use of sex and gender-related information as a basis for social inferences. Adults make best guesses about other people on the basis of sex and their stereotypes about what they believe is masculine and feminine (e.g., Deaux & Lewis, 1984).[2] Adults make predictions about someone they do not know the sex of on the basis of a single masculine or feminine attribute (e.g., Deaux & Lewis, 1984). For instance, a person described as having a masculine physical attribute, such as broad shoulders, is more likely to be attributed another masculine characteristic, such as being assertive, rather than a feminine characteristic (e.g., being nurturant). In some cases, individuating information, such as interests, and gender stereotypes about masculinity and femininity may overpower sex in making predictions (e.g., Locksley, Borgida, Brekke, & Hepburn, 1980).

In contrast to adults, children are more likely to rely on a person's sex than on gender-related information to make predictions about others, but the extent of the reliance on sex depends on their age. For instance, in one study children were told about unfamiliar boys and girls who were described as having masculine, feminine, or neutral interests (Martin, 1989). Then the children were asked to rate how much they would like each child and how much each target child would like to play with other masculine and feminine toys. Developmental trends were apparent. The 4- to 6-year-old children in the sample focused only on the target child's sex, and they disregarded all the extra information about the child's interests. For instance, one boy was described as liking

---

[2]Here, masculinity and femininity refer to the network of associations that individuals hold about the full range of characteristics associated with each sex.

to play with a kitchen set and having a best friend who was a girl. Even ~~˙ ˡ˖ⁿ ᵂᵃˢ~~ described as having feminine interests, the young ~~˖˖ˡⁱⁿᵉ~~ activities, such as play-

~~ᵂ˸˖~~

Other studies generally ~~˖˖~~ of sex- and gender-related information for making ~~ˢᵒ˖ⁱ˖˖~~, (Biernat, 1991a; Lobel, Bempechat, Gewirtz, Shoken-Topaz, & Bashe, 1993; but cf. Berndt & Heller, 1986). The kind of individuating information, however, appears to make a difference in whether it is used by children. Children seem to be more likely to consider individuating information if it is very extreme in terms of gender typing, such as a boy wearing lipstick (Zucker, Wilson-Smith, Kurita, & Stern, 1995).

The results from these inference studies as well as from other inference studies (e.g., Biernat, 1991b) suggest that over time children are able to separate the notions of what it means to be a boy or girl from the attributes that are considered masculine and feminine. That is, they come to understand that there is variation within each sex; for instance, they realize that some women have feminine interests and some women have masculine interests.

The pervasive nature of gender effects can be seen in children's toy choices, playmate preferences, and their use of sex as a basis for making judgments about others. In each case, age changes and the strength of the gender-typed patterns are more obvious than are individual differences in these effects—all of which suggests a powerful organizational role of gender in young children's lives.

DEVELOPMENTAL ISSUES ABOUT MULTIDIMENSIONALITY

Social and developmental psychologists have approached the issue of multidimensionality from different angles. In contrast to the adult literature that focuses on identifying the meaning of masculinity and femininity and on exploring the predictive value of personality variables, such as instrumentality and expressiveness, the literature on young children focuses on the predictive value of gender identity, gender constancy, and gender stereotypes.

These differences have been theoretically driven. In the literature on children, interest is on the origins of gender-typed behavior and thinking. To unravel the issue of origins, one must understand whether gender typing develops as a whole or different aspects develop at different times. For instance, are cognitions about gender a driving force, and do they organize all other aspects of gender? Because of the interest in the origins of gender-typed behavior, researchers have investigated the extent to which children use gender cognitions of any sort to drive their behavior and thinking and, if they do, which sorts of cognitions they use. For instance, what roles do gender identity and gender constancy play in motivating children to adopt gender-typed behaviors? Cognitive-social learning views (e.g. Bussey & Bandura, 1992) presuppose that gender cognitions play a small role in driving behavior and are not involved in the origins of gender-typed behavior, whereas cognitive theories propose that they play a larger role. For developmental schema theorists (Martin & Halverson, 1981), the focus is on recognizing one's own sex as a major motivator of acquiring other aspects of gender. Also gender stereotypes are expected to guide behavior and thinking. For cognitive development theorists (Kohlberg, 1966), the concern is on the predictive value of gender constancy, that is, children knowing that sex does not change over time or appearances. Surprisingly little interest has been paid to personality variables, possibly because such variables are difficult to measure in very young children and when they are measured, boys and girls often show few differences in them.

The original criticisms of the idea that cognitions influence children's behavior, on the basis of the available evidence at that time, were focused on two broad concerns (Huston, 1985). First, individual differences in gender cognitions did not always correlate with individual differences in gender-typed behavior; second was the order-of-development issue. In some studies, gender-typed behavior has been found to precede gender cognitions in development by about 6 months. For example, gender-typed toy play has been found in 2-year-olds, but ~~·~~ ~~· ᵗᵒ~~~ ᵇᵃᵛᵉ not been evident until 2 1/2

predicts other aspₑcₜₛ ᵥᵣ ᵨ
Huston, 1985; Perry et al., 1984; Signorella, Bigler, & Lıᵦₑₙ, ₁,,,,,,
other gender cognitions do. Specifically, a basic understanding of gender appears important for initiating gender development (e.g., Constantinople, 1973; Fagot, 1985; Serbin & Sprafkin, 1986; Spence, 1985). This basic understanding involves children recognizing their own sex and the sex of others. A number of psychologists have argued that when children recognize their sex and others', they then become motivated to learn more about gender (Fagot & Leinbach, 1985; Martin, 1993; Martin & Halverson, 1981). Knowing their own group membership should motivate children to pay more attention to gender-relevant information and should increase the likelihood of children applying gender knowledge to guide their behavior. Being able to recognize the sex of others provides one with the opportunities to directly observe and learn about the behaviors of human males and females (Fagot, 1985; Martin, 1993).

The importance of knowing one's sex has not been tested as much as gender constancy or gender stereotyping, but some relevant information does exist. Martin and Little (1990) found that young children who recognize their own sex and the sex of other children had more knowledge about stereotypes about clothing (but not toys) and showed more gender-typed preferences for toys and peers than children who did not recognize or label sex as accurately. Fagot and her colleagues have also found that children who better recognized the sexes showed stronger same-sex peer preferences (Fagot, 1985) and adopted gender-typed behaviors (Fagot & Leinbach, 1985; Fagot, Leinbach, & O'Boyle, 1992). Longitudinal studies show that children who learned to identify the sexes early tended to adopt gender-typed behaviors later on (Fagot & Leinbach, 1989).

The methods used to measure gender cognitions also need to be considered. Issues about methods have muddied the waters of understanding the extent of interrelatedness in aspects of gender, especially for young children. For instance, for gender stereotype measures, the wording of questions makes a significant difference in the meaning and interpretation of the findings (Signorella et al., 1993). Also most measures of gender stereotyping are too simplistic and need to be further refined to capture developmental changes in how they are used (Martin, Wood, & Little, 1990). Most often, very simple associations are tapped, for instance, between a gender label and attribute (e.g., "Who usually cooks, boys or girls?"). Not surprisingly, children show high levels of knowledge on these measures at an early age, and little individual variability is found with these sorts of measures. Ideally, psychologists need measures that assess stereotypes in more complex ways and that capture the probabilistic nature and range of stereotypes and their salience to children (Martin, 1991, 1993).

The most typical strategy for assessing the predictive value of aspects of gender is by using correlational analyses. However, predicting within-sex individual differences may be difficult for strongly gender-related behaviors because there is often such a restricted range in the behaviors of interest (Maccoby, 1990). For instance, most children prefer same-sex playmates, and little variability is seen in children's play preferences when aggregated over a long time period. A focus on individual differences may restrict researchers to trying to explain why one girl shows relatively lower levels of sex segregation—60% of her time—versus another girl who shows higher levels—75% of her time. The number of children who show consistent and strong other-sex playmate preferences is limited. Also one group of children who often play with the other sex, tomboys, may really only play with boys in very constrained circumstances, such as in a particular sport.

The timetable of children's acquisition of differing aspects of gender needs to be reconsidered. As testing methods for young children have become more sophisticated and less reliance is placed on verbal testing, studies now reveal that infants and toddlers know more about gender

~~~~~~~~~ previously thought. Six-month-old infants who were

recognize as novel a highly

1994). By 24 months, toddlers

stereotypes about activities associated with the sexes (Serbin,

Dubois, & Eichstedt, 1997). Of course, psychologists still do not know how these very rudimentary discriminations translate into gender concepts.

Recent studies also suggest that toddlers use gender concepts. To study the use of gender schemas, Patricia Bauer (1993) presented children with action sequences, such as shaving or diapering a teddy bear. After a delay, she then observed whether children imitated the gender-consistent versus gender-inconsistent sequences. Toddler boys but not toddler girls were more likely to imitate gender-consistent sequences. Some of the boys even refused to play with the diapering props, suggesting that they had a clear concept of who was supposed to be doing the diapering—and it is not boys.

In summary, the developmental issues about multidimensionality largely focus on assessing the roles of different types of gender cognitions on the development of other aspects of gender in young children; unlike the adult literature, little attention has been paid to personality variables as predictors of gender development. Although earlier research suggested that cognitions did not relate to behavior very well, newer research hints that cognitions about the sexes may play an important organizing role in gender development.

NEW DIRECTIONS FOR STUDYING GENDER CONCEPTS

Many questions about gender development are still left unanswered. To better understand the role of cognitive factors in gender development, researchers may want to consider some new directions for research on gender concepts.

One direction is to think more broadly and flexibly about gender concepts and to identify both broad and narrow gender concepts. For instance, children may develop very broad and abstract notions about the sexes. One may think of children as being gender theoreticians who develop ideas about the sexes, revise them on occasion, and then apply these theories to help make sense of the social world.

Martin et al. (1995) conducted several studies of gender theories. We began with the notion that children develop two simple theories: a within-group similarity theory, in which they assume that children of the same sex share similarities, on the basis of having the same "essence," and a between-group differences theory, in which they assume that children of different sexes are not alike because they have fundamentally different essences. To test these theories, we collected a set of novel toys that were unfamiliar to children. Children were shown each toy and were asked to rate how much they liked it, how much they thought girls would like it, and how much they thought boys would like it. One possibility was that children would generalize from their own preferences to all other children. However, the pattern we expected was gender centric, that is, based on gender theories. A girl may say that because she likes a toy, other girls also will like the toy but boys will not.

Preschoolers' toy preferences showed the gender-centric pattern (Martin et al., 1995). Children exhibited smaller absolute differences between their own liking of a toy and their predictions for same-sex children than with other-sex children. When the profile of each child's individual toy preferences was compared with their profile of beliefs about others' preferences, a gender-centric pattern also was evident. There were high positive correlations between children's own liking of toys and their predictions of liking for same-sex others. In both cases, the children's theory of within-gender group similarity was stronger than the theory of between-group differences. Surprisingly, even undergraduate students showed the same tendencies when asked to rate unfamiliar objects, suggesting that people may continue to hold these theories into adulthood (Martin et al., 1995).

From these findings, it appears that children develop abstract the-
~ries about the sexes that go beyond the specific and explicit gender
‸ ⸱⸱⸱⸱⸱⸱ ⸱⸱⸱⸱⸱⸱ gender theories may derive from

have investigated ɪᴏɪᴋ ᴛʜᴇꜱᴇ
have considered whether these kinds of gender concepts ʀᴇʟᴀᴛᴇ ᴛᴏ
aspects of gender. Taylor (1996) conducted a clever study with young
children in which she asked them to imagine a young girl who is raised
on an island only by men or a young boy raised on an island only by
women. Children were then asked whether the child would grow up to
be malelike or femalelike in a number of ways. Generally, children from
4 to about 9 years old tended to believe in biological influences; that
is, they thought that because a boy is a boy, he will want to play football
and be a firefighter, even if he is raised by women. Children older than
9 years of age were more likely to recognize the influence of social
factors on these children.

Martin and Parker (1995) investigated adults' folk theories about
the origins of sex and race differences. A sample of 464 undergraduate
students was asked to rate the extent to which biological factors, socialization factors, and differences in opportunities relate to sex and
race differences. These students acknowledged that socialization, opportunities, and biology each contributed to sex and race differences,
although they believed that sex differences were due somewhat more
to socialization than to opportunities or biology (Martin & Parker,
1995). We also found evidence of a link between these beliefs and beliefs
in biological determinism. The more adults believed that biological factors played a role in sex differences, the more they said they thought it
would be difficult to eliminate sex differences. Folk beliefs weakly related to their views of the sexes: Adults who believed strongly in biological influences were more likely to perceive the sexes as differing in

the personalities, appearance, and interests, although this did not account for much of the variance in these scores.

A third direction for future research is to consider the processes underlying the use of gender concepts. Many researchers have started to take this approach. For instance, Bigler's (1995) research on how children stereotype peers in their classes illustrates that the functional use of a category and physical markers about category membership are used in conjunction to produce stereotyping effects. Powlishta's (1995) work on in-group and out-group issues has been helpful for identifying the ways that children use membership in gender groups as a source of information.

Process-oriented methods can be used to assess how people form stereotypes about novel social groups. Martin and Bullock (1986) tried this technique with adults. Over a 2-week period, adults watched and listened to five travelogues about two groups of creatures from another planet. We were interested in assessing what they learned about the groups and how this information changed over time. The most significant finding was that adults exaggerated the physical differences between the two groups and minimized physical similarities.

The classic example of stereotyping is that people learn about someone's group but know nothing else about the person, yet they are willing to make extensive attributions about the person. How and when do people make generalization from group labels to group members? Novel group methods also are useful for investigating how stereotypes are applied. In one set of studies, preschool children were shown two groups of humanoid creatures from outer space (Martin, 1987). One group was labeled *Gongos* and one *Bleeps*. These groups were similar in most aspects of appearance, but they differed in their skin color and head shape. Children made two sorts of judgments. First, they were asked to make inductive inferences: They were told a characteristic about a group member and asked whether other members of the same group and of the other group also had that particular characteristic. If children were to use group theories, they might believe that Bleeps are similar to one another, that Gongos are similar to one another, but that Gongos and Bleeps would be different. Although the effects were not strong in these studies and varied depending on the type of judgment, a tendency to generalize was found. For instance, children told about a

` ` `··· ·····ded to say that other Gongos would be very

` ` `¹ ·····dgment

using unua....... ᵧ .

The fourth promising direction is to consiuci .u. _ __ cated manner when and how gender cognitions will be activated and used to process information and guide behavior (see Deaux & Major, 1987). Some situations should make gender much more salient and more likely to be used for information processing, such as classrooms where gender has been made salient (see Bigler, 1995; and chapter 6, this volume). Some people are likely to have more salient gender concepts and apply them to more situations than do other people. In only a few developmental studies have researchers examined individual differences in salience, but those few studies suggest that salience varies across individuals and relates to the individuals' information processing (e.g., Levy & Carter, 1989).

CONCLUSIONS

Thinking of gender as a puzzle with many pieces does not go far enough to capture the current thinking about gender. Instead, gender is better conceived of as being many puzzles, each with many pieces and the potential of having different origins. This way of thinking about gender better captures its complexity and provides a starting point for researchers to develop new and better theories about gender. In doing so, however, care must be taken to not go too far in the interpretation of the multidimensional and multifactorial view. The strong version of the multidimensionality argument implies no unity among the various aspects of gender. However, some areas of unity are evident, both in children and adults. Both adults and children develop gendered self concepts that are coherent in many ways yet fuzzy in their boundaries. Coherence may be fostered in part by gender-related cognitions, especially those about gender identity and group membership, which provide organization for behavior. Researchers and theoreticians are left with a Herculean challenge: to understand the aspects of gender that provide coherence and predictability while recognizing the flexible and dynamic nature of gender.

REFERENCES

Bauer, P. J. (1993). Memory for gender-consistent and gender-inconsistent event sequences by twenty-five-month-old children. *Child Development, 64*, 285–297.

Beauvois, C., & Spence, J. T. (1987). Gender, prejudice, and categorization. *Sex Roles, 16*, 89–100.

Bem, D. J. (1996). Exotic becomes erotic: A developmental theory of sexual orientation. *Psychological Review, 103*, 320–335.

Bem, S. L. (1974). The measurement of psychological androgyny. *Journal of Consulting and Clinical Psychology, 42*, 155–162.

Bem, S. L. (1981). Gender schema theory: A cognitive account of sex typing. *Psychological Review, 88*, 354–364.

Berenbaum, S. A., & Hines, M. (1992). Early androgens are related to childhood gender-typed toy preferences. *Psychological Science, 3*, 203–206.

Berenbaum, S. A., & Snyder, E. (1995). Early hormonal influences on childhood gender-typed activity and playmate preferences: Implications for the development of sexual orientation. *Developmental Psychology, 31*, 889–898.

Berndt, T. J., & Heller, K. A. (1986). Gender stereotypes and social inferences: A developmental study. *Journal of Personality and Social Psychology, 50*, 889–898.

Biernat, M. (1991a). Gender stereotypes and the relationship between masculinity and femininity: A developmental analysis. *Journal of Personality and Social Psychology, 61*, 351–365.

Biernat, M. (1991b). A multicomponent, developmental of analysis sex-typing. *Sex Roles, 24*, 567–586.

Bigler, R. S. (1995). The role of classification skill in moderating environmental influences on children's gender stereotyping: A study of the functional use of gender in the classroom. *Child Development, 66,* 1072–1087.

˜ ˉ ˙˄˃˕˒ ˄ ˁ (1983). The effects of sex-typed labeling

˙ ˉ ˢ

ɒussεy, ɪ˶., ˭ ˍˍˍ

development. *Child Development, 63,* 1236–1250.

Caldera, Y. M., Huston, A. C., & O'Brien, M. (1989). Social interactions and play patterns of parents and toddlers with feminine, masculine, and neutral toys. *Child Development, 60,* 70–76.

Carter, D. B. (1987). The roles of peers in sex role socialization. In D. B. Carter (Ed.), *Current conceptions of sex roles and sex typing: Theory and research* (pp. 101–121). New York: Praeger.

Constantinople, A. (1973). Masculinity–femininity: An exception to a famous dictum? *Psychological Bulletin, 80,* 389–407.

Cowan, G., & Hoffman, C. D. (1986). Gender stereotyping in young children: Evidence to support a concept-learning approach. *Sex Roles, 14,* 211–224.

Deaux, K. (1993). Commentary: Sorry, wrong number: A reply to Gentile's call [Special section]. *Psychological Science, 4*(2), 125–126.

Deaux, K., & Lewis, L. L. (1984). Structure of gender stereotypes: Interrelationships among components and gender label. *Journal of Personality and Social Psychology, 46,* 991–1004.

Deaux, K., & Major, B. (1987). Putting gender into context: An interactive model of gender-related behavior. *Psychological Review, 94,* 369–389.

Di Pietro, J. A. (1981). Rough and tumble play: A function of gender. *Developmental Psychology, 17,* 50–58.

Downs, A. C., & Langlois, J. H. (1988). Sex typing: Construct and measurement issues. *Sex Roles, 18,* 87–100.

Ellis, S., Rogoff, B., & Cromer, C. C. (1981). Age segregation in children's social interactions. *Developmental Psychology, 17,* 399–407.

Fabes, R. A. (1994). Physiological, emotional, and behavioral correlates of sex segregation. In W. Damon (Series Ed.) & C. Leaper (Vol. Ed.), *Childhood sex segregation: Causes and consequences* (New Directions for Child Development series, No. 65, pp. 19–34). San Francisco: Jossey-Bass.

Fagan, J. F., & Singer, L. T. (1979). The role of simple feature differences in infants' recognition of faces. *Infant Behavior and Development, 2,* 39–45.

Fagot, B. I. (1985). Changes in thinking about early sex role development. *Developmental Review, 5,* 83–98.

Fagot, B. I. (1995). Parenting boys and girls. In M. H. Bornstein (Ed.), *Handbook of parenting. Vol. 1: Children and parenting* (pp. 163–183). Mahwah, NJ: Erlbaum.

Fagot, B. I., & Hagan, R. (1991). Observations of parent reactions to sex-stereotypic behaviors: Age and sex effects. *Child Development, 62,* 617–628.

Fagot, B. I., & Leinbach, M. D. (1985). Gender identity: Some thoughts on an old concept. *Journal of the American Academy of Child Psychiatry, 24,* 684–688.

Fagot, B. I., & Leinbach, M. D. (1989). The young child's gender schema: Environmental input, internal organization. *Child Development, 60,* 663–672.

Fagot, B. I., Leinbach, M. D., & Hagan, R. (1986). Gender labeling and the adoption of gender-typed behaviors. *Developmental Psychology, 22,* 440–443.

Fagot, B. I., Leinbach, M. D., & O'Boyle, C. (1992). Gender labeling, gender stereotyping, and parenting behaviors. *Developmental Psychology, 28,* 225–230.

Gelman, S. A., Collman, P., & Maccoby, E. E. (1986). Inferring properties from categories versus inferring categories from properties. *Child Development, 57,* 396–404.

Hines, M., & Kaufman, F. R. (1994). Androgen and the development of human sex-typical behavior: Rough-and-tumble play and sex of preferred playmates in children with congenital adrenal hyperplasia (CAH). *Child Development, 65,* 1042–1053.

Hort, B. E., & Leinbach, M. D. (1993, April). *Children's use of metaphorical cues in gender-typing of objects.* Paper presented at the meetings of the Society for Research in Child Development, New Orleans, LA.

Hort, B. E., Leinbach, M. D., & Fagot, B. I. (1991). Is there coherence among components of gender acquisition? *Sex Roles, 24,* 195–208.

‘‘‘‘‘) ‘‘‘ ‘‘‘‘‘‘‘ In E. M. Hetherington (Ed.), *Handbook of*

Комьргь, ᴸ. (-- ‚

concepts and attitudes. In E. E. Maccoby (Ed.), *The developmen ᵤⱼ ᵤᵤ. differences* (pp. 82–173). Stanford, CA: Stanford University Press.

La Freniere, P., Strayer, F. F., & Gauthier, R. (1984). The emergence of same-sex affiliative preferences among preschool peers: A developmental/ ethological perspective. *Child Development, 55,* 1958–1965.

Langlois, J. H., & Downs, A. C. (1980). Mothers, fathers and peers as socialization agents of gender-typed play behaviors in young children. *Child Development, 50,* 1219–1222.

Leaper, C. (1994). Exploring the consequences of sex segregation on social relationships. In W. Damon (Series Ed.) & C. Leaper (Vol. Ed.), *Childhood sex segregation: Causes and consequences* (New Directions for Child Development series, No. 65, pp. 67–86). San Francisco: Jossey-Bass.

Leinbach, M. D., & Fagot, B. I. (1993). Categorical habituation to male and female faces: Gender schematic processing in infancy. *Infant Behavior and Development, 16,* 317–332.

Leinbach, M. D., Hort, B. E., & Fagot, B. I. (1997). Bears are for boys: Metaphorical associations in young children's gender stereotypes. *Cognitive Development, 12,* 107–130.

Levy, G. C., & Carter, D. B. (1989). Gender schema, gender constancy, and gender-role knowledge: The roles of cognitive factors in preschoolers' gender-role stereotype attributions. *Developmental Psychology, 25,* 444–449.

Liss, M. B. (1983). Learning gender-related skills through play. In M. B. Liss (Ed.), *Social and cognitive skills: Sex roles and children's play* (pp. 147–167). New York: Academic Press.

Lobel, T. E., Bempechat, J., Gewirtz, J., Shoken-Topaz, T., & Bashe, E. (1993). The role of gender-related information and self endorsement of traits in preadolescents' inferences and judgments. *Child Development, 64,* 1285–1294.

Lobliner, D. B., & Bigler, R. S. (1993, April). *A cognitive-developmental approach to social stereotyping: The role of categories and inferences.* Paper presented at the Society for Research in Child Development, New Orleans, LA.

Locksley, A., Borgida, E., Brekke, N., & Hepburn, C. (1980). Sex stereotypes and social judgment. *Journal of Personality and Social Psychology, 39,* 821–831.

Lytton, H., & Romney, D. M. (1991). Parents' differential socialization of boys and girls: A meta-analysis. *Psychological Bulletin, 109,* 267–296.

Maccoby, E. E. (1988). Gender as a social category. *Developmental Psychology, 24,* 755–765.

Maccoby, E. E. (1990). Gender and relationships: A developmental account. *American Psychologist, 45,* 513–520.

Maccoby, E. E., & Jacklin, C. N. (1987). Gender segregation in childhood. In H. Reese (Ed.), *Advances in child development and behavior* (Vol. 20, pp. 239–287). New York: Academic Press.

Martin, C. L. (1987, August–September). *Learning to stereotype: Children's generalization of social information.* Paper presented at the 95th Annual Convention of the American Psychological Association, New York, NY.

Martin, C. L. (1989). Children's use of gender-related information in making social judgments. *Developmental Psychology, 25,* 80–88.

Martin, C. L. (1991). The role of cognition in understanding gender effects. In H. Reese (Ed.), *Advances in child development and behavior* (Vol. 23, pp. 113–149). San Diego, CA: Academic Press.

Martin, C. L. (1993). New directions for investigating children's gender knowledge. *Developmental Review, 13,* 184–204.

Martin, C. L. (1994). Cognitive influences on the development and maintenance of gender segregation. In W. Damon (Series Ed.) & C. Leaper (Vol. Ed.), *New directions for child development: The development of gender relationships* (pp. 35–51). San Francisco: Jossey-Bass.

Martin, C. L., & Bullock, M. (1986, August). *Learning stereotypes: Biases in judging characteristics.* Paper presented at the 94th Annual Convention of the American Psychological Association, Washington, DC.

Martin, C. L., Eisenbud, L., & Rose, H. (1995). Children's gender-based reasoning about toys. *Child Development, 66,* 1453–1471.

[illegible] & Fabes, R. A. (1997, April). *Building gender stereotypes in the* [illegible]

Martin, C. L., & Halverson, C. F. (1987). The roles of [illegible] acquisition. In D. B. Carter (Ed.), *Current conceptions of sex roles and sex typing: Theory and research* (pp. 123–137). New York: Praeger.

Martin, C. L., & Little, J. K. (1990). The relation of gender understanding to children's gender-typed preferences and gender stereotypes. *Child Development, 61,* 1427–1439.

Martin, C. L., & Parker, S. (1995). Folk theories about sex and race differences. *Personality and Social Psychology Bulletin, 21,* 45–57.

Martin, C. L, Wood, C. H., & Little, J. K. (1990). The development of gender stereotype components. *Child Development, 61,* 1891–1904.

Meaney, M. J., Stewart, J., & Beatty, W. W. (1985). Sex differences in social play: The socialization of sex roles. In J. S. Rosenblatt, C. Beer, C. M. Bushnell, & P. Slater (Eds.), *Advances in the study of behavior* (Vol. 15, pp. 1–58). Orlando, FL: Academic Press.

Miller, C. L. (1987). Qualitative differences among gender-stereotyped toys: Implications for cognitive and social development in girls and boys. *Sex Roles, 16,* 473–487.

Moller, L. C., & Serbin, L. A. (1996). Antecedents of toddler sex segregation: Cognitive consonance, gender-typed toy preferences and behavioral compatibility. *Sex Roles, 35,* 445–460.

O'Brien, M., & Huston, A. C. (1985). Development of sex-typed play behavior in toddlers. *Developmental Psychology, 21,* 866–871.

Perry, D. G., White, A. J., & Perry, L. C. (1984). Does early sex typing result from children's attempts to match their behavior to sex role stereotypes? *Child Development, 55,* 2114–2121.

Pomerleau, A., Bolduc, D., Malcuit, G., & Cossette, L. (1990). Pink or blue: Environmental gender stereotypes in the first two years of life. *Sex Roles, 22,* 359–367.

Poulin-Dubois, D., Serbin, L. A., Kenyon, B., & Derbyshire, A. (1994). Infants' intermodal knowledge about gender. *Developmental Psychology, 30,* 436–442.

Powlishta, K. K. (1995). Intergroup processes in children: Social categorization and sex role development. *Developmental Psychology, 31,* 781–788.

Rheingold, H. L., & Cook, K. V. (1975). The contexts of boys' and girls' rooms as an index of parent's behavior. *Child Development, 46,* 445–463.

Roopnarine, J. L. (1986). Mothers' and fathers' behaviors toward the toy play of their infant sons and daughters. *Sex Roles, 14,* 59–68.

Rothbart, M., & Taylor, M. (1992). Category labels and social reality: Do we view social categories as natural kinds? In G. Semin & K. Fiedler (Eds), *Language, interaction and social cognition* (pp. 11–36). London: Sage.

Ruble, D. N., & Martin, C. L. (1998). Gender development. In W. Damon (Series Ed.) & N. Eisenberg (Vol. Ed.), *Handbook of child psychology. Vol. 3: Social, emotional and personality development* (5th ed., pp. 933–1016). New York: Wiley.

Serbin, L. A., Moller, L. C., Gulko, J., Powlishta, K. K., & Colburne, K. A. (1994). The emergence of sex segregation in toddler playgroups. In W. Damon (Series Ed.) & C. Leaper (Vol. Ed.), *Childhood sex segregation: Causes and consequences* (New Directions for Child Development series, No. 65, pp. 7–17). San Francisco: Jossey-Bass.

Serbin, L. A., Poulin-Dubois, D., & Eichstedt, J. A. (1997, April). *The construction of gender concepts between 12 and 24 months.* Paper presented at the meetings of the Society for Research in Child Development, Washington, DC.

Serbin, L. A., & Sprafkin, C. (1986). The salience of gender and the process of sex-typing in three to seven year olds. *Child Development, 57,* 1188–1199.

Serbin, L. A., Sprafkin, C., Elman, M., & Doyle, A. B. (1984). The early development of sex differentiated patterns and social influence. *Canadian Journal of Social Science, 14,* 350–363.

Shell, R., & Eisenberg, N. (1990). The role of peers' gender in children's naturally occurring interest in toys. *International Journal of Behavioral Development, 13,* 373–388.

Signorella, M. L., Bigler, R. S., & Liben, L. S. (1993). Developmental differences

deregger (Vol. Ed.), *Nebraska Symposium on Motivation. Vol. 32. Psychology* and gender (pp. 59–95). Lincoln: University of Nebraska Press.

Spence, J. T. (1993). Gender-related traits and gender ideology: Evidence for a multifactorial theory. *Journal of Personality and Social Psychology, 64,* 624–635.

Spence, J. T., & Hall, S. K. (1996). Children's gender-related self-perceptions, activity preferences, and occupational stereotypes: A test of three models of gender constructs. *Sex Roles, 35,* 659–692.

Spence, J. T., & Helmreich, R. L. (1978). *Masculinity and femininity: Their psychological dimensions, correlates, and antecedents.* Austin: University of Texas Press.

Taylor, M. G. (1996). The development of children's beliefs about social and biological aspects of gender differences. *Child Development, 67,* 1555–1571.

Thorne, B. (1986). Girls and boys together, but mostly apart. In W. W. Hartup & K. Rubin (Eds.), *Relationship and development* (pp. 167–184). Hillsdale, NJ: Erlbaum.

Whiting, B. B., & Edwards, C. P. (1988). *Children of different worlds.* Cambridge, MA: Harvard University Press.

Zucker, K. J., Wilson-Smith, D. N. W., Kurita, J. A., & Stern, A. (1995). Children's appraisal of gender-typed behavior in their peers. *Sex Roles, 33,* 703–725.

4

A Shifting Standards Perspective

One of Janet Taylor Spence's many contributions to the understanding of gender is her argument that the gender construct is multifactorial or multidimensional in nature. Under the rubric of gender are the constructs of gender roles, gender stereotypes, gendered behavior, gender belief systems, sex typing, sexual orientation, gender identity, gender schematicity, and gender-related attitudes (e.g., traditionality, feminism, dislike of women). As Spence has noted, measures of these constructs are often unrelated to each other (Edwards & Spence, 1987; Spence, 1985, 1993; Spence & Sawin, 1985; see also Frable, 1989): With sex-typed personality traits, for example, individuals do not necessarily favor traditional roles for women or recall words in a gendered fashion; those who apply gender stereotypes to others are not necessarily sex-typed themselves. Furthermore, no single meaning of *masculinity* and *femininity* can be mapped onto oneself and others (Spence & Sawin, 1985), and much evidence suggests that measures of masculinity and femininity (or perhaps more appropriately, instrumentality and expressiveness) reflect independent as opposed to bipolar dimensions (Bem, 1974; Block, 1973; Carlson, 1971; Constantinople, 1973; Spence, Helmreich, & Stapp, 1975).

This chapter focuses on gender stereotypes and the processes by which they are used in evaluating individual women and men. Echoing Spence's theme of complexity in the gender construct, we recognize that gender stereotypes are also multidimensional in nature and that gender stereotyping effects appear in a variety of forms. After examining the diverse judgment patterns that have emerged in the literature on gender stereotyping, we describe the "shifting standards model" as a framework for understanding the assimilative as well as the sometimes absent and contrastive influences of gender stereotypes on social judgment.

GENDER STEREOTYPES AND STEREOTYPING

The multidimensionality of gender stereotypes is reflected in common definitions and perspectives. For example, Ashmore and Del Boca (1979) defined gender stereotypes very broadly as "structured sets of beliefs about the personal attributes of women and men" (p. 222), and these beliefs were assumed to include pictorial, behavioral, and affective components. Deaux and Lewis (1983, 1984) have distinguished among traits, roles, physical characteristics, occupations, and assumptions about sexual orientation as components of gender stereotypes; emotional dispositions may be reflected in stereotypes as well (Deaux & LaFrance, 1998). For Eckes (1994), the empirically derived set of components that comprise gender stereotypes are personality traits, attitudes and beliefs, overt behaviors and behavioral preferences, and physical appearance. Representations of these components reside under the general umbrella of gender stereotypes but may function relatively independently as they affect the impressions formed of individual women and men (see also Biernat, 1991). Gender stereotypes also likely contain information about the perceived variability within the categories of male and female (e.g., Park & Judd, 1990) as well as inferential links among the various components (Ashmore & Del Boca, 1979).

Studies of gender subtypes further indicate that representations of women and men are complex, differentiated, and in some cases overlapping, even though perhaps always tinged by the broader gender category (Clifton, McGrath, & Wick, 1976; Deaux, Winton, Crowley, & Lewis, 1985; Eckes, 1994; Edwards, 1992; Noseworthy & Lott, 1984; Six & Eckes, 1991; Taylor, 1981; Thompson & Pleck, 1987). For example, ~~~~~~ likely have cognitive representations of both businesswomen

in the diverse patterns of effects that emerge in research on gender-based person perception and impressions.

Diverse Patterns of Gender Stereotyping Effects

Perhaps the most common pattern is that gender stereotypes affect judgments of individuals in an *assimilative* fashion—men and women are judged consistently with broad gender stereotypes. This pattern is typically seen in research in which nothing or little else is known about a target person besides her or his gender or when individuating information about the person is irrelevant or ambiguous with regard to gender stereotypes (e.g., Hamilton & Sherman, 1994; Heilman, 1984; Heilman, Block, Martell, & Simon, 1989; Locksley, Borgida, Brekke, & Hepburn, 1980; Locksley, Hepburn, & Ortiz, 1982; Martin, 1989; Nelson, Biernat, & Manis, 1990; Rasinski, Crocker, & Hastie, 1985). For example, Locksley et al. (1980, Study 2) found that a male target was judged to be more assertive than a female target when only names were provided (Tom and Nancy). In another study, Nelson et al. found that photographs of male targets were consistently judged taller than photos of female targets, even when the targets were actually matched (across gender) in height, when participants were told of this matching, and when participants were offered a cash reward for accuracy. This tendency was especially marked when the targets were pictured in sitting as opposed to standing poses, which render height cues more ambiguous.

Under other conditions, however, a different pattern emerges. Considerable research indicates that the effects of gender stereotypes are *nullified* or "swamped" when perceivers have access to unambiguous or highly diagnostic individuating information (Biernat, 1991; Berndt & Heller, 1986; Deaux & Lewis, 1984; Dipboye & Wiley, 1977; Glick, Zion, & Nelson, 1988; Kunda & Thagard, 1996; Locksley et al., 1980).[1] Thus, in both children (Biernat, 1991) and adults (Deaux & Lewis, 1984), target individuals—male and female—who are described as having "feminine" physical characteristics (e.g., soft voice, dainty, delicate) are predicted to engage in feminine role behaviors and occupations (e.g., cares for children, decorates the home, works as a school teacher) to a much greater extent than masculine roles and occupations. Gender as a category is much less influential than gendered individuating information in making such inferences. Indeed, in Kunda and Thagard's (1996) meta-analysis of stereotyping research (which includes studies on gender as well as a variety of other group stereotypes), the average effect size for individuating information was much stronger ($r = .71$) than was the effect for stereotypes, even when no individuating information accompanied the category/stereotype information ($r = .25$).

In addition to assimilative and null effects, some gender stereotyping research indicates *contrastive* influences of gender stereotypes—that is, male and female targets are judged counterstereotypically, as when a woman is perceived to be more masculine than a man. Like null effects, this pattern generally occurs when unambiguous (typically stereotype-disconfirming) information is provided. For example, par-

---

[1]A related line of research looks at the *dilution effect*—the tendency for nondiagnostic individuating information to reduce or dilute the impact of stereotypes on judgments of individuals (Nisbett, Zukier, & Lemley, 1981; Zukier, 1982; Zukier & Jennings, 1984). For example, Nisbett et al. found that when no individuating information was provided, judges expected that an engineering student would be able to withstand more electric shock than a music major (i.e., assimilation to a stereotype about college majors). However, with the addition of individuating information about the target (e.g., that he was Catholic), the influence of the stereotype was significantly reduced. More recent research indicates that such apparently nondiagnostic individuating information may have diluted the influence of the stereotype because it had "typical diagnosticity": Although irrelevant to electric shock tolerance, the knowledge that someone is Catholic has broad relevance or implications across many judgment domains (Fein & Hilton, 1992; Hilton & Fein, 1989). These latter authors demonstrated that the impact of stereotypes is not diluted in the presence of "clearly irrelevant" individuating information, as we indicated above.

ticipants in a study by Abramson, Goldberg, Greenberg, and Abramson (1977) judged female targets (particularly, female attorneys) to be more vocationally competent than analogous male targets (see also Williams, ⁓ ⁓ ⁓ that men in feminine occupations are

candidates were ⁓⁓⁓⁓ visory position than male candidates (Dipboye & Wiley, 1977), a woman's performance in an emergency was viewed as better than the same performance by a man (Taynor & Deaux, 1973), and men described as incompetent were evaluated as less competent and less intelligent than similarly incompetent women (Deaux & Taynor, 1973).

The Confirmatory Influence of Gender Stereotypes

In short, the literature suggests that gender stereotypes may affect judgments of individual men and women in complex and seemingly contradictory ways: Impressions may be assimilated to, contrasted from, or uninfluenced by a target's gender. However, before taking these latter two patterns at face value and concluding that the average effect of gender stereotypes is null, it is worth examining them more closely. Our premise is that despite their surface features, both the absent and contrastive judgment effects described above may nonetheless be steeped in the (confirmatory) influence of gender stereotypes.

First, even in studies that demonstrate relatively little influence of gender stereotypes relative to diagnostic individuating information, some findings continue to document the important role gender stereotypes play in impressions. For example, Deaux and Lewis (1984, Study 3) found that target gender consistently affected subsequent impressions, even in the presence of unambiguous personality trait information: "Emotional, kind, understanding, and helpful" targets were judged to have other feminine qualities to a greater extent than "active and self-confident" individuals who "never gave up easily" and "stood up well under pressure" (attributes from Spence, Helmreich, & Stapp's, 1974, Personal Attributes Questionnaire [PAQ]). But independent of this, female targets were judged to be more feminine and less masculine (in roles, occupational preferences, and physical attributes) than were comparable male targets. Biernat (1991) also found that despite a strong influence of gendered individuating information, participants' judgments were still highly affected by a target's gender category; this effect was reliable and stable across all age groups included in the sample (kindergarten through college).

Second, in other studies, researchers have found no effects of gender stereotypes on some dependent measures but strong effects on others. For example, Glick et al. (1988) found that personality and job suitability judgments were equivalent for male and female applicants who were both described as having "worked during summers in retail sales at a sporting goods store, had a work–study job with the campus grounds maintenance crew, and been captain of the [men's or women's] varsity basketball team" (p. 180). However, participants were nonetheless significantly more likely to interview the man than the woman for a traditionally masculine job and the woman than the man for a traditionally feminine job.

Similarly, a number of researchers have found that behavioral predictions may be affected by gender stereotypes, even when trait judgments are not: Berndt and Heller (1986) reported no effects of an actor's sex on judgments of personality traits (e.g., aggressive, emotional) but strong effects on estimates of future behavioral choices (e.g., Will the boy choose to fix a bicycle or bake brownies?), particularly among young respondents (kindergarten through sixth grade; see Kunda & Thagard, 1996, for a further discussion of the effects of stereotypes on behavioral predictions).

For the remainder of this chapter, we focus on a perspective that attempts to integrate and explain these diverse patterns of gender stereotyping effects; it offers additional reasons to suspect that null and contrastive influences of gender stereotypes on impressional judgments are more apparent than real. This is the shifting standards model of Biernat and her colleagues (Biernat, 1995; Biernat & Kobrynowicz, 1997; Biernat & Manis, 1994; Biernat, Manis, & Nelson, 1991). Before turning ~~~~ ~~~~~~ ~~ ~~~ ~~~~~ ~~ ~~~~ ~~~~ ~~ ~~~~~~~~~~~~ the general

sense, the shifting standards model adds additional complexity to the intricate structural and process features of gender stereotyping described earlier, highlighting that the influence of gender stereotypes can be measured in different ways (in shorthand for now, either "objectively" or "subjectively") with very different effects.

THE SHIFTING STANDARDS MODEL

The shifting standards model makes the argument that gender stereotypes, in addition to serving as interpretive frameworks (as is frequently assumed in the stereotyping literature; see von Hippel, Sekaquaptewa, & Vargas, 1995), function as standards of comparison. That is, holding a gender stereotype (e.g., that men are more aggressive than women) leads the perceiver to judge individual men and women relative to within-group reference points on the stereotyped dimension: A man is judged relative to men in general, and a woman is judged relative to other women. The result is that subjective evaluations of individuals from different social groups may sometimes reveal equivalent perceptions (e.g., an individual man and woman may both be described as aggressive), when underlying this apparent equivalence are gender-typed perceptions and impressions. Given that she is compared with a lower aggressiveness standard, an aggressive woman is presumably surpassing the expectations for her sex, whereas an aggressive man is meeting the expectations for his sex. Even though the judgment is equivalent, the meaning differs by sex; furthermore, were the two individuals directly compared, the label aggressive would likely translate into the choice of the man as the objectively more aggressive of the two (Kobrynowicz, 1997). Viewing this example from a different angle, Biernat and Manis (1994, Study 4) found that specific aggressive behaviors were more likely to be seen as diagnostic of aggression in a woman (Linda) than in a man (Larry), presumably because of low standards of aggression for women.

The stereotype that men are more athletic than women provides yet another example. When male and female softball players were described as highly competent batters (e.g., batting .450 for their coed softball teams), women were judged better than were men on a *very poor player* to *very good player* rating scale—a contrast effect (Biernat & Vescio, 1998). This gender difference presumably occurred because .450 was well above (low) female standards. Does this evidence suggest that gender stereotyping on the softball field was overcome? The answer is *no* because in this same study, Biernat and Vescio documented a bias against the highly competent female—she was less likely than the comparable male to be placed in the top of the batting order.

A central theme of the shifting standards model is that because the language of judgment and evaluation is typically subjective in nature, perceivers are able to impose their own meaning on judgment units. The source of meaning derives, at least in part, from group stereotypes. The terms *good* or *bad, tall* or *short, emotional* or *unemotional,* therefore, denote different things when they are applied to men than to women: They imply, for example, "emotional, for a woman" or "short, for a man," even when these tags are not explicit. Thus, respondents' judgments of target individuals on subjective (e.g., Likert-type or semantic-differential) rating scales may mask the influence of underlying stereotypes, in that judgment units are interpreted in relation to those very stereotypes. In general, we argue that whenever respondents are supplied with a subjective judgment scale on which to rate individual group members, they adjust the end anchors of the scales so as to reflect the expected distribution of group members on the attribute being judged (see Parducci, 1963, 1965; Upshaw, 1962, 1969; and Volk-mann, 1951, for evidence of this theme in psychophysical and other judgment domains). This scale adjustment is imposed for each group judged, and in that sense, standards and judgment unit meanings shift.

information about credentials) were judged to have equal likelihood of success on the job (when rated on a 1 [*very unlikely to be successful*] to 9 [*very likely to be successful*] scale). This study is described above as evidence for the null effects of gender stereotypes under some conditions. However, if the shifting standards account is correct, these null effects do not indicate that gender stereotypes are ignored or "swamped"; instead, it is precisely because stereotypes are imposed on the judgment task that the male and female targets are judged comparably. Success on the job for a female worker may mean something quite different from success on the job for a male worker (Biernat & Kobrynowicz, 1997); that meaning derives from the gender stereotype that men are more career-oriented than are women. The broader statement that derives from the shifting standards model is this: Research on gender stereotyping likely underestimates the strength of stereotyping effects. Researchers miscalculate the influence of gender stereotypes on judgments of individual targets whenever they ask respondents to make their evaluations in "slippery," subjective language.

The shifting standards model also suggests a method for overcoming the interpretational difficulty that arises from the use of subjective rating scales: Participants should be provided with judgment scales that do not allow them to shift or adjust the meaning of judgment units. We have referred to response scales of this sort as objective, "externally anchored," or "common rule" scales. Essentially, a judgment scale is *objective* if its response units have a constant meaning, regardless of the attributes of the target to which they are applied. For example, one could judge height in subjective *short* to *tall* units or in feet and inches. Short and tall are subjective terms, but an inch is objective because it is applied equally well to men and women, with no change in meaning (an inch is an inch). In our research on height judgments, we have shown, for example, that men and women who are described as equally tall (a null effect of gender stereotypes) are nonetheless perceived to differ in feet and inches—tall for a man translates into a height of about 6' 3.5" (1.92 m), whereas tall for a woman translates to about 5' 9" (1.75 m; Biernat et al., 1991; see also Roberts & Herman, 1986). Because they cannot shift in meaning across rating categories, objective rating units (inches, pounds, minutes, dollars) are more likely than subjective rating units to reveal evidence of (assimilative) gender stereotyping effects.

Below, we review some research from our laboratory that documents this effect in a variety of judgment domains, using a number of different methodologies. These studies indicate that even when some judgment evidence suggests that gender stereotypes have been overcome or overridden, stereotypes are nonetheless lurking—coloring perceivers' impressions of individual men and women.

Comparing Subjective and Objective Judgments of Women and Men

In initial research examining whether subjective judgments mask the influence of gender stereotypes, participants judged the heights and weights of a series of photographed women and men (Biernat et al., 1991). Thus, in this work, Biernat et al. examined the (accurate) gender stereotypes that on average, men are taller and weigh more than women. Results clearly indicate that when judgments were made in objective units (feet and inches, pounds), they were consistent with these stereotypes; when judgments were made in subjective units (*short–tall, light–heavy*), stereotyping effects were significantly reduced. Such a pattern is consistent with the notion that subjective judgments of men's and women's heights and weights are based on within-category comparisons. Men and women might each be judged as equally "heavy" when objectively the man might be perceived to weigh about 40 pounds (18.14 kg) more. The pattern of stronger evidence of stereotyping on

(information was provided that the average person [males and females included] can lift between 70 and 170 pounds (31.75–77.11 kg) up off the ground). Similar to the results described above, objective estimates indicated significant gender stereotyping effects (men, on average, were judged capable of lifting more weight than women lift), but subjective strength estimates significantly reduced this pattern. This Target Sex × Response Scale interaction was reliable for judgments of both White and Black targets.

Still, these findings appear on judgment dimensions that are not in the typical province of stereotyping researchers. Biernat et al. (1991) did, however, examine one dimension that is more closely linked to the concerns of gender researchers: gender-based perceptions of income and earning potential. Using the same photographic stimuli described earlier, participants were asked to judge the personal income of a series of 40 men and women on either objective or subjective scales. In the objective condition, participants estimated targets' yearly personal income (in dollars), whereas in the subjective condition, participants rated how "financially successful" the individual was, on a 1 (*financially very unsuccessful*) to 7 (*financially very successful*) rating scale. Male targets were judged to earn significantly more money (in dollars) than were female targets. However, the subjective judgments revealed a surprising reversal of this pattern, a contrast effect. The same women who were objectively judged to earn, on average, about $9,000 less per year than the target men were subjectively seen as more financially successful than the men. The contrast, we argue, is due to differential standards for financial success in women than in men—women can earn less and still be seen as relatively successful as compared with other women.[2]

Gender beliefs about height, weight, strength, and income have one quality that distinguishes them from many other gender-related conceptions: They are accurate stereotypes. They nonetheless conform to Ashmore and Del Boca's (1979) definition of gender stereotypes, and they nicely reflect the physical characteristics and role components of gender stereotypes described by Deaux and Lewis (1984). However, we also have evidence that shifting standards effects operate on judgment dimensions that reflect the more traditional traitlike conception of gender stereotypes.

For example, the stereotype that women are more verbally able than men presumably leads perceivers to judge individual women and men relative to within-sex judgment standards on this dimension; these standards are higher for women than for men. Biernat and Manis (1994, Study 2) asked participants to view high school yearbook photographs of 20 men and 20 women. Accompanying each photograph were two vocabulary definitions that the pictured individual had presumably provided in an oral vocabulary test. These definitions were included to provide some basis for judging verbal skills, and they had earlier been pretested for perceived thought disturbance (verbal skill) so that they could be matched on this dimension across target sex. Half of the participants judged verbal skill subjectively, using a 1 (*very low verbal ability*) to 7 (*very high verbal ability*) judgment scale, whereas the other half estimated the letter grade that they believed each individual earned in their high school English courses. Biernat and Manis conceptualized letter grades as relatively objective or externally anchored in nature, in that their assignment is presumably based on standards of performance that do not fluctuate for members of different groups—an A means

---

[2]Recall that subjective height and weight judgments reveal a reduction of stereotyping effects, whereas subjective financial status judgments show a reverse-stereotyping effect (contrast). Elsewhere, it has been argued that contrast is more likely to occur when stereotypes are strong, such that little overlap is perceived in the distributions of men and women on the dimension of interest, and when individuating information is stereotype inconsistent (see Biernat et al., 1991; and Biernat, Vescio, & Manis, 1998).

an "A," regardless of who has received it (in a pretest sample, 91% of undergraduates also believed letter grades to be objective as opposed to subjective in nature).

~~Ex~~ ~~indicate that~~ when verbal ability estimates were made in

~~of the study~~

centage of women than of men with high verbal ability. Twenty-nine percent indicated no perceived group difference, and 25% indicated that they thought men were more verbally able than women. Analyses within each group of participants indicate that the signature shifting standards pattern (stronger stereotyping on objective than subjective judgments) was only reliable among individuals who endorsed the stereotype. This lends further credence to the model's suggestion that stereotypes are responsible for the use of within-gender judgment standards.

A study of gender stereotypes regarding competence also provides evidence of standard shifts (Biernat & Manis, 1994, Study 1). In addition, this study suggests that rather than holding global stereotypes that women are less competent than men, perceivers are more likely to view competence as context specific: Men are more competent than are woman at masculine tasks; women are more competent than men at feminine tasks. This study was based on the famous Goldberg (1968) "Joan McKay–John McKay" research, in which female participants judged written work to be higher in quality when it was attributed to a male rather than female author. In 1989, Swim, Borgida, Maruyama, and Myers published a meta-analysis of 20 years of research in the Joan–John tradition and found that in fact, the male–female evaluative bias was negligible (effect size [d] was around $-.07$). Biernat and Manis suggested that one reason for this null effect of gender stereotypes might be that researchers have typically provided their respondents with subjective scales on which to make their evaluations. If competence is assessed in a within-sex fashion, subjective judgments may mask the influence of gender stereotypes.

In Biernat and Manis's (1994) study, participants read an excerpt of a magazine article that was attributed to either Joan T. McKay or John T. McKay and concerned either a masculine (e.g., bass fishing), feminine (e.g., trends in eye makeup), or neutral (e.g., the mind–body problem) topic. Participants were asked to evaluate the quality, monetary worth, and interest level of the article, either using objective or subjective response scales (e.g., monetary worth in dollars that an editor would pay for the article or on a *very little money* to *lots of money* rating scale).

When judgments were made in objective units, evidence of gender stereotyping was clear: Feminine articles were better when written by Joan than by John, masculine articles were better when written by John than by Joan, and neutral articles were judged equivalently, regardless of the author's sex. Subjective judgments produced results consistent with the meta-analysis findings: Author's sex had no impact on evaluation. This suggests, then, that participants judged the article quality using an Author's Sex × Context evaluative framework. Despite a willingness to pay authors more when their sex "matched" the article topic (John deserves more than Joan for his article on bass fishing), this "translated" into equivalent subjective evaluations (for a woman, Joan's article on fishing is pretty good; for a man, John's article on eye makeup is okay).

In an additional study on gender stereotypes and competence, this time in a work setting, participants evaluated the resume of "Katherine Anderson" or "Kenneth Anderson," who had applied for either a masculine (executive chief of staff) or feminine (executive secretary) position (Biernat & Kobrynowicz, 1997). In reality, the job description provided to participants was identical across positions, only the title was changed. Pretesting indicated that when the title "chief of staff" was attached to the description, the job was perceived to be more masculine, higher in status, and more likely to command a high salary than the same position appended with the "secretary" title. Consistent with the previously described methodology, half the participants evaluated the applicant on objective rating scales (e.g., assigned letter grade, percentage likelihood of promotion in the position) and half on subjective scales (e.g., *poor quality* to *high quality, competent* to *incompetent*).

Results in this study were comparable with those in the Joan

cant for the feminine job as "very good, for a man, and the female applicant for the masculine job as "very good, for a woman."

In this work, as in the other research described above, we conceptualize objective evaluations as more likely than subjective evaluations to reflect perceivers' true mental representations of targets. The reason is that objective ratings are relatively impervious to the shifts or adjustments of response unit meaning that can render cross-gender comparisons untenable. The research has shown that these mental representations of individual targets are consistently influenced by gender stereotypes, even when ratings on subjective response scales may indicate otherwise.

Rankings and Paired-Choice Comparisons

Another means of testing and establishing the point that objective judgments provide a better reflection of perceivers' mental representations comes from research in which participants directly compare (e.g., rank order) men and women on a single response continuum. Rank ordering requires the use of a common rule scale for all individuals in the ranking pool, regardless of their social group membership (i.e., separate rankings for women and men are not possible). In this sense, rank orderings and paired-choice comparisons meet our criteria of objectivity—units have a constant meaning (e.g., position 1 is position 1), regardless of who is assigned to it.

In one study on paired-choice comparisons, participants read descriptions of two targets, one male and one female, who were each described as having engaged in a series of five aggressive behaviors (e.g., responding to someone's insult with an even worse insult, asking a person sitting nearby at a ballgame not to smoke; Kobrynowicz, 1997). In Locksley et al.'s (1980) well-known research on perceptions of assertiveness, male and female targets who each engaged in assertive behaviors were judged to be equally assertive, suggesting that gender stereotypes were ignored. However, in this study (Kobrynowicz, 1997), clear patterns of gender stereotyping emerged when participants made paired-choice comparisons of the aggressive female and the aggressive male targets. Specifically, despite the equivalence in their behaviors, the male target was chosen as the more aggressive of the pair in 67% of cases. Furthermore, respondents were also asked to indicate which member of the pair had "more of" a series of other attributes. These were the 40 items of Spence, Helmreich, and Holahan's (1979) Extended Personal Attributes Questionnaire (EPAQ). Paired-choice judgments on each of these trait sets indicate strong influences of gender stereotypes. As can be seen in Table 1, the female target was chosen significantly more often than the male target on negative feminine, positive feminine,

Table 1
Paired Choice Comparisons on EPAQ Trait Sets of Aggressive Female and Male Targets

EPAQ trait set	% female over male choice
Feminine–negative	65
Feminine–positive	63
Masculine–negative	42
Masculine–positive	30
Neutral–negative	60
Neutral–positive	45

Note. Data from Kobrynowicz (1997). EPAQ = Extended Personal Attributes Questionnaire (Spence et al., 1979).

and negative neutral attributes and significantly less often than the male target on negative masculine and positive masculine attributes. In other words, impressions of these equivalently behaving individuals were markedly gender typed.[3]

pattern—greater evidence of stereotyping on objective (in this case, rank orders) than subjective judgment scales—is evident in a "real-world" context, in which meaningful, consequential judgments are made of live targets. To do this, they conducted a study of perceptions of leadership competence at an U.S. Army training facility in Fort Leavenworth, Kansas.

Participants in this study were 100 U.S. Army captains who were attending a required 9-week leadership training course. Most of the participants were male ($n = 89$) and White ($n = 79$). For the duration of this course, the Army assigned captains to 12- or 13-person groups; the Army's policy is to establish these groups such that each includes at least one woman, several ethnic minorities, and individuals from different branches of the Army (e.g., combat arms, combat support, combat service support). At three times during the 9-week course, Biernat et al. (in press) asked participants to both rank and rate their group mates (including themselves) on their overall effectiveness as "leaders/commanders."

Considerable research documents that leadership competence is a

---

[3]The 40 items of the EPAQ were intentionally developed and included in the instrument because they were stereotyped—the typical man and woman were perceived to differ on these attributes. In Kobrynowicz's study, a specific aggressive female target and a specific aggressive male target were perceived to differ as well. Without both group and individual judgments in the same study, however, we cannot assess whether the general tendency toward gender stereotyping was intensified or reduced on these dimensions in the case of targets who displayed the masculine attribute of aggressiveness.

marked component of gender stereotypes (Bem, 1974; Eagly, Karau, & Makhijani, 1995; Eagly, Makhijani, & Klonsky, 1992), and Eagly et al.'s (1995) meta-analysis indicates that studies conducted in military settings are particularly likely to find gender bias in perceptions of leadership effectiveness ($d = .42$, with men faring better than women). The shifting standards model suggests, then, that leadership ability is likely to be evaluated on a within-gender basis. Therefore, Biernat et al. (in press) anticipated that subjective evaluations, which are prone to gender-based standard shifts, would tend to mask the effects of stereotyping but that rank orderings—because they force the arrangement of men and women on a single continuum—would document a strong influence of the gender stereotype that men are better leaders than are women.

Biernat et al. (in press) examined the effects of the captains' sex on the leadership evaluations they received from their group mates (excluding themselves) by first controlling for a variety of status factors (including "merit," as indicated by number and prestige of captains' earned medals and badges, previous combat deployment, years at rank of captain, branch of service, and race). By this method, any effects of target sex could not be attributed to differences between men and women on these dimensions. At each temporal period, male captains were ranked as better leaders than were female captains, and this tendency increased over time; however, subjective rating differences between women and men were never significant. In short, these data provide decisive evidence that rank orderings may reveal evidence of stereotyping effects, even when trait ratings do not, and that the shifting standards model applies to meaningful judgments of real-world targets.

Translating Language From Subjective to Objective

Implicit in research on the shifting standards model is the notion that subjective evaluations are differentially translated into objective estimates for women and for men—for example, a subjective rating of 4 on verbal ability is interpreted to mean a higher grade in English courses if a target is female rather than male. However, in none of the work described thus far have perceivers been explicitly asked to decode subjective language into objective estimates. But we did ask this explicit question in a study of gender stereotypes about parenting—namely, that mothers do more for their children than do fathers (Kobrynowicz

children? How many days a week does the parent make lunch for the children? How many school functions does the parent attend? How many of the children's "favorite things" does the parent know? etc.). In each of the broad categories of activities—emotional needs, physical needs, and centrality of the children in the parent's life—mothers were judged to engage in parenting behaviors with greater frequency than were fathers. This was true in the case of both the very good and all right parents. Both evaluative labels translated into more frequent behaviors for mothers than for fathers, presumably because mothers are held to a higher standard of involvement with children than are fathers (see Chesler, 1991).

In summary, the shifting standards perspective argues that because stereotypes function as standards of comparison, their effects on judgments of individual men and women may be particularly "stealthy." Subjective language of the sort used in everyday conversation and in much of stereotyping research serves to mask the differences people perceive between men and women at a representational level because the meaning of subjective language is discerned relative to group expectations. Thus, the conclusion that some have come to—that stereotypes are easily overridden by individuating information—may not be accurate. This is not to deny that perceivers do attend to individuating information; for example, verbally able targets are consistently judged higher in verbal ability than nonable targets, and applicants with strong credentials are evaluated more favorably than those with weak credentials. But, nonetheless, stereotypes continue to exert a (sometimes hidden) influence on the judgment process.

EXTENSIONS OF THE SHIFTING STANDARDS MODEL

Self Standards

Our research on stereotype-based shifting standards in the judgment of individual men and women has led us to the question of whether people use gender-based standards in judgments of themselves. This is admittedly not a novel issue, as years of research on social comparison processes suggests that people compare themselves (i.e., assess their opinions and abilities) with similar others (Festinger, 1954; see also Goethals & Darley, 1977; and Wood, 1989) and that "similarity" is often based on social category membership, such as gender (e.g., Buunk & VanYperen, 1991; Major, 1989, 1993; Major & Forcey, 1985; Major & Testa, 1989; Zanna, Goethals, & Hill, 1975). Major and Testa, for example, found that women and men tend to make within-sex rather than cross-sex comparisons of their jobs and wages.

Furthermore, there is considerable evidence that as a consequence of self-categorization processes, individuals engage in *self-stereotyping*—ascribing to themselves the attributes of their group (e.g., Biernat, Vescio, & Green, 1996; Hardie & McMurray, 1992; Haslam, Oakes, Turner, & McGarty, 1996; Hogg & Turner, 1987; Lau, 1989; Lorenzi-Cioldi, 1991; Simon, Glässner-Bayerl, & Stratenwerth, 1991; Simon & Hamilton, 1994; Turner, 1982; Turner, Hogg, Oakes, Reicher, & Wetherell, 1987). To the extent, then, that the self is considered a member of a stereotyped group and to the extent that a comparison of the self to in-group others occurs, the processes previously outlined for stereotype-based judgment of others may also apply to the self. That is, the use of within-category judgment standards may lead to reductions of self-stereotyping effects on subjective compared with objective judgment scales.

In the study of U.S. Army captains described earlier, Biernat et al.

(in press) examined how individual's self-judgments of leadership competence, on both ratings and rankings, were affected by gender. In both groups including only one woman ("solos") and those including two women captains' gender clearly mattered. At Time 1, for example,

periods later in the training course, groups with solo women continued to show this pattern, suggesting that the presence of a solo woman in a group may have exacerbated the tendency to use within-category judgment standards, especially over time. In the groups that included two women, however, this pattern disappeared. These findings are generally consistent with research suggesting that solo contexts, relative to nonsolo contexts, produce increased (a) salience of the relevant category cue, (b) attention to the solo member, and (c) stereotyping (see Biernat & Vescio, 1993; Kanter, 1977; Pettigrew & Martin, 1987; and Taylor, Fiske, Etcoff, & Ruderman, 1978).

Qualitative Differences in Judgments of Women and Men

All the work we have discussed thus far has focused on the quantitative differences that people perceive between men and women—for example, men are more aggressive than women, and women have more verbal ability than do men. However, stereotypic beliefs also are likely to differ in qualitative ways as well. For example, women may not simply be perceived as more "emotional" than men, but one may think of their emotionality as qualitatively different than that of men; men may not only be thought of as more athletic than women, but the expected form of their athleticism may differ. One way to examine this qualitative difference is to look at the language people "spontaneously" use to describe male and female targets. In the study by Kobrynowicz (1997) mentioned earlier, participants were provided with descriptions of male and female targets who had each engaged in a series of five aggressive behaviors and then were asked to indicate the first word that came into their minds to describe the target. The data presented in Table 2 reflect the great diversity in these descriptions. The modal first word description of the aggressive woman was "bitch" or "bitchy"; the modal response for the man was "aggressive" (with "asshole" and "jerk" close behind). Independent judges rated the genderedness of each of these words; words used to describe the female target were significantly more likely to indicate femaleness than were those assigned to the male target. These data only scratch the surface of the many subtle ways in which men and women are perceived as qualitatively different, despite equivalent behavior descriptions.

CONCLUSION

The construct of *gender* is complex, gender stereotypes are complex, and gender stereotyping effects appear to be complicated and often contradictory. Nonetheless, with the appropriate methods, we can clarify this complexity. Indeed, one of the lessons Spence conveyed throughout her career is that complexity of this sort can be understood by listening to how individuals talk about gender (Spence, 1985; Spence & Sawin, 1985) and through the use of multiple methods and measures (Spence, 1993; Spence & Hall, 1996). In this chapter, we argued that the diverse patterns of gender stereotyping effects documented in the literature—assimilation, contrast, and apparent null effects—can all be understood, within the shifting standards paradigm, as reflecting the powerful, but sometimes hidden, influence of gender stereotypes as interpretive frameworks and as standards of comparison. What hides this influence is research methodology that allows respondents to subjectively construe the meaning of evaluative language.

It is also the case that various situational factors may operate to increase the likelihood that gender stereotypes will influence impressions of individual men and women (e.g., the relative ratio of women to men in a work setting [Crocker & McGraw, 1982; Kanter, 1977]; environments that prime the concept of women as sex objects [Borgida,

Table 2

First-Word Descriptions of "Aggressive" Female and Male Targets

	Female target ($n = 27$)		Male target ($n = 26$)	
Cocky	—		2	(7.7%)
Confident	2	(7.4%)	—	
Conservative	—		1	
Controlling	1		—	
Demanding	1		1	
Dominant	—		1	
Egotistical	—		1	
Fun	1		—	
Inconsiderate	1		1	
Jerk	—		3	(11.1%)
Normal	—		1	
Overaggressive	1		—	
Pushy	2	(7.4%)	1	
Reckless	—		1	
Rude	2	(7.4%)	2	(7.7%)
Self-centered	1		—	
Selfish	1		1	
Smart	—		1	
Snob	1		—	
Snobby	1		—	
Snotty	1		—	
Stuck-up	1		—	
Tricky	1		—	

Note. Data from Kobrynowicz (1997). — = term was not mentioned.

Rudman, & Manteufel, 1995; McKenzie-Mohr & Zanna, 1990; Rudman & Borgida, 1995], and in laboratory settings, whether a picture of the target is available or not [Beckett & Park, 1995]). Such factors may tip the impressional balance in a stereotypic direction, even if other factors (e.g., the presence of much individuating information) work against it. Our message here is simple and pessimistic: Gender stereotypes continue to color perceptions of individual men and women, even when it appears they do not.

REFERENCES

Abramson, P. R., Goldberg, P. A., Greenberg, J. H., & Abramson, L. M. (1977). The talking platypus phenomenon: Competency ratings as a function of sex and professional status. *Psychology of Women Quarterly, 2,* 114–124.

Ashmore, R. D., & Del Boca, F. K. (1979). Sex stereotypes and implicit personality theory: Toward a cognitive-social psychological conceptualization. *Sex Roles, 5,* 219–248.

Beckett, N. E., & Park, B. (1995). Use of category versus individuating information: Making base rates salient. *Personality and Social Psychology Bulletin, 21,* 21–31.

Bem, S. L. (1974). The measurement of psychological androgyny. *Journal of Consulting and Clinical Psychology, 42,* 155–162.

Berndt, T. J., & Heller, K. A. (1986). Gender stereotypes and social inferences: A developmental study. *Journal of Personality and Social Psychology, 50,* 889–898.

Biernat, M. (1991). Gender stereotypes and the relationship between masculinity and femininity: A developmental analysis. *Journal of Personality and Social Psychology, 61,* 351–365.

Biernat, M. (1995). The shifting standards model: Implications of stereotype accuracy for social judgment. In Y. T. Lee, L. J. Jussim, & C. R. McCauley (Eds.), *Stereotype accuracy: Toward appreciating group differences* (pp. 87–114). Washington, DC: American Psychological Association.

Biernat, M., Crandall, C. S., Young, L. V., Kobrynowicz, D., & Halpin, S. M. (in press). All that you can be: Stereotyping of self and others in a military context. *Journal of Personality and Social Psychology.*

Biernat, M., & Kobrynowicz, D. (1997). Gender- and race-based standards of competence: Lower minimum standards but higher ability standards for devalued groups. *Journal of Personality and Social Psychology, 72*, 544–557.

Biernat, M., & Manis, M. (1994). Shifting standards and stereotype-based judgments. *Journal of Personality and Social Psychology, 66*, 5–20.

sas, Lawrence.

Biernat, M., Vescio, T. K., & Green, M. L. (1996). Selective self-stereotyping. *Journal of Personality and Social Psychology, 71*, 1194–1209.

Biernat, M., Vescio, T. K., & Manis, M. (1998). Judging and behaving toward members of stereotyped groups: A shifting standards perspective. In C. Sedikides, J. Schopler, & C. Insko (Eds.), *Intergroup cognition and intergroup behavior* (pp. 151–175). Hillsdale, NJ: Erlbaum.

Block, J. H. (1973). Conceptions of sex role: Some cross-cultural and longitudinal perspectives. *American Psychologist, 28*, 512–526.

Borgida, E., Rudman, L. A., & Manteufel, L. L. (1995). On the courtroom use and misuse of gender stereotyping research. *Journal of Social Issues, 51*, 181–192.

Brewer, M. B. (1996). When stereotypes lead to stereotyping: The use of stereotypes in person perception. In C. N. Macrae, C. Stangor, & M. Hewstone (Eds.), *Stereotypes and stereotyping* (pp. 254–275). New York: Guilford Press.

Buunk, B. P., & VanYperen, N. W. (1991). Referential comparisons, relational comparisons, and exchange orientation: Their relation to marital satisfaction. *Personality and Social Psychology Bulletin, 17*, 709–717.

Carlson, R. (1971). Sex differences in ego functioning. *Journal of Consulting and Clinical Psychology, 37*, 267–277.

Chesler, P. (1991). Mothers on trial: The custodial vulnerability of women. *Feminism and Psychology, 1*, 409–425.

Clifton, A. K., McGrath, D., & Wick, B. (1976). Stereotypes of women: A single category? *Sex Roles, 2*, 135–148.

Constantinople, A. (1973). Masculinity–femininity: An exception to the famous dictum? *Psychological Bulletin, 80,* 389–407.

Costrich, N., Feinstein, J., Kidder, L., Marecek, J., & Pascale, L. (1975). When stereotypes hurt: Three studies of penalties for sex-role reversals. *Journal of Experimental Social Psychology, 11,* 520–530.

Crocker, J., & McGraw, M. M. (1982). What's good for the goose is not for the gander: Solo status as an obstacle to occupational achievement for males and females. *American Behavioral Scientist, 27,* 357–369.

Deaux, K., & LaFrance, M. (1998). Gender. In D. T. Gilbert, S. T. Fiske, & G. Lindzey (Eds.), *The handbook of social psychology* (4th ed., pp. 788–827). New York: McGraw-Hill.

Deaux, K., & Lewis, L. L. (1983). Assessments of gender stereotypes: Methodology and components. *Psychological Documents, 13,* 25 (Ms. 2583).

Deaux, K., & Lewis, L. L. (1984). Structure of gender stereotypes: Interrelationships among components and gender label. *Journal of Personality and Social Psychology, 46,* 991–1004.

Deaux, K., & Taynor, J. (1973). Evaluation of male and female ability: Bias works two ways. *Psychological Reports, 32,* 261–262.

Deaux, K., Winton, W., Crowley, M., & Lewis, L. L. (1985). Level of categorization and content of gender stereotypes. *Social Cognition, 3,* 145–167.

Dipboye, R. L., & Wiley, J. W. (1977). Reactions of college recruiters to interviewee sex and self-presentation style. *Journal of Vocational Behavior, 10,* 1–12.

Eagly, A. H., Karau, S. J., & Makhijani, M. G. (1995). Gender and the effectiveness of leaders: A meta-analysis. *Psychological Bulletin, 117,* 125–145.

Eagly, A. H., Makhijani, M. G., & Klonsky, B. G. (1992). Gender and the evaluation of leaders: A meta-analysis. *Psychological Bulletin, 111,* 3–22.

Eagly, A. H., & Steffen, V. J. (1984). Gender stereotypes stem from the distribution of women and men into social roles. *Journal of Personality and Social Psychology, 46,* 735–754.

Eckes, T. (1994). Explorations in gender cognition: Content and structure of female and male subtypes. *Social Cognition, 12,* 37–60.

Edwards, G. H. (1992). The structure and content of the male gender role stereotype: An exploration of subtypes. *Sex Roles, 27,* 533–551.

Edwards, V. J., & Spence, J. T. (1987). Gender-related traits, stereotypes, and schemata. *Journal of Personality and Social Psychology, 53,* 146–154.

Fein, S., & Hilton, J. L. (1992). Attitudes toward groups and behavioral intentions toward individual group members: The impact of nondiagnostic information. *Journal of Experimental Social Psychology, 28,* 101–124.

Human Relations,

Goethals, G. R., & Darley, J. M. butional approach. In J. Suls & R. Miller (Eds.), *Social comparison processes: Theoretical and empirical perspectives* (pp. 259–278). Washington, DC: Hemisphere.

Goldberg, P. (1968). Are women prejudiced against women? *Transaction, 5,* 178–186.

Hamilton, D. L., & Sherman, J. W. (1994). Stereotypes. In R. S. Wyer & T. K. Srull (Eds.), *Handbook of social cognition* (Vol. 2, pp. 1–68). Hillsdale, NJ: Erlbaum.

Hardie, E. A., & McMurray, N. E. (1992). Self stereotyping, sex role ideology, and menstrual attitudes: A social identity approach. *Sex Roles, 27,* 17–37.

Haslam, S. A., Oakes, P. J., Turner, J. C., & McGarty, C. (1996). Social identity, self-categorization, and the perceived homogeneity of ingroups and outgroups: The interaction between social motivation and cognition. In R. M Sorrentino & E. T. Higgins (Eds.), *Handbook of motivation and cognition. Vol. 3: The interpersonal context* (pp. 182–222). New York: Guilford . Press.

Heilman, M. E. (1984). Information as a deterrent against sex discrimination: The effects of applicant sex and information type on preliminary employment decisions. *Organizational Behavior and Human Performance, 33,* 174–186.

Heilman, M. E., Block, C. J., Martell, R. F., & Simon, M. C. (1989). Has anything changed? Current characterizations of men, women, and managers. *Journal of Applied Psychology, 74,* 935–942.

Hilton, J. L., & Fein, S. (1989). The role of typical diagnosticity in stereotype-based judgments. *Journal of Personality and Social Psychology, 57,* 201–211.

Hogg, M. A., & Turner, J. C. (1987). Intergroup behaviour, self-stereotyping and the salience of social categories. *British Journal of Social Psychology, 26,* 325–340.

Kanter, R. M. (1977). *Men and women of the corporation.* New York: Basic Books.

Kobrynowicz, D. (1997). *Stealthy stereotypes: Revealing the ubiquitous but hidden effects of gender stereotypes on judgments of individuals.* Unpublished doctoral dissertation, University of Kansas, Lawrence.

Kobrynowicz, D., & Biernat, M. (1997). Do the same traits imply the same behavior? Shifting standards in the interpretation of trait concepts. *Journal of Experimental Social Psychology, 33,* 579–601.

Kunda, Z., & Thagard, P. (1996). Forming impressions from stereotypes, traits, and behaviors: A parallel-constraint-satisfaction theory. *Psychological Review, 103,* 28–308.

Lau, R. R. (1989). Individual and contextual influences on group identification. *Social Psychology Quarterly, 5,* 220–231.

Locksley, A., Borgida, E., Brekke, N., & Hepburn, C. (1980). Sex stereotypes and social judgment. *Journal of Personality and Social Psychology, 39,* 821–831.

Locksley, A., Hepburn, C., & Ortiz, V. (1982). Social stereotypes and judgments of individuals. *Journal of Experimental Social Psychology, 18,* 23–42.

Lorenzi-Cioldi, F. (1991). Self-stereotyping and self-enhancement in gender groups. *European Journal of Social Psychology, 21,* 403–417.

Major, B. (1989). Gender differences in comparisons and entitlement: Implications for comparable worth. *Journal of Social Issues, 45,* 99–115.

Major, B. (1993). Gender, entitlement, and the distribution of family labor. *Journal of Social Issues, 49,* 141–159.

Major, B., & Forcey, B. (1985). Social comparisons and pay evaluations: Preferences for same-sex and same-job wage comparisons. *Journal of Experimental Social Psychology, 21,* 393–405.

Major, B., & Testa, M. (1989). Social comparison processes and judgments of entitlement and satisfaction. *Journal of Experimental Social Psychology, 25,* 101–120.

Martin, C. L. (1989). Children's use of gender-related information in making social judgments. *Developmental Psychology, 25,* 80–88.

McKenzie-Mohr, D., & Zanna, M. P. (1990). Treating women as sexual objects: ˙ ˙   ˙ ˙˙ ˙˙˙˙˙˙ pornography. *Per-*

59, 664–675.

Nisbett, R. E., Zukier, H., & Lemley, R. E. (1981). The dilution effect: Nondiagnostic information weakens the implications of diagnostic information. *Cognitive Psychology, 13,* 248–277.

Noseworthy, C. M., & Lott, A. J. (1984). The cognitive organization of gender-stereotypic categories. *Personality and Social Psychology Bulletin, 10,* 474–481.

Parducci, A. (1963). Range–frequency compromise in judgment. *Psychological Monographs, 77*(2, No. 565).

Parducci, A. (1965). Category judgment: A range frequency model. *Psychological Review, 72,* 407–418.

Park, B., & Judd, C. M. (1990). Measures and models of perceived group variability. *Journal of Personality and Social Psychology, 59,* 173–191.

Pettigrew, T., & Martin, J. (1987). Shaping the organizational context for Black American inclusion. *Journal of Social Issues, 43,* 41–78.

Pratto, F., & Bargh, J. A. (1991). Stereotyping based upon apparently individuating information: Trait and global components of sex stereotypes under attention overload. *Journal of Experimental Social Psychology, 27,* 26–47.

Rasinski, K. A., Crocker, J., & Hastie, R. (1985). Another look at sex stereotypes and social judgments: An analysis of the social perceiver's use of subjective probabilities. *Journal of Personality and Social Psychology, 49,* 317–326.

Roberts, J. V., & Herman, C. P. (1986). The psychology of height: An empirical review. In C. P. Herman, M. P. Zanna, & E. T. Higgins (Eds.), *Physical appearance, stigma, and social behavior: The Ontario Symposium* (Vol. 3, pp. 113–140). Hillsdale, NJ: Erlbaum.

Rudman, L. A., & Borgida, E. (1995). The afterglow of construct accessibility: The cognitive and behavioral consequences of priming men to view women as sexual objects. *Journal of Experimental Social Psychology, 31,* 493–517.

Simon, B., Glässner-Bayerl, B., & Stratenwerth, I. (1991). Stereotyping and self-stereotyping in a natural intergroup context: The case of heterosexual and homosexual men. *Social Psychology Quarterly, 54,* 252–266.

Simon, B., & Hamilton, D. L. (1994). Self-stereotyping and social context: The effects of relative in-group size and in-group status. *Journal of Personality and Social Psychology, 66,* 699–711.

Six, B., & Eckes, T. (1991). A closer look at the complex structure of gender stereotypes. *Sex Roles, 24,* 57–71.

Spence, J. T. (1985). Gender identity and its implications for the concepts of masculinity and femininity. In R. A. Dienstbier (Series Ed.) & T. B. Sonderegger (Vol. Ed.), *Nebraska Symposium on Motivation and Achievement. Vol. 32: Psychology and gender* (pp. 59–95). Lincoln: University of Nebraska Press.

Spence, J. T. (1993). Gender-related traits and gender ideology: Evidence for a multifactorial theory. *Journal of Personality and Social Psychology, 64,* 624–635.

Spence, J. T., & Hall, S. K. (1996). Children's gender-related self-perceptions, activity preferences, and occupational stereotypes: A test of three models of gender constructs. *Sex Roles, 35,* 659–692.

Spence, J. T., Helmreich, R. L., & Holahan, C. K. (1979). Negative and positive components of psychological masculinity and femininity and their relationship to self-reports of neurotic and acting out behaviors. *Journal of Personality and Social Psychology, 37,* 1673–1682.

Spence, J. T., Helmreich, R., & Stapp, J. (1974). The Personal Attributes Questionnaire: A measure of sex-role stereotypes and masculinity–femininity. *JSAS Catalog of Selected Documents in Psychology, 4,* 43–44 (Ms. 617).

Spence, J. T., Helmreich, R. L., & Stapp, J. (1975). Ratings of self and peers on sex-role attributes and their relations to self-esteem and conceptions of masculinity and femininity. *Journal of Personality and Social Psychology, 32,* 29–39.

Spence, J. T., & Sawin, L. L. (1985). Images of masculinity and femininity: A reconceptualization. In V. O'Leary, R. Unger, & B. Wallston (Eds.), *Sex, gender, and social psychology* (pp. 35–65). Hillsdale, NJ: Erlbaum.

Swim. I., Borgida, E., Maruyama, G., & Myers, D. G. (1989). Joan McKay versus

Psychological Bulle-

sonality and Social Psychology, 30, 118.

Taynor, J., & Deaux, K. (1973). When women are more deserving than men: Equity, attribution and perceived sex difference. *Journal of Personality and Social Psychology, 32,* 381–390.

Thompson, E. H., Jr., & Pleck, J. H. (1987). The structure of male role norms. In M. S. Kimmel (Ed.), *Changing men: New directions in research on men and masculinity* (pp. 25–36). Newbury Park, CA: Sage.

Turner, J. C. (1982). Towards a cognitive redefinition of the social group. In H. Tajfel (Ed.), *Social identity and intergroup relations* (pp. 15–40). Cambridge, England: Cambridge University Press.

Turner, J. C., Hogg, M. A., Oakes, P. J., Reicher, S. D., & Wetherell, M. (1987). *Rediscovering the social group: A self-categorization theory.* Oxford, England: Basil Blackwell.

Upshaw, H. S. (1962). Own attitude as an anchor in equal-appearing intervals. *Journal of Abnormal and Social Psychology, 64,* 85–96.

Upshaw, H. S. (1969). The Personal Reference Scale: An approach to social judgment. In L. Berkowitz (Ed.), *Advances in experimental social psychology* (Vol. 4, pp. 315–371). New York: Academic Press.

Volkmann, J. (1951). Scales of judgment and their implications for social psychology. In J. H. Rohrer & M. Sherif (Eds.), *Social psychology at the crossroads* (pp. 273–294). New York: Harper.

von Hippel, W., Sekaquaptewa, D., & Vargas, P. (1995). On the role of encoding processes in stereotype maintenance. In M. P. Zanna (Ed.), *Advances in experimental social psychology* (Vol. 27, pp. 177–254). New York: Academic Press.

West, C., & Zimmerman, D. H. (1987). Doing gender. *Gender and Society, 1,* 125–151.

Williams, C. L. (1992). The glass escalator: Hidden advantages for men in the "female" professions. *Social Problems, 39,* 253–267.

Wood, J. V. (1989). Theory and research concerning social comparisons of personal attributes. *Psychological Bulletin, 106,* 231–248.

Zanna, M., Goethals, G. R., & Hill, J. (1975). Evaluating a sex-related ability: Social comparison with similar others and standard setters. *Journal of Experimental Social Psychology, 11,* 86–93.

Zukier, H. (1982). The dilution effect: The role of the correlation and the dispersion of predictor variables in the use of nondiagnostic information. *Journal of Personality and Social Psychology, 43,* 1163–1174.

Zukier, H., & Jennings, D. L. (1984). Nondiagnosticity and typicality effects in prediction. *Social Cognition, 2,* 187–198.

5

Multidimensionality of Gender

I began graduate school just as Spence, Helmreich, and Stapp (1974) and Bem (1974) were simultaneously publishing their scales of instrumental and expressive personality traits (the Personal Attributes Questionnaire [PAQ] and the Bem Sex Role Inventory [BSRI], respectively). Bem had hypothesized a causal relation between the degree of stereotyping in one's self-descriptions on these gender-related trait dimensions and significant gender-related behaviors. This hypothesis was later elaborated to include the notion of an overarching gender schema (Bem, 1981; for a summary see Bem, 1985).

Spence, however, went on to propose a more elaborate theory of gender identity (e.g., Spence, 1985) and to investigate empirically the interrelations of various measures of gender schemata. Her work on multifactorial models of gender schemas has strongly influenced my recent thinking and research. In this chapter, I examine the developmental implications of Spence's model. The first questions I address are

I acknowledge the contributions made by my frequent collaborators Lynn S. Liben and Rebecca S. Bigler to the ideas expressed here; I thank Ronni Greenwood, Sharon Hall, Kristen Johnston, and Janet Taylor Spence for providing additional information; and I thank Judith Langlois and Janet Taylor Spence for their comments on this chapter.

Why is there a need to consider multiple components of gender schemas and What are some of those components? The developmental implications of Spence's theory are then identified and tested through meta-analysis.

IS THERE ONE GENDER SCHEMA?

Bem's (1981) gender schema theory in its various incarnations proposes a very attractive hypothesis for anyone who would like to see less gender-based categorization and decision making in society. Bem (1981) maintained that "sex typing derives, in part, from a generalized readiness to process information on the basis of sex-linked associations that constitute the gender schema" (p. 355). She further proposed that the way to raise "gender-aschematic" children is to teach them that gender refers only to certain physical characteristics (e.g., Bem, 1983).

One of the clear implications of Bem's (1981) theory is that one should be able to identify those persons who view the world through a gender schema. Such persons, whom she called *gender schematic,* should be more likely to organize information on the basis of gender. Organizing by gender should be reflected in standard measures of category use in memory, such as clustering in free recall. Gender-based organization of information should also lead to bias in both recognition and recall favoring gender-stereotype-consistent information. Bem (e.g., 1981) identified gender schematics through their "sex-typed" scores on the BSRI: women with high scores on expressivity and low scores on instrumentality and men with the reverse pattern.

Numerous attempts to replicate Bem's (1981) initial finding that gender schematics show a consistent pattern of gender bias in information processing have been unsuccessful in adults (e.g., see Edwards & Spence, 1987). In an example from my own work (Signorella, 1992), I asked college students to recall either gender-related pictures or words. Because the stimulus materials had no direct self-relevance to the participants, I hypothesized that contrary to Bem's theory, BSRI scores would not predict memory. Rather I expected that a measure of participants' tendencies to assign traits to others on the basis of gender would be a better predictor of whether the participants could remember gender-stereotyped materials or cluster those materials in recall. These hypotheses were supported, in that the gender stereotyping of the traits

the BSRI, are not likely to predict measures of attitudes toward others, such as whether one thinks that both sexes should possess a trait or choose an occupation (e.g., Spence & Helmreich, 1980).

WHAT ARE THE COMPONENTS OF GENDER SCHEMAS?

The implication of the failure to find a single, simple, and sovereign gender schema is a need to examine separately the various aspects of gender schemas. Huston (1983), for example, identified multiple components of gender schemas and was an early advocate in the developmental area for research using multiple measures (see also Ruble & Martin, 1998). Figure 1 displays some of the components that Huston and Ruble and Martin have identified and that I discuss here.

Rebecca Bigler, Lynn Liben, and I (Signorella, Bigler, & Liben, 1993) also used some of Huston's and others' similar categories for our meta-analysis of gender schemas about others (see also Bigler, 1997). The developmental literature is characterized by considerable conceptual and methodological confusion concerning the components of gender schemas. One of the first distinctions we felt was important to make was between schemas about others versus self schemas. Children can be asked about their own preferences and about what people in general do, yet both types of questions are characterized in the same vague terms, such as *stereotyping* or *sex typing*. In some cases, the various

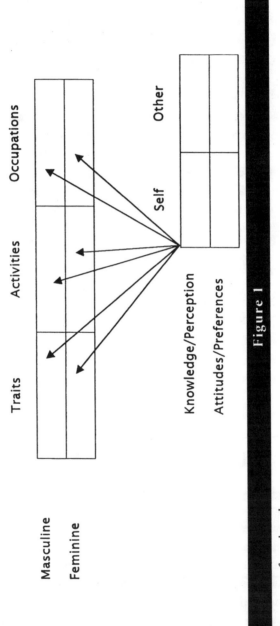

Figure 1

Components of gender schemas.

measures are deliberately used interchangeably, under the assumption of an overriding characteristic called sex typing, not unlike Bem's (1981) gender schema. It appears, however, that this was inappropriate, given

the sexes. The concept *attitudes* refers to a more affective judgment about who should perform the activities or possess the traits.

Developmental Patterns in Gender Schemas About Others

Once separated, interesting differences in the developmental trends emerged between these two types of measures (Signorella et al., 1993). Knowledge was assessed by either forced-choice questions requiring children to choose one or the other sex or by explicit questions about who is "usually" or "likely" to do an activity. The meta-analysis shows that children were increasingly accurate with age in identifying societal stereotypes, as would be anticipated.

Attitudes were assessed by unconstrained measures in which children were not forced to choose one sex or the other in conjunction with being asked who "should" or "can" do an activity or possess a trait. The analysis of attitude measures revealed a peak in stereotyped responding around kindergarten, followed by a decline through elementary school (Signorella et al., 1993). Whether stereotyping in such measures continues to decline through adolescence is still an open question (Ruble & Martin, 1998) because of fewer available studies and less consistent findings with adolescents.

Many questions remained from the Signorella et al. (1993) meta-analysis. First, were we justified in labeling as attitudes those types of measures in which children were allowed to make a nonstereotyped response to the question Who should or can do an activity or possess a trait? Such measures are often referred to in the developmental literature by the more neutral name of "flexibility" (e.g., Serbin, Powlishta, & Gulko, 1993) because children demonstrate flexibility when they assign items to both sexes. Further data are needed to determine if flexibility is primarily a cognitive aspect of stereotyping or has a substantial affective component (i.e., an attitude; cf. Martin, 1993; and Ruble & Martin, 1998). Pretest data from my gender and memory study (Signorella, 1992) showed that college students who had more liberal scores on the Attitudes Toward Women Scale (AWS; Spence & Helmreich, 1972) assigned more traits to both sexes. I also have data showing that children and adolescents with more liberal scores on an adapted AWS (Galambos, Petersen, Richards, & Gitelson, 1985) are more likely to assign activities to both sexes (Signorella, Frieze, & Hershey, 1997). These data support the hypothesis that flexibility represents attitudes toward stereotypes, but an alternative hypothesis that still needs to be ruled out is that both flexibility measures and scales such as the AWS share a cognitive flexibility component.

Self-Schema Measures

A second major gap exists with self-schema measures. The developmental trends do not appear to be as consistent as are observed with knowledge or flexibility measures; they may also depend on the particular component assessed (e.g., see Ruble & Martin, 1998). Another little noticed issue is that both Huston (1983) and Ruble and Martin used separate categories for self-perception versus self-preference or attitudes. Measures such as the BSRI or PAQ would fall under the self-perception category because individuals are asked how they view themselves or what personality attributes they possess. Perhaps self-perceptions are parallel to the knowledge individuals have about stereotypes for people in general. In contrast, a preference or attitude measure would ask the person what he or she would like to be, such as a measure of "ideal self" (e.g., Newcombe & Dubas, 1992). Similarly, for activities, a self-perception or knowledge measure might assess how frequently one participates in an activity (e.g., Bigler et al., 1997; Signorella et al., 1997), whereas a preference measure would assess how much one likes or prefers the activity (e.g., Spence & Hall, 1996). It is possible that one's aspirations and values (i.e., the more affective aspects of self-schemas) predict a different aspect of behavior than do one's self-knowledge, as

sible categories (except itself), there are 276 unique pairs of gender schema components that could be investigated. Needless to say, there has not been anything close to complete coverage of these many areas. Becker and Schram (1994) noted that such missing information prevents complete testing of complex models but that identifying the areas of incomplete data can also provide directions for future research.

DEVELOPMENTAL IMPLICATIONS OF SPENCE'S THEORY

Spence (e.g., 1985) has also argued for the early importance of one of the components of gender schemas, one's gender identity or "basic phenomenological sense of one's maleness or femaleness that parallels awareness and acceptance of one's biological sex and is established early in life" (p. 91). Spence argued that as one of the earliest gender schemas acquired, gender identity drives the development of other gender-related characteristics in only young children. Older children and adults should show "considerable diversity within each sex" (p. 91) because of the multiple influences on the components of gender schemas. As a consequence, older children and adults would have fewer significant relations among various measures of gender schemata.

Spence's (1985) gender identity theory does not specify at what age the weaker relations among measures are observed or whether age-related decreases in the interrelations are linear. However, at least two reasonable hypotheses can be made based on other aspects of gender schema development. Children establish a gender identity by 24 to 36 months (Ruble & Martin, 1998), thus suggesting that the strongest relations among gender schemata might be observed in preschoolers. Alternatively, Spence and Hall (1996) suggested that the increase in stereotype flexibility observed during elementary school might signal the period in which the interrelations among gender schemas are weakened. I tested Spence's (e.g., 1993) multifactorial theory and the developmental implications using meta-analysis (cf. Becker & Schram, 1994).

A META-ANALYSIS OF AGE CHANGES IN THE INTERRELATIONS OF GENDER SCHEMATA

Using the scheme in Figure 1 as a guide, I searched the literature for studies in which more than one measure of gender schemas had been administered to children or adolescents. Unfortunately, only a small number of studies have more than one usable gender schema measure. Although I agree with Ruble and Martin (1998) about the recent and laudable increase in the tendency for researchers to use multiple measures in investigations of children and adolescents (e.g., Biernat, 1991b; Downs & Langlois, 1988; Katz & Ksansnak, 1994; Serbin et al., 1993), the change has been too recent to provide many studies in which two or more gender schema measures are used. In addition, even if more than one measure is used, the relevant data for a meta-analysis also must be reported, which may not be the case (e.g., Pigott, 1994). Table 1 shows the subset of gender schema measures analyzed in the meta-analysis.

Standard meta-analytic techniques were used to test for the significance of the associations between pairs of gender schema measures (e.g., see Cooper & Hedges, 1994), and all were computed using DSTAT (Johnson, 1989). Average effect sizes and other meta-analytic statistics were only computed if there were five or more independent effects available and only if those effects came from more than one study. The analyses were performed using d, the unbiased estimate of effect size produced by weighting g by the variance of the sample size. Effects are displayed in Table 1 as *r* because of that latter statistic's common use to represent associations between continuous measures.

The statistic Q_w, or within-groups Q was used as a test of the homogeneity of the *d*s from a set or subset of studies (see Table 1). A

ᴛᴦᴀˢᴛ ᴏᴎly ᴎ ᴛʜᴇʀᴇ ᴡᴇʀᴇ ᴛʜʀᴇᴇ ᴏʀ ᴍᴏʀᴇ ages in a sample of effect sizes. If the age contrast was significant, the relation between average age and effect size was also graphed, as significance can be obtained with various patterns. The magnitudes of the effect sizes may have become larger or smaller with age, or the sign of the effects may have changed, such as the developmental shift from positive to negative correlations reported by Biernat (1991a) between masculine and feminine self-ratings.

Sex-related effects for samples with significant heterogeneity were tested with the between-groups Q, or Q_B, which tests the differences in the distribution of *d* between groups. If there was a significant sex effect, the results were reported separately by sex (see Table 1). If within either sex there continued to be significant heterogeneity of effect sizes, the age contrast was performed on the sex subgroup (as long as there were different ages represented in the samples).

Several general points about Table 1 should be noted. First, some of the components originally identified in Figure 1 had to be eliminated, combined, or altered (see also Table 1's note).[1] There remained 16 cat-

---

[1]One type of measure excluded is knowledge of others. Such measures are more typically used with preschoolers, as knowledge of stereotypes reaches ceiling levels by elementary school (Ruble & Martin, 1998) and there were no comparisons with a sufficient number of samples to make the meta-analytic comparisons. Although correlates of knowledge measures (called forced choice) were previously examined in the Signorella et al. (1993) meta-analysis, Table 11 from that meta-analysis shows that there is only one category (toy preferences) of relevance to the present study and that $n = 6$ was obtained only through combining disparate measures. The other major exclusion is measure of preschooler toy preference, which is most often correlated with the above-mentioned knowledge measures.

Table 1
Meta-Analysis of Gender Schema Components by Children's Age

Schema pair	k^a	N	r	Q_w	Age^b
For masculine activities and					
Self-preference					
Self-preference for feminine activities	11	1,500	.08*	60.6*	sm
Self-knowledge of masculine traits	9	1,449	.11*	33.9*	na
Self-knowledge of feminine traits	9	1,449	−.03	64.1*	na
Boys	4[c]	618	.08*	21.7*	na
Girls	4[c]	686	−.08*	8.4	na
For feminine activities and					
Self-knowledge of masculine traits	9	1,449	.01	13.8	na
Self-knowledge of feminine traits	9	1,449	.18*	136.6*	na
For nontraditional occupations[d] and					
Self-knowledge of nontraditional occupations[d]	5[e]	233	.74*	57.0*	lg
Attitudes toward others' activities/occupations[f]	6	734	.12*	5.8	—
For masculine occupations and					
Self-knowledge of masculine activities	6	452	.36*	21.3*	na
Self-knowledge of feminine activities	6	452	.43*	24.4*	na
Boys	3	220	.32*	6.5	na
Girls	3	232	.52*	3.4	na

Attitudes toward others' activities[f]	8	502	†	ns
Boys	4	248	†	sm
Girls	4	254	†	ns
For feminine occupations and				
Self-knowledge of masculine activities	6	452	†	na
Boys	3	220		na
Girls	3	232		na
Self-knowledge of feminine activities[f]	6	452	†	na
Attitudes toward others' activities[f]	8	504	†	na
Boys	4	248	†	na
Girls	4	256		na
Self-knowledge				
Of masculine traits and				
Self-knowledge of feminine traits	20	2,170	†	ns
Boys	9[c]	873	†	ns
Girls	10[c]	1,152	†	ns
Self-knowledge of masculine activities	9	525	†	ns
Self-knowledge of feminine activities	9	524	†	ns
Attitudes toward others' activities/occupations[f]	11	850	†	lg
Boys	5	280	†	sm
Girls	6	570		—
Attitudes toward others' activities[f]	10	558	†	ns

(table continues)

117

Table 1 (continued)

Schema pair	k^a	N	r	Q_w	Age^b
Self-knowledge (continued)					
Attitudes toward others' occupations^f	9	942	.06*	38.7*	na
Of feminine traits and					
Self-knowledge of masculine activities	9	522	.06*	36.2*	p/n
Self-knowledge of feminine activities	9	520	.32*	23.4*	ns
Attitudes toward others' activities/occupations^f	11	843	.05	49.0*	n/p
Boys	5	280	.22*	11.5*	n/p
Girls	6	563	-.03	13.1*	n/p
Attitudes toward others' activities	10	553	.07*	32.5*	ns
Boys	4^c	169	.19*	10.5*	n/p
Girls	5^c	351	.01	14.4*	ns
Attitudes toward others' occupations^f	9	942	.04	28.3*	na
Of masculine activities and					
Self-knowledge of feminine activities	13	18,225	.26*	52.8*	sm
Boys	6	13,460	.27*	12.7*	sm
Girls	7	4,765	.23*	26.7*	sm
Attitudes toward others' activities^f	9	525	.11*	56.4*	ns
Boys	4	169	-.13*	6.5	—
Girls	5	356	.22*	21.9*	ns

Attitudes toward others' occupations[f]	10	18,150	na
Boys	5	13,510	na
Girls	5	640	na
Of feminine activities and			
Attitudes toward others' activities[f]	9	524	*ns*
Boys	4	169	—
Girls	5	355	—
Attitudes toward others' occupations[f]	10	18,150	na
Boys	5	13,510	na
Girls	5	4,640	na
Attitudes toward others' occupations and attitudes toward others' activities[f]	7	492	na

Note. Sm = smaller; lg = larger; — = no follow-up tests because of nonsignifican[...] [...]egative; n/p = [...] negative to positive.

[a]Of independent samples. [b]Results of the contrast using average age on effect size. [...]uded from the [...] sex comparison because data were only reported for the sexes combined. [d]Respon[...] [...] scored by the stereotyping of the choice (masculine or feminine); higher scores indicated nontrad[...] [...]omparison was possible because there was only one effect size for boys. [f]Measures of attitudes towa[...] [...]cross masculine and feminine items. Such measures are often reported in that way and for an obvi[...] [...]elation between the masculine and feminine items of measures of attitude toward others (see Bigle[...] [...]la et al., 1997). Higher scores indicated nontraditional (i.e., nonstereotyped) responses.

*p < .05.

egories of measures that were used in at least one study—a possible 120 unique pairs of measures. Only 26 comparisons met the criteria of five or more effects from two or more separate studies. Self-knowledge of masculine and feminine traits and self-knowledge of masculine and feminine activities were among the better represented measures. Thus, to examine the multidimensional nature of gender schemas, more researchers need to examine and report on more aspects of gender schemas.

For the key test of age changes in the interrelations, it should first be noted that out of the 58 effect sizes displayed in Table 1, 26 could not be tested for age differences because of little or no variation in the participants' ages. Out of the remaining 32 effects, 19 showed no significant age differences (including those for which homogeneity of effect sizes was retained, thus precluding any further testing). The remaining 13 effects that did show an age difference consisted of 6 showing a smaller magnitude of effect with age, 2 showing a larger magnitude of effect with age, 4 that changed sign from negative to positive, and 1 that changed sign from positive to negative. Thus, no consistent age-related pattern emerged.

A major limitation in the age analyses was that most of the studies included in the meta-analysis had either elementary schoolchildren or adolescents as the participants, with the majority in fourth to sixth grade. Although preschoolers have been tested frequently on measures of gender schemata, it is not typically in the same way as with older children. There also seems to be more variation in the way the preschool measures are used, resulting in fewer studies with common measures.

Finally, there were some sex-related differences in the patterns of the correlations. One set of correlations seemed to form an understandable pattern. With only a few exceptions, nonstereotyped attitudes were correlated with characteristics associated with the other sex. For girls, less stereotyped attitude scores (or higher flexibility) were associated with self-perceptions of masculine traits, self-reports of participating in masculine activities and not participating in feminine activities, a liking for masculine occupations, and a disliking for feminine occupations.

For boys, less stereotyped attitude scores (or higher flexibility) were associated with self-perceptions of feminine traits, self-reports of participating in feminine activities, and a liking for feminine occupations. This pattern may indicate that attitudes (or flexibility) are an aspect of

measure also did on another, regardless of the stereotyping of the items. One possible explanation would be the "generalized acquiescence bias" (Spence & Hall, 1996, p. 683) detected by the authors in their data. Such a bias, in which the participants endorse everything indiscriminately, cannot be evaluated in the present meta-analysis. Another possibility is that there is a general tendency for those children who are more active in general to be interested in many different occupations and to have instrumental personality characteristics (Kelly & Smail, 1986; Spence & Hall, 1996).

CONCLUSIONS

The developmental implications of Spence's (e.g., 1985) gender identity theory were tested with a meta-analysis. Available data on the interrelations of gender schema measures were examined to determine if gender schemas become more differentiated with age. No clear age-related patterns emerged. However, the interpretation of the lack of age differences must await future research because there was little age variation present in these samples. Even the significant age effects that occurred must be interpreted with caution because of small numbers of samples and restricted age ranges. Thus, no sufficient data exist yet to test adequately the developmental aspect of Spence's theory. It will be important for future research to provide such data. Notably missing and crucial to a complete test of a developmental change in the interrelations of gender schema measures are sufficient data on preschoolers. It is possible, however, to use the available data to evaluate the various gender schema approaches. Spence and Hall (1996), for example, outlined the one-factor, two-factor, and multifactorial theories.

The one-factor model (e.g., Bem, 1981) argues for a single gender schema, with some individuals overapplying this schema (gender schematics) and others rarely using it (aschematics). The present data do not support the one-factor model. The only possible evidence was the tendency for children with less stereotyped (i.e., nontraditional) attitudes toward others to report participation in other-sex activities, possession of other-sex traits, and preference for other-sex occupations. Most of those correlations, however, were quite small. Furthermore, those same attitudes toward others did not consistently predict same-sex preferences or knowledge, as also would be expected in the one-factor model. Finally, it is hard to see how the pattern of positive correlations observed among the self-schema measures could be consistent with the one-factor model. First, there should have been more sex differences in these correlations. Second, the sex differences present in the data show cross-gender relations opposite to what would be predicted by the one-factor theory (boys with higher feminine trait scores said they participated in more masculine activities). Consistent with this interpretation, Spence and Hall (1996) tested the one-factor model in their data using Masculine × Feminine interaction terms in multiple regression and found no supporting evidence.

The two-factor model argues for independent factors of masculinity and femininity that only predict behaviors within their own gender. Thus, masculine scales correlate with one another, feminine scales correlate with one another, but feminine and masculine scales are not correlated. The present data show instead a general tendency for all such scales (masculine and feminine) to be positively correlated, thus contradicting the two-factor model.

The last theory to consider, Spence's (1993) multifactorial theory, is the best fit to the present data. Many of the correlations are extremely small, and as discussed earlier, there are few consistent or easily interpretable patterns. Spence and her colleagues (e.g., Spence & Hall, 1996;

Spence & Helmreich, 1980) have been careful to note that "it is not our view that gender-related measures are never related to one another" (Spence & Hall, 1996, p. 686) but that

. ~~-- -- ----------. .. .~ ....p~.....~ ~~ ~~ ~~ .~.

the sake of completeness; it is also important because the accumulating evidence suggests that children have many gender schemas with diverse developmental trends and loose interconnections.

REFERENCES

References marked with an asterisk indicate studies included in the meta-analysis.

Becker, B. J., & Schram, C. M. (1994). Examining explanatory models through research synthesis. In H. Cooper & L. V. Hedges (Eds.), *The handbook of research synthesis* (pp. 357–382). New York: Russell Sage Foundation.

Bem, S. L. (1974). The measurement of psychological androgyny. *Journal of Consulting and Clinical Psychology, 42,* 155–162.

Bem, S. L. (1981). Gender schema theory: A cognitive account of sex typing. *Psychological Review, 88,* 354–364.

Bem, S. L. (1983). Gender schema theory and its implications for child development: Raising gender-aschematic children in a gender-schematic society. *Signs, 8,* 598–616.

Bem, S. L. (1985). Androgyny and gender schema theory: A conceptual and empirical integration. In R. A. Dienstbier (Series Ed.) & T. B. Sonderegger (Vol. Ed.), *Nebraska Symposium on Motivation. Vol. 32: Psychology and gender* (pp. 179–226). Lincoln: University of Nebraska.

Biernat, M. (1991a). Gender stereotypes and the relationship between masculinity and femininity: A developmental analysis. *Journal of Personality and Social Psychology, 61,* 351–365.

Biernat, M. (1991b). A multicomponent, developmental analysis of sex typing. *Sex Roles, 24,* 567–586.

Bigler, R. S. (1997). Conceptual and methodological issues in the measurement of children's sex typing. *Psychology of Women Quarterly, 21,* 53–70.

*Bigler, R. S., Liben, L. S., Lobliner, D. B., & Yekel, C. A. (1997). *The structure of gender schemata: Relations among multifactorial measures in children and adults.* Manuscript submitted for publication, University of Texas at Austin.

*Boldizar, J. P. (1991). Assessing sex typing and androgyny in children: The Children's Sex Role Inventory. *Developmental Psychology, 27,* 505–515.

Cooper, H., & Hedges, L. V. (Eds.). (1994). *The handbook of research synthesis.* New York: Russell Sage Foundation.

Downs, A. C., & Langlois, J. H. (1988). Sex typing: Construct and measurement issues. *Sex Roles, 18,* 87–100.

Edwards, V. J., & Spence, J. T. (1987). Gender-related traits, stereotypes, and schemata. *Journal of Personality and Social Psychology, 53,* 146–154.

*Galambos, N. L., Almeida, D. M., & Petersen, A. C. (1990). Masculinity, femininity, and sex role attitudes in early adolescence: Exploring gender intensification. *Child Development, 61,* 1905–1914.

*Galambos, N. L., Petersen, A. C., Richards, M., & Gitelson, I. B. (1985). The Attitudes Toward Women Scale for Adolescents: A study of reliability and validity. *Sex Roles, 13,* 343–356.

*Greenwood, R. M., & Hall, S. K. (1997, April). *An examination of the multifactorial theory of gender across three ethnic groups.* Paper presented at the festschrift to honor Janet Taylor Spence, Austin, TX.

Huston, A. C. (1983). Sex-typing. In P. H. Mussen (Ed.), *Handbook of child psychology. Vol. 4: Socialization, personality, and social development* (4th ed., pp. 387–467). New York: Wiley.

Johnson, B. T. (1989). *DSTAT: Software for the meta-analytic review of research literatures.* Hillsdale, NJ: Erlbaum.

*Johnston, K. E. (1997). *Influences on preschoolers' toy preferences for the self and others: Evidence for a multifactorial gender schema model.* Unpublished master's thesis, Pennsylvania State University.

Katz, P. A., & Ksansnak, K. R. (1994). Developmental aspects of gender role flexibility and traditionality in middle childhood and adolescence. *Developmental Psychology, 30*, 272–282.

*Kelly A & Smail B (1986) Sex stereotypes and attitudes to science among

spectives. *Monographs of the Society for Research in Child Development, 58*(2, Serial No. 232), 75–85.

Newcombe, N., & Dubas, J. S. (1992). A longitudinal study of predictors of spatial ability in adolescent females. *Child Development, 63*, 37–46.

Pigott, T. D. (1994). Methods for handling missing data in research synthesis. In H. Cooper, & L. V. Hedges (Eds.), *The handbook of research synthesis* (pp. 163–175). New York: Russell Sage Foundation.

*Repetti, R. L. (1984). Determinants of children's sex stereotyping: Parental sex-role traits and television viewing. *Personality and Social Psychology Bulletin, 10*, 457–467.

Rosenthal, R. (1991). *Meta-analytic procedures for social research* (rev. ed.). Beverly Hills, CA: Sage.

Ruble, D. N., & Martin, C. L. (1998). Gender development. In W. Damon (Series Ed.) & N. Eisenberg (Vol. Ed.), *Handbook of child psychology. Vol. 3: Social, emotional and personality development* (5th ed., pp. 933–1016). New York: Wiley.

*Serbin, L. A., Powlishta, K. K., & Gulko, J. (1993). The development of sex typing in middle childhood. *Monographs of the Society for Research in Child Development, 58*(2, Serial No. 232), 1–74.

Signorella, M. L. (1992). Remembering gender-related information. *Sex Roles, 27*, 143–156.

Signorella, M. L., Bigler, R. S., & Liben, L. S. (1993). Developmental differences in children's gender schemata about others: A meta-analytic review. *Developmental Review, 13*, 147–183.

*Signorella, M. L., Frieze, I. H., & Hershey, S. W. (1997, April). *Interrelations of gender-related attitudes, preferences, and self-descriptions in female children and adolescents.* Paper presented at the meeting of the Society for Research in Child Development, Washington, DC.

*Silvern, L. E., & Katz, P. A. (1986). Gender roles and adjustment in elementary-school children. *Sex Roles, 14,* 181–202.

Spence, J. T. (1985). Gender identity and its implications for the concepts of masculinity and femininity. In R. A. Dienstbier (Series Ed.) & T. B. Sonderegger (Vol. Ed.), *Nebraska Symposium on Motivation. Vol. 32: Psychology and gender* (pp. 59–95). Lincoln: University of Nebraska.

Spence, J. T. (1993). Gender-related traits and gender ideology: Evidence for a multifactorial theory. *Journal of Personality and Social Psychology, 64,* 624–635.

*Spence, J. T., & Hall, S. K. (1996). Children's gender-related self-perceptions, activity preferences, and occupational stereotypes: A test of three models of gender constructs. *Sex Roles, 35,* 659–692.

Spence, J. T., & Helmreich, R. L. (1972). The Attitudes Toward Women Scale: An objective instrument to measure the attitudes toward the rights and roles of women in contemporary society. *JSAS Catalog of Selected Documents in Psychology, 2,* 66–67 (Ms. 153).

*Spence, J. T., & Helmreich, R. L. (1978). *Child Test Battery: Instructions for administration.* Unpublished manuscript, University of Texas at Austin.

Spence, J. T., & Helmreich, R. L. (1980). Masculine instrumentality and feminine expressiveness: Their relationships with sex role attitudes and behaviors. *Psychology of Women Quarterly, 5,* 147–163.

Spence, J. T., Helmreich, R. L., & Stapp, J. (1974). The Personal Attributes Questionnaire: A measure of sex-role stereotypes and masculinity–femininity. *JSAS Catalog of Selected Documents in Psychology, 4,* 43–44 (Ms. 617).

PART THREE

Modern Sexism and

6

Psychological Interventions
Designed to Counter Sexism in

S ince the beginning of the Women's Movement in the early 1970s, psychologists have increasingly argued that the endorsement of sex-stereotypic beliefs carries many dysfunctional consequences for children and adults (e.g., Bem, 1974; Block, 1973; Saario, Jacklin, & Tittle, 1973). Many of these consequences are reviewed in other chapters in this volume. Among children, gender stereotyping is associated with the inability to accurately remember events, stories, and interactions with people (e.g., Liben & Signorella, 1980; Martin & Halverson, 1983) and the imposition of limitations on the expression of personal interests and skills (e.g., Bussey & Bandura, 1992). As a result, a good deal of interest has been generated in the development of interventions to reduce sex typing in children. For over 2 decades now, developmental researchers have studied children's responses to interventions designed to change their sex-typed attitudes and behavior (e.g., Flerx, Fidler, & Rogers, 1976; Guttentag & Bray, 1976; Katz & Walsh, 1991). The developmental literature on this topic is diverse and extensive but can be characterized perhaps by one generalization—experimental interventions have had only limited impact on children's sex typing (e.g., see Katz, 1986; Liben & Bigler, 1987; and Serbin & Unger, 1986).

The developmental literature on sex-typing interventions is too extensive and broad to examine in detail here. Instead, the primary purpose of this chapter is to review the limitations that characterize previous interventions aimed at changing children's sex-typed beliefs and to argue that the failure to design more effective interventions is due, in large part, to the lack of breadth and sophistication in the theoretical models on which intervention strategies are based. I begin the chapter with a discussion of the goals and methods of intervention and a review of the types of limitations that characterize empirical data from extant intervention studies. Next, I discuss several of the theoretical assumptions that underline the research on countering sexism in children. Finally, I make several specific suggestions for expanding the theoretical models on which to base the development of additional intervention strategies.

INTERVENTION GOALS

Theoretically, an intervention might seek to achieve many types of change. For example, Huston (1983) presented a matrix of sex-typing constructs that includes over 20 dimensions, any of which could be the target of change through experimental intervention. Some of these constructs are the topic of considerable intervention research, whereas others receive far less attention. At a broad level, intervention goals can be categorized into those attempting to change children's gender attitudes versus their own sex-typed behavior (see Signorella, chapter 5, this volume). In this chapter, I focus on interventions designed to change children's sex-typed beliefs about others (rather than their own sex-typed behavior). There are at least two reasons for focusing on children's beliefs about gender.

First, the goal of changing children's sex-typed beliefs is less controversial than the goal of changing children's sex-typed traits or behaviors. The endorsement of rigid beliefs about the appropriate roles and traits for men and women (e.g., only men can be brave or only women can be nurses) is now widely regarded as undesirable. The manipulation of children's sex-typed behavior (e.g., peer and toy preferences) is less widely accepted—both in the case of those children who are highly sex typed and those children who are "cross-gender identified" (e.g., see Bem, 1993). Second, it is likley that children's gender attitudes about others are more malleable than their own sex-typed

operationalized as a reduction in the number of traits, occupations, toys, or activities that children view as appropriate for only one gender (e.g., Barclay, 1974; Flerx et al., 1976).

Two other types of attitude change could be considered as attitude intervention goals, but so far they have not been the topic of empirical research with children. Recent research suggests that intergroup processes are involved in the process of sex typing (e.g., Bigler, 1995; Fishbein, 1996; Powlishta, 1995a, 1995b). According to intergroup theories (e.g., Tajfel, 1970), the mere categorization of individuals into groups (e.g., male and female) produces increased perception of between-group differences and within-group similarity. The study of the perception of variability within and between gender groups is relatively new in the developmental literature, but it shows promise of providing a more complex picture of children's gender-related beliefs (Bigler, 1995; Powlishta, 1995a, 1995b). Intervention attempts might therefore be designed to increase children's perception of variability within gender groups, to reduce children's perception of the variability between gender groups, or both. Further discussion of intergroup theory as a basis for intervention design follows later in this chapter.

In addition, interventions might seek to alter the degree to which children view gender as a salient and important social category; Bem (1983, 1993), for example, has argued that interventions should attempt to minimize the psychological significance of gender among children. This goal touches on core ideologies concerning the meaning of gender and gender differences and, hence, is the subject of considerable and heated debate (see James, 1997). The debate pits those theorists holding a "difference" model of gender, (i.e., the view that men and women are inherently, broadly, and essentially different) against those theorists holding a "similarity" model (i.e., the view that men and women are highly similar and flexible in their behavior). To the extent that gender is viewed as an "essentialist," important, and legitimate social category, individuals are likely to believe that diminishing its psychological significance is undesirable and unlikely to succeed. For example, some parent groups have fought to ban new educational materials and reinstate older material that depict traditional sex roles for girls and boys (e.g., see Holden, 1987). To date, no empirical data evaluating the outcome of interventions aimed at altering children's view of the significance of gender as a social category have been reported.

INTERVENTION TECHNIQUES

In addition to the different types of intervention goals, researchers have used a broad array of specific strategies for reducing sex typing in children. Researchers have developed home-based interventions involving toys and stories and school-based interventions involving cooperative learning and role playing (e.g., Johnson, Johnson, & Scott, 1978; Kourilsky & Campbell, 1984). Perhaps the most-often studied technique is the presentation of counterstereotypic information through symbolic as well as live models (e.g., Ashton, 1983; Flerx et al., 1976; Weeks & Porter, 1983). Unfortunately, few researchers have compared the effectiveness of different techniques, and little is known about the exact components of intervention that facilitate gender attitude change.

Interventions also differ considerably in their scope. Some interventions have a fairly focused and narrow content (e.g., Hurwitz & White, 1977), whereas others include exposure to a broad range of experiences and activities (e.g., Guttentag & Bray, 1976). Liben and Bigler (1987) reported that more narrowly focused intervention, which tend to use posttest measures that are highly similar to the intervention material, document greater attitude change than do broader interventions.

EMPIRICAL LIMITATIONS OF PREVIOUS INTERVENTIONS

Several traditional reviews of the developmental literature on sex-typing

The Prevalence of Nonsignificant Effects

Although significant effects of intervention programs are occasionally reported, they are typically embedded within a context of nonsignificant effects both across and within studies. Across studies, it appears that there is a substantial *file-drawer problem* (the tendency for studies that report nonsignificant findings to go unpublished) in the field of intervention research (Rosenthal, 1979). My colleagues and I are currently in the process of compiling published as well as unpublished (e.g., master's theses and dissertations) studies of the effectiveness of gender stereotyping interventions for use in a meta-analytic review of the literature (Bigler, Signorella, & Liben, 1998). Our literature search revealed a substantial body of unpublished intervention work that reports nonsignificant differences between experimental and control groups.

Even within studies, it is very common to find that those effects reported as significant are often just a few of many nonsignificant effects. For example, the program Freestyle (Johnston & Ettema, 1982) is widely cited as a successful gender-stereotyping intervention. The intervention consists of 13 half-hour videocassettes featuring (a) activities designed to foster interest in nontraditional careers, (b) behavioral skills designed to foster nontraditional traits (e.g., assertiveness for girls and helpfulness for boys), and (c) egalitarian adult work and family roles. A careful inspection of the results indicates that although several statistically significant changes in sex typing did occur, many aspects of

133

children's sex typing remained unchanged after exposure to the program materials. For example, boys' attitudes about the sex appropriateness of occupations remained unaffected by the program. At pretest, boys rated 80% of a list of occupations as "male" jobs and 20% as "female" jobs. At posttest, boys related 79% of these occupations as male jobs and 21% as female jobs.

In addition to the failure of interventions to generalize across multiple measures within studies, it is also very common for significant effects to be reported for only some of the participants in the experimental conditions. For example, significant intervention effects are sometimes reported only for children at certain developmental levels or ages (e.g., Katz & Walsh, 1991). Unfortunately, no consistent age effects are readily discernible across intervention studies. Another common finding is that girls alter their gender attitudes as a result of exposure to intervention programs more so than do boys (e.g., Ashton, 1983; Kourilsky & Campbell, 1984; Raskin & Israel, 1981). Several hypotheses for the sex difference in the response to intervention have been proposed. It may be, for example, that boys have more to gain by maintaining the status quo and, thus, are reluctant to accept more egalitarian attitudes (e.g., see Fishbein, 1996). It is also possible that boys are less responsive to interventions than are girls because the majority of interventions are conducted by female experimenters (Katz & Walsh, 1991).

The Weakness of Long-Term Effects

Long-term measures of attitude change are relatively rare in the intervention literature. When posttest attitude measures are given after a substantial time delay (e.g., several days or weeks), initially significant effects often disappear. For example, Flerx et al. (1976) reported that the egalitarian effects produced by reading nonsexist story books disappeared when children were tested 1 week after the story manipulations ended. In addition, a 9-month follow-up of the Freestyle program by Johnston and Ettema (1982) showed erosion in at least some of the areas of prior success.

The Limitation of Effect Sizes

Ideally, the goal of gender stereotyping interventions is the elimination of gender-biased responding (e.g., the assignment of traits or roles

The experimental intervention taught children a cognitive strategy for deciding who could perform sex-typed occupations. Specifically, children were taught the irrelevance of gender, coupled with the relevance of two criteria: a person's liking some job function and a person's learning how to perform some job function. The experimental intervention produced significant decreases in children's gender stereotyping, yet the overall level of gender stereotyping remained fairly high among children in both the treatment and control groups. For example, children in the experimental group gave egalitarian responses to only 13.4 of the 26 posttest occupational items; the comparable mean for children in the control group was 10.4 of the 26 items. In summary, the statistically significant effects reported in sex-typing interventions rarely translate into practically or educationally meaningful outcomes.

Summary of Effects

Despite the variety of sex-typing interventions reported in the developmental literature, most interventions are largely ineffective in altering children's sex-typed beliefs. What accounts for the weakness of previous intervention attempts? I argue that extant interventions are only marginally successful because of the paucity of sophisticated developmental theoretical models of attitude change on which these interventions are based. The theoretical underpinnings of intervention studies of social stereotyping in children is weaker, for example, than that of intervention studies of social stereotyping in adults (e.g., Hewstone, Macrae, Griffiths, Milne, & Brown, 1994). Furthermore, the theoretical basis of the intervention literature on gender stereotyping is much less sophisticated than the theoretical grounding of research aimed at reducing racial prejudice (e.g., see Eberhardt & Fiske, 1996; and Hewstone, 1996).

In contrast to the social psychological and racial prejudice research, developmental studies of interventions designed to change children's gender attitudes are grounded primarily within one theoretical model—learning theory. The epistemological tradition of learning theory carries with it many assumptions about children's learning (and, hence, unlearning) of sex-typed beliefs and behaviors. Many of these implicit assumptions are at least partially responsible for the paucity of intervention effects. In addition, simplistic assumptions about the structure and measurement of children's gender schemata have contributed to the weakness of experimental intervention findings.

THEORETICAL ISSUES RELEVANT TO INTERVENTION DESIGN

The Passive Versus Active Nature of Sex-Role Learning

One assumption that underlies many intervention studies is that children are relatively passive absorbers of environmental messages about gender, including the intervention material to which they are exposed. This assumption is rooted in the epistemology tradition of learning theory, which posits that individuals are passive recipients of the reality of the external world. In contrast, Piagetian (1970) theory holds that knowledge is actively constructed by the individual. Stimuli acquire meaning, therefore, as much from the internal world as from the external world of the child.

One implication of this view is that what a child takes away from an intervention may not be what the investigators intended. Specifically, children may distort or entirely forget material presented as part of intervention programs. Furthermore, this memory bias may be greatest among those children with the most sex-typed attitudes. A great deal of developmental research now supports the idea that high gender stereotyping children show poorer memory for counterstereotypic material than their low gender stereotyping peers (Bigler & Liben, 1993; Signorella & Liben, 1984).

Again, an example from my work with Liben (Bigler & Liben, 1990) is illustrative of the constructive nature of children's i f

ngnter?" One young boy enthusiastically replied "Yes!" "How do you know?" the experimenter asked. "Because *he* follows our rules," the boy replied.

In addition to the tendency to distort counterstereotypic material, children show two other forms of memory bias that are likely to limit the effectiveness of intervention efforts. A recent meta-analysis indicates that children show better memory for same-sex characters (male vs. female) and same-sex stereotypic material (masculine vs. feminine) than for other-sex characters or other-sex stereotypic material (Signorella et al., 1997). So, for example, boys remember male characters better than female characters and material related to traditionally masculine activities and roles better than they remember that related to traditionally feminine activities and roles. This suggests that it may be particularly difficult to induce children to attend to and remember counterstereotypic information and to expand their knowledge and performance of traits and roles to include items that are culturally stereotyped as appropriate for the other sex.

The data presented by Martin (chapter 3, this volume) on children's memory for novel toys labeled "for boys" or "for girls" are consistent with this suggestion. Martin reports that children remembered those toys labeled as appropriate for their own sex better than those labeled as appropriate for the other sex. Perhaps more dramatic, however, is the finding that children did not remember toys labeled as appropriate for "both boys and girls" any better than those toys labeled as appropriate for members of the other sex exclusively. This finding suggests that the egalitarian presentation of materials and information in schools and other settings may do little to counteract children's sex typing.

General Versus Age-Specific Cognitive Mechanisms

Another assumption that stems from the epistemological tradition of learning theory is that the mechanisms involved in attitude formation and change (e.g., reinforcement and observational learning) are the same across all ages—and across children and adults. The implication of such an assumption is that the same intervention strategies are appropriate (and effective) among children of different ages. In contrast, cognitive-developmental theories hold that there are logical constraints on children's thinking. Piaget (1970) outlined a host of developmental constraints on children's cognitive processes, many of which are likely to be involved in children's gender stereotyping and responses to intervention efforts.

One cognitive characteristic of young children that may be relevant is *centration*, the tendency to attend to one particular dimension of a stimulus to the exclusion of other equally relevant dimensions. This phenomenon is traditionally illustrated by reference to the conservation of continuous quantity problem, in which two identical beakers are filled to the same level with liquid. The liquid from one beaker is then poured into a third beaker, taller and thinner than the original beakers. Young children, when asked whether there is still the same amount to drink in the two beakers, respond negatively, explaining that the new beaker has more because the liquid is higher. The child centers on the liquid's height, ignoring the equally relevant dimension of the beaker's width (e.g., see Piaget, 1970).

This cognitive constraint is likely to be relevant to social perception. A child might, for example, focus on an individual's gender and might be unable to consider equally important characteristics of the individual (e.g., his or her skills and interests). The young child's inability to use multiple classification skills (Piaget, 1965) becomes relevant as well. A child who has difficulty categorizing people and objects along multiple dimensions may have difficulty understanding and remembering an individual who is a member of two (stereotypically) nonoverlapping categories (e.g., women and scientists).

Recent empirical work supports the notion that cognitive constraints affect children's gender attitudes as well as child ...

... these same and novel target children. Regardless of the number of counterstereotypic attributes assigned to the targets, children based their inferences on the targets' gender. Thus, when making inferences about the activity preferences of female characters who had been described (as part of the intervention) as liking to hunt, fix bicycles, play with rockets, and so forth, the majority of children selected primarily those attributes stereotypically associated with the feminine sex role (e.g., liking to baby sit and bake cookies).

Finally, Bigler and Liben (1993) reported that children with less advanced multiple classification skills showed higher levels of gender stereotyping and poorer memory for counterstereotypic gender information than did children with more advanced multiple classification skills. Each of these studies suggests that many forms of intervention (including the modeling of counterstereotypic information) may be ineffective among young children because they (a) center on the gender (rather than traits or interests) of stimulus persons and (b) lack the ability to attend to multiple attributes of individuals.

Compliance With Authority Versus Internal Motivation

Another assumption that underlies many intervention studies is that children are motivated to adopt and internalize the messages presented as part of intervention lessons. In other words, experimenters assume that children will be receptive to the intervention message. There are a host of reasons to expect that this may not be the case. For example, gender stereotypes are likley to have emotional–motivational as well as cognitive and behavioral components. Unfortunately, little developmental research has addressed the emotional or motivational aspects of the acquisition and maintenance of sex-stereotypic beliefs and behavior. These aspects may, however, interfere with the internalization of the cognitive and behavioral changes targeted by intervention.

In addition, developmentalists generally agree that children are motivated to make sense of the world through the use of cognitive categorization. Because gender represents a perceptually salient and socially important category, children form categories on the basis of gender and develop a broad associative network of attributes and roles that are associated with men and women in their culture (e.g., Bem, 1983; Martin & Halverson, 1981). Some interventions designed to reduce sex typing are likely to present material that contradicts the content of children's gender stereotypes. That is, children may develop sex-typed beliefs as a result of exposure to multiple sex-typed models; these beliefs may be incompatible with the messages embedded in an intervention. For example, although an intervention may teach that women can or even should be scientists (e.g., Bigler & Liben, 1990), a child's personal experience, or memory for this experience, may consist of having seen only male scientists. Under these circumstances, children may be particularly unlikely to show an attitude change.

In keeping with this notion, Lee and Bigler (1988) found that children construct beliefs about social groups on the basis of exemplars of behavior rather than explicit statements concerning the group's attributes. Lee and Bigler presented elementary school-aged children with space creatures (e.g., "Plutonians") that differed in color (e.g., red and blue). Children were told that the two colors of Plutonians were equivalent along some dimension (e.g., they were equally smart). Children were then exposed to story books that presented information that either contradicted or confirmed the original egalitarian statement. Later, children were asked to make judgments about the characteristics of the Plutonians. Results indicated that when the stories contradicted the egalitarian statements, children based their judgments on the information presented in the stories (rather than on the egalitarian statements that contradicted the story information).

Unidimensional Versus M~~ultidi~~

~~ly to both~~ the self and ~~others.~~ According to Bem (1979, 1981), some (but not all) individuals are *gender schematic*, which means that they systematically organize information about themselves, other people, and objects along gender lines. From this perspective, one would expect considerable consistency in stereotyping across varying substantive contents or context and between individuals' gender-related beliefs and behavior. Bem (1993) stated, for example, that "the gendered personality ... has a readiness to superimpose a gender-based classification on every heterogeneous collection of human possibilities that presents itself" (p. 154). This theoretical position assumes that changing one aspect of a child's gender schemata should produce changes in other aspects as well. According to this account, exposing children to models of women and men in nontraditional occupational roles should, for example, increase children's egalitarian beliefs about activities and traits and their interest in pursuing nontraditional jobs as adults.

In contrast, Janet Spence and her colleagues have argued against the notion of monolithic concepts, such as sex-role identification or gender schemata, and have proposed instead that gender-related phenomena are multifactorial in nature, with different factors having substantial independence (Spence, 1985; Spence & Helmreich, 1978; Spence & Sawin, 1984). From this perspective, one would not necessarily expect consistency in gender-related beliefs or behaviors across different contexts or substantive topics or between gender-related beliefs about others and gender-related preferences for the self. Edwards and Spence

(1987) stated, for example, that "instrumental and expressive traits ... are expected to have little or no relation with behaviors and other [gender-related] characteristics that are not directly affected by instrumentality and expressiveness" (p. 147).

Empirical data now overwhelmingly support Spence's (1985, 1993) theoretical position that gender schemata are multidimensional and multifactorial. Young children's gender knowledge, attitudes, and behavior are often only weakly related, if related at all (Bigler, Liben, Lobliner, & Yekel, 1998; Serbin, Powlishta, & Gulko, 1993; Spence & Hall, 1996). This finding has important implications for designing interventions to reduce gender stereotypic beliefs and behavior. Previous researchers have often attempted to change children's gender attitudes within one domain (e.g., occupations), with the goal of affecting other aspects of children's sex typing, including gender attitudes within other domains (e.g., toys), gender-related behavior (e.g., see Liben & Bigler, 1987), and occupational goals (e.g., Bigler & Liben, 1990). The majority of studies do not find such effects or only weak effects. In summary, empirical evidence supports the notion, which is based on multifactorial and multidimensional models of gender schemata, that changes in an individual's sex-typed beliefs within a particular domain do not necessarily affect the individual's sex-typed beliefs within other domains or his or her sex-typed behavior.

DIRECTIONS FOR FUTURE INTERVENTION RESEARCH

I argued that intervention strategies designed to reduce gender stereotyping and discrimination in children are based on a restricted and simplistic set of theoretical models about gender role learning and gender schemata structure and that the resulting interventions are generally ineffective in reducing gender bias. To develop more effective intervention strategies, researchers need to look to other theoretical models of sex typing and to models of stereotyping and discrimination more broadly.

Cognitive-Developmental Theories

As reviewed earlier, several tenets of cognitive-developmental theory (e.g., Piaget, 1970) appear useful for explaining the weakness of pre-

revision (e.g., Crocker, Fiske, & Taylor, 1984; Hamilton, 1981; Roth-bart, 1981). According to the *bookkeeping* model (Rothbart, 1981), as stereotype-inconsistent information is presented, the perceiver gradually adjusts and revises his or her stereotypic belief relevant to the new information. So, for example, exposure to increasing numbers of female physicists should result in increasingly egalitarian beliefs about women across time. According to the *conversion* model, highly salient and convincing stereotype-inconsistent information produces sudden (rather than gradual) changes in attitudes. For example, exposure to a very highly competent female physicist should result in sudden and dramatic decreases in sex stereotyping. Finally, according to the *subtyping* model, as stereotype-inconsistent information is presented, the original stereotype becomes differentiated into subtypes, with one particular subtype representing the disconfirming evidence. So according to this model, exposure to a female physicist should leave overall levels of gender stereotyping unaffected but should produce a stereotype of female scientists that is embedded within the gender stereotype.

To date, no researchers have empirically examined whether these models of attitude change are applicable to children and, more important, how developmental constraints on children's logical thought might affect the use of these various cognitive processes. Understanding the cognitive processes involved in the revision of children's gender attitudes seems crucial for designing more effective intervention strategies.

Intergroup Theories

As discussed earlier, intergroup processes are increasingly being implicated in children's gender stereotyping and discrimination (e.g., Bigler,
1995; Fishbein, 1996; Powlishta, 1995a, 1995b) and, hence, might reasonably be considered an important target for intervention. Thus, intergroup theories of the development of intergroup bias and discrimination represent another important source for developing additional
models of gender attitude change.

One of the major theoretical accounts of intergroup behavior was
proposed by Tajfel, Flament, Billig, and Bundy in 1971. Intergroup theory (Tajfel et al., 1971) asserts that the mere act of categorizing individuals into social groups is sufficient to produce intergroup prejudice
and discrimination. Several consequences of social categorization under
"minimal" group condition (i.e., when social categories are uninfor-
mative, irrelevant, or completely unfounded) are well documented
within the social psychological literature (see Brewer, 1979; Hamilton
& Trolier, 1986; and Messick & Mackie, 1989). Social categorization is
shown to produce increased perception of between-group differences
and within-group similarity (e.g., Doise, Deschamps, & Meyer, 1978),
increased perception of out-group homogeneity (e.g., Park & Rothbart,
1982; Quattrone & Jones, 1980), and increased intergroup bias, including both in-group favoritism and out-group discrimination (e.g., Allen
& Wilder, 1975; Brewer & Silver, 1978).

Intervention based on intergroup theory might take several forms.
For example, it may be possible to reduce gender bias by creating salient
and important categories that cross gender (i.e., that include both boys
and girls). Consistent with this hypothesis, some social psychological
research suggests that cross-classification reduces bias against out-group
members (e.g., Deschamps & Doise, 1978; Vanbeselaere, 1987). In addition, a recent developmental study by Bigler, Jones, and Lobliner
(1997) reports that elementary schoolchildren whose teachers made extensive use of novel, perceptually salient social categories (e.g., red and
green color groups) in the classroom showed reduced bias against
other-sex peers. That is, children rated other-sex peers as more likable

when a perceptually salient social category that was important in the classroom included both boys and girls.

It might also be possible to alter children's perception of variability within and between gender groups through ╌╌╌╌ ╌ ╌ ╌ ╌

CONCLUSION

In this chapter, I argued that previous attempts to reduce children's sex typing are relatively ineffective. Furthermore, I argued that extant interventions are based on narrow and simplistic theoretical models of attitudes and attitude change in children. I suggested several additional possible theoretical perspectives on which to base intervention designs. It is clear, however, that gender stereotyping is pervasive among children and is resistant to change. It is possible that highly effective intervention might, therefore, require combinations of strategies that are based on several different theoretical foundations. For example, optimally effective interventions might include exposure to gender counterstereotypic models (e.g., women scientists), training in attending to the multiple features of these models (e.g., their gender and occupation), and practice in detecting within-group differences (e.g., differences between female scientists and female beauticians) and between-group similarities (e.g., similarities between male and female scientists).

It is also possible, however, that psychological interventions are necessarily limited in their impact, given the wider cultural messages that children receive about gender. Fishbein (1996), for example, has argued that intergroup bias is rooted in the evolutionary–genetic heritage of human beings and that whenever two separate groups are identified, children (and adults) will show prejudice and bias toward their own group. A recent intergroup study by Bigler et al. (1997) supports the notion that when perceptually salient social groups are pointed out by the environment, children show biases toward their in-group and against the out-group. This theoretical and empirical work suggests that children inevitably develop gender stereotypes and biases when they live in cultures where (a) gender is viewed as an important social category that is routinely used to distinguish among individuals and (b) the male and female populations are viewed as inherently different (e.g., as a result of biological differences). Thus, societal changes concerning the messages that children receive about the meaning and importance of gender may be necessary before psychological strategies for overcoming sex typing are likely to be highly effective.

REFERENCES

Ashton, E. (1983). Measures of play behavior: The influence of sex-role stereotyped children's books. *Sex Roles, 9,* 43–47.

Allen, V. L., & Wilder, D. A. (1975). Categorization, belief similarity, and group discrimination. *Journal of Personality and Social Psychology, 32,* 971–977.

Barclay, L. K. (1974). The emergence of vocational expectations in preschool children. *Journal of Vocational Behavior, 4,* 1–4.

Bem, S. L. (1974). The measurement of psychological androgyny. *Journal of Consulting and Clinical Psychology, 42,* 155–162.

Bem, S. L. (1979). Theory and measurement of androgyny: A reply to the Pedhazur-Tetenbaum and Locksley-Colten critiques. *Journal of Personality and Social Psychology, 37,* 1047–1054.

Bem, S. L. (1981). Gender schema theory: A cognitive account of sex typing. *Psychological Review, 88,* 354–364.

Bem, S. L. (1983). Gender schema theory and its implications for child development: Raising gender-aschematic children in a gender-schematic society. *Signs: Journal of Women in Culture and Society, 8,* 598–616.

Bem, S. L. (1993). *The lenses of gender: Transforming the debate on sexual inequality.* New Haven, CT: Yale University.

Bigler, R. S. (1995). The role of classification skill in moderating environmental influences on children's gender stereotyping: A study of the functional use of gender in the classroom. *Child Development, 66,* 1072–1087.

Bigler, R. S., Jones, L. C., & Lobliner, D. B. (1997). Social categorization and the formation of intergroup attitudes in children. *Child Development, 68,* 530–543.

Bigler, R. S., & Liben, L. S. (1990). The role of attitudes and interventions in gender-schematic processing. *Child Devel̵~~~~ ~~ ~~~*

Bigler, R. S., Signorella, M. L., & Liben, L. S. (1998). *The effectiveness of interventions aimed at reducing gender stereotyping in children: A meta-analytic review.* Manuscript in preparation, University of Wisconsin—Madison.

Block, J. H. (1973). Conceptions of sex role: Some cross-cultural and longitudinal perspectives. *American Psychologist, 28,* 512–526.

Brewer, M. B. (1979). In-group bias in the minimal intergroup situation: A cognitive-motivational analysis. *Psychological Bulletin, 86,* 307–324.

Brewer, M. B., & Silver, M. (1978). Ingroup bias as a function of task characteristics. *European Journal of Social Psychology, 8,* 393–406.

Bussey, K., & Bandura, A. (1992). Self-regulatory mechanisms governing gender development. *Child Development, 63,* 1236–1250.

Crocker, J., Fiske, S. T., & Taylor, S. E. (1984). Schematic bases of belief change. In J. R. Eisner (Ed.), *Attitudinal judgment* (pp. 197–226). New York: Springer-Verlag.

Deschamps, J. C., & Doise, W. (1978). Crossed category memberships in intergroup relations. In H. Tajfel (Ed.), *Differentiation between social groups* (pp. 141–158). London: Academic Press.

Doise, W., Deschamps, J. C., & Meyer, G. (1978). The accentuation of intra-category similarities. In H. Tajfel (Ed.), *Differentiation between social groups: Studies in the social psychology of intergroup relations.* New York: Academic Press.

Eberhardt, J. L., & Fiske, S. T. (1996). Motivating individuals to change: What is a target to do? In N. Macrae, C. Stangor, & M. Hewstone (Eds.), *Foundations of stereotypes and stereotyping* (pp. 369–414). New York: Guilford.

147

Edwards, V. J., & Spence, J. T. (1987). Gender-related traits, stereotypes, and schemata. *Journal of Personality and Social Psychology, 53,* 146–154.

Fishbein, H. D. (1996). *Peer prejudice and discrimination.* Boulder, CO: Westview Press.

Flerx, V. C., Fidler, D. S., & Rogers, R. W. (1976). Sex-role stereotypes: Developmental aspects and early interventions. *Child Development, 47,* 998–1007.

Foss, C. J., & Slaney, R. B. (1986). Increasing nontraditional career choices in women: Relation of attitudes toward women and responses to a career intervention. *Journal of Vocational Behavior, 28,* 191–202.

Guttentag, M., & Bray, H. (1976). *Undoing sex stereotypes.* New York: McGraw-Hill.

Hamilton, D. L. (1981). Stereotyping and intergroup behavior: Some thoughts on the cognitive approach. In D. L. Hamilton (Ed.), *Cognitive processes in stereotyping and intergroup behavior* (pp. 333–353). Hillsdale, NJ: Erlbaum.

Hamilton, D. L., & Trolier, T. K. (1986). Stereotypes and stereotyping: An overview of the cognitive approach. In J. F. Dovidio & S. L. Gaertner (Eds.), *Prejudice, discrimination, and racism* (pp. 127–163). Orlando, FL: Academic Press.

Hewstone, M. (1996). Contact and categorization: Social psychological intervention to change intergroup relations. In N. Macrae, C. Stangor, & M. Hewstone (Eds.), *Foundations of stereotypes and stereotyping* (pp. 323–368). New York: Guilford.

Hewstone, M., Macrae, N., Griffiths, R., Milne, A. N., & Brown, R. (1994). Cognitive models of stereotype change: (5). Measurement, development, and consequences of subtyping. *Journal of Experimental Social Psychology, 30,* 505–526.

Holden, C. (1987). Textbook controversy intensified nationwide. *Science, 235,* 19–21.

Hurwitz, R. E., & White, M. A. (1977). Effect of sex-linked vocational information on reported occupational choices of high school juniors. *Psychology of Women Quarterly, 2,* 149–156.

Huston, A. C. (1983). Sex-typing. In E. M. Hetherington (Vol. Ed.) & P. H. Mussen (Series Ed.), *Handbook of child psychology. Vol. 4: Socialization, personality, and social development* (pp. 387–486). New York: Wiley.

James, J. B. (1997). What are the social issues involved in focusing on difference in the study of gender? *Journal of Social Issues, 53,* 213–232.

Johnson, D. W., Johnson, R. T., & Scott, L. (1978). The effects of cooperative and individualized instruction on student ...

Katz, P. A. (1986). Modification of children's gender-stereotyped behavior: General issues and research considerations. *Sex Roles, 14,* 591–601.

Katz, P. A., & Walsh, P. V. (1991). Modification of children's gender-stereotyped behavior. *Child Development, 62,* 338–351.

Katz, P. A., & Zalk, S. R. (1978). Modification of children's racial attitudes. *Developmental Psychology, 14,* 447–461.

Kourilsky, M., & Campbell, M. (1984). Sex differences in a simulated classroom economy: Children's beliefs about entrepreneurship. *Sex Roles, 10,* 53–65.

Lee, J., & Bigler, R. S. (1998). *Verbal versus nonverbal influences in the acquisition of gender and racial stereotypes.* Unpublished undergraduate honor's thesis, University of Texas at Austin.

Liben, L. S., & Bigler, R. S. (1987). Reformulating children's gender schemata. In L. S. Liben & M. L. Signorella (Eds.), *Children's gender schemata* (pp. 89–105). San Francisco: Jossey-Bass.

Liben, L. S., & Signorella, M. L. (1980). Gender-related schemata and constructive memory in children. *Child Development, 51,* 11–18.

Martin, C. L., & Halverson, C. (1981). A schematic processing model of sex typing and stereotyping in children. *Child Development, 52,* 1119–1134.

Martin, C. L., & Halverson, C. F. (1983). The effects of sex-typing schemas on young children's memory. *Child Development, 52,* 1119–1132.

Messick, D. M., & Mackie, D. M. (1989). Intergroup relations. *Annual Review of Psychology, 40,* 45–81.

Park, B., & Rothbart, M. (1982). Perception of out-group homogeneity and levels of social categorization: Memory for subordinate attributes of in-group and out-group members. *Journal of Personality and Social Psychology, 42,* 1051–1068.

Piaget, J. (1965). *The child's conception of number.* New York: Norton.

Piaget, J. (1970). Piaget's theory. In P. H. Mussen (Ed.), *Carmichael's manual of child psychology* (pp. 703–732). New York: Wiley.

Powlishta, K. K. (1995a). Gender bias in children's perception of personality traits. *Sex Roles, 32,* 17–28.

Powlishta, K. K. (1995b). Intergroup processes in childhood: Social categorization and sex role development. *Developmental Psychology, 31,* 781–788.

Quattrone, G. A., & Jones, E. E. (1980). The perception of variability within in-groups and out-groups: Implications for the law of small numbers. *Journal of Personality and Social Psychology, 38,* 141–152.

Rosenthal, R. (1979). The "file drawer problem" and tolerance of null results. *Psychological Bulletin, 86,* 638–641.

Raskin, P. A., & Israel, A. C. (1981). Sex role imitation in children: Effects of sex of child, sex of model, and sex role appropriateness of modeled behavior. *Sex Roles, 7,* 1067–1077.

Rothbart, M. (1981). Memory processes and social beliefs. In D. L. Hamilton (Ed.), *Cognitive processes in stereotyping and intergroup behavior* (pp. 145–181). Hillsdale, NJ: Erlbaum.

Saario, T. N., Jacklin, C. N., & Tittle, C. K. (1973). Sex role stereotyping in the public schools. *Harvard Educational Review, 43,* 386–414.

Serbin, L. A., Powlishta, K. K., & Gulko, J. (1993). The development of sex typing in middle childhood. *Monographs of the Society for Research in Child Development, 58*(Serial No. 232).

Serbin, L. A., & Unger, R. K. (1986). Social change: Introduction. *Sex Roles, 14,* 561–566.

Signorella, M. L., Bigler, R. S., & Liben, L. S. (1997). A meta-analysis of children's memories for own-sex and other-sex information. *Journal of Applied Developmental Psychology, 18,* 429–445.

Signorella, M. L., & Liben, L. S. (1984). Recall and reconstruction of gender-related pictures: Effects of attitude, task difficulty, and age. *Child Development, 55,* 393–405.

Spence, J. T. (1985). Gender identity and its implications for the concepts of masculinity and femininity. In R. A. Dienstbier (Series Ed.) & T. B.

Sonderegger (Vol. Ed.), *Nebraska Symposium on Motivation Vol. 32: Psychology and gender* (pp. 59–95). Lincoln: University of Nebraska Press.

Spence, J. T. (1993). Gender-related traits and gender ideology: Evidence for a multifactorial theory. *Journal of Personality and Social Psychology, 64*

~~~~~~, j. 1., & ~awin, L. L. (1984). Images of masculinity and femininity: A reconceptualization. In V. O'Leary, R. Unger, & B. Wallston (Eds.), *Sex, gender, and social psychology* (pp. 35–66). Hillsdale, NJ: Erlbaum.

Tajfel, H. (1970). Experiments in intergroup discrimination. *Scientific American, 223*, 96–102.

Tajfel, H., Flament, C., Billig, M., & Bundy, R. (1971). Social categorization and intergroup behaviour. *European Journal of Social Psychology, 1*, 149–178.

Vanbeselaere, N. (1987). The effects of dichotomous and crossed social categorization upon intergroup discrimination. *European Journal of Social Psychology, 17*, 143–156.

Weeks, M. O., & Porter, E. P. (1983). A second look at the impact of nontraditional vocational role models and curriculum on the vocational role preferences of kindergarten children. *Journal of Vocational Behavior, 23*, 64–71.

7

Linking Gender to Educational, Occupational and Recreational

Jacquelynne S. Eccles, Bonnie Barber, and
Debra Jozefowicz

Despite recent efforts to increase the participation of women in advanced educational training and high-status professional fields and such male-dominated recreational activities as athletics, women and men are still concentrated in different educational programs, occupational fields, and recreational activities. Most important for this chapter, women are still underrepresented in many high-status occupational fields, particularly those associated with physical science, engineering, and applied mathematics (Eccles, 1987; National Science Foundation, 1996; Vetter & Babco, 1986). The differences in educational and occupational attainment are even evident among highly gifted individuals in this country (see Benbow, 1988; Benbow & Minor, 1986; Eccles & Harold, 1992; and Terman & Oden, 1947). Why? Many factors, ranging from outright discrimination to the processes associated with gender-role socialization, undoubtedly contribute to these gendered patterns of

We wish to thank all of our colleagues and former students who have worked with them in developing the studies summarized in this chapter. These include Carol Midgley, David Reumen, Douglas Mac Iver, David Klingel, Allan Wigfield, Janis Jacobs, and Kim Updegraf. This work has been supported by grants from the National Institute of Mental Health, the National Institute for Child Health and Development, and the National Science Foundation.

educational and occupational choices. Discussing all possible mediating variables is beyond the scope of a single chapter. Instead, we focus on a set of social and psychological factors that was first outlined in a book edited by Janet Taylor Spence in 1983, *Perspectives on Achievement and Achievement Motives* (see Eccles [Parsons] et al., 1983).

In that same volume, Spence and Helmreich (1983) summarized their theoretical and empirical work on several facets of achievement motivation and the facets' relations to academic performance in college students and career success among members of several professions. The original impetus of this work came from skepticism about the widely accepted hypotheses that women fail to develop the kind of intrinsic motivation that is necessary to enter and succeed in demanding occupations and that this lack is a major cause of the discrepancy between women's and men's academic choices and vocational attainment. Their data essentially disconfirmed these ideas about gender (e.g., Spence & Helmreich, 1978, 1983). In our approach to gender differences in educational and occupational choice, we have built on this critical work in two fundamental ways: First, their work sensitized us to the need to understand women's behavior from a choice perspective rather than a deficit perspective; second, Spence's approach to conceptualization and measurement of personality has guided our theoretical and methodological work. Spence's subsequent work on gender roles (e.g., Spence, 1993) has informed our stress on the role of values as critical to understanding gendered behaviors. These influences are evident throughout this chapter.

This chapter focuses on a model of achievement-related choices and the ongoing Michigan Study of Adolescent Life Transitions (MSALT) study. After reviewing the support for this model, we provide a brief overview of recent evidence supporting the power of the most proximal predictors of achievement-related choices, expectations for success and subject task value. In the final section, we discuss more specifically how gender roles relate to the model and how gender roles can lead to different educational and occupational choices.

A MODEL OF ACHIEVEMENT-RELATED CHOICES

Over the past 20 years, Eccles and her colleagues have studied the motivational and social factors influencing such achievement goals and

~~~~~, ~~~ ~~~~~~~~~ theory (see Crandall, 1969; Spence & Helmreich, 1978; and Weiner, 1974), they elaborated a comprehensive theoretical model of achievement-related choices that could be used to guide subsequent research efforts.

This model, depicted in Figure 1, links achievement-related choices directly to two sets of beliefs: the individual's expectations for success and the importance or value the individual attaches to the various options perceived as available. The model also specifies the relation of these beliefs to cultural norms, experiences, aptitudes, and those personal beliefs and attitudes that are commonly assumed to be associated with achievement-related activities by researchers in this field (see Eccles, 1987; Eccles [Parsons] et al., 1983; and Meece, Eccles [Parsons], Kaczala, Goff, & Futterman, 1982). In particular, the model links achievement-related beliefs, outcomes, and goals to interpretative systems like causal attributions, the input of *socializers* (primarily parents, teachers, and peers), gender-role beliefs, self-perceptions and the self concept, and perceptions of the task itself.

For example, consider course enrollment decisions. The model predicts that people will most likely enroll in courses that they think they can master and that have high task value for them. Expectations for success (and a sense of domain-specific personal efficacy) depend on the confidence the individual has in his or her intellectual abilities and on the individual's estimations of the difficulty of the course. These beliefs are shaped over time by the individual's experiences with the subject matter and subjective interpretation of those experiences (e.g.,

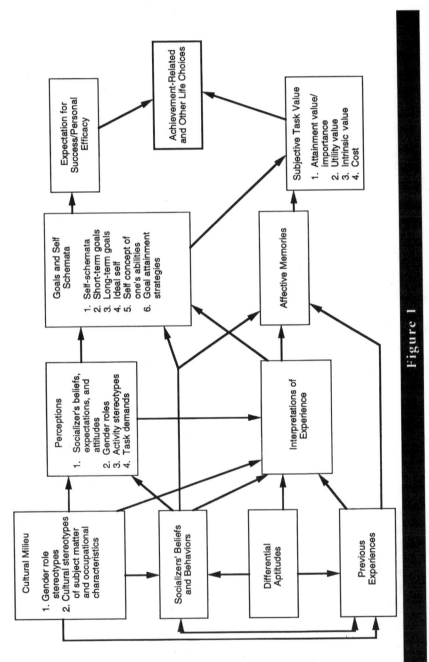

Figure 1

Theoretical model of achievement-related choices developed by Eccles (Parsons) et al. (1983).

Does the individual think that her or his successes are a consequence of high ability or lots of hard work?). Likewise, it is assumed that several factors influence the value of a particular course to the individual: For example, does an individual ~~enjoy study~~ ... ...

~~, ... as the decision to~~

enroll in an accelerated math program or to major in education rather than engineering, are made within the context of a complex social reality that presents each individual with a wide variety of choices; each of which has both long-range and immediate consequences. Consequently, the choice is often between two or more positive options or between two or more options that all have both positive and negative components. For example, the decision to enroll in a physics course is typically made in the context of other important decisions, such as whether to take advanced English or a second foreign language, whether to take a course with one's best friend, whether it is more important to spend one's senior year working hard or having fun, and so forth.

Consider, for example, two high school students: Mary and Barbara. Both young women enjoy mathematics and have always done very well in the subject. Both have been offered the opportunity to participate in an accelerated math program at the local college during their next school year. Barbara is also very interested in gymnastics and hopes to win a sport scholarship to college. To accomplish this goal, she needs to train every afternoon for 4 hr. In contrast, Mary hopes to major in biology in college and plans a career as a research scientist. Taking the accelerated math course involves driving to and from the college. Because the course is scheduled for the last period of her school day, it will take the last two periods as well as 1 hr of afterschool time to take the course. What will the young women do? In all likelihood, Mary will enroll in the program because she likes math and thinks that the effort required to both take the class and master the material is worthwhile and important for her long-range career goals. Barbara's decision is more complex. She may want to take the class but may also think that the time required is too costly, especially given the demands of her gymnastic training schedule. Whether she takes the college course will depend, in part, on the advice she gets at home and from her counselors. If they stress the importance of the math course, then its subjective worth to her is likely to increase. If its subjective worth increases sufficiently to outweigh its subjective cost, then Barbara will probably take the course, despite its cost in time and effort.

Thus, building on the work of Spence and Helmreich (e.g., 1983; Spence, 1993), the model is based on the assumption that women's and men's behaviors are determined by a complex set of factors. The fact that women and men may differ in their choices is likely to reflect gender differences in a wide range of predictors, mediated primarily by differences in self-perceptions, values, and goals rather than motivational strength, drive, or both. Such an approach changes the issue from "Why don't women make the same choices as men?" to "Why do women make the choices they do?" This change, in turn, moves us beyond a deficit model of women's behavioral choices and focuses our attention on both the positive and negative reasons why women and men make the choices they do. This change also leads us to question whether differences favoring men necessarily reflect a strength for men and a deficit for women. For example, like others, both Spence and Eccles have consistently found that men score higher than do women on measures of interpersonal competitiveness. Both have also found, however, that this characteristic does not necessarily lead to either better performance or more intrinsically motivated behavioral choices. Consequently, whereas others have interpreted such a gender difference as one of the "strengths" that facilitate men's achievement (e.g., Goldberg, 1973), our approach makes this an empirical question in need of appropriate, contextually sensitive, causal modeling.

In summary, as outlined in Figure 1, we assume that achievement-related choices (e.g., educational and occupational choices), whether made consciously or unconsciously, are guided by the following: (a) one's expectations for success on and sense of personal efficacy for the various options, (b) the relation of the options to both one's short- and long-range goals and one's core self identity and basic psychological needs, (c) one's gender role related personal ...

Before going on however, we want to provide information about the particular study we focus on in our summaries of our findings. These analyses were done using data from the MSALT. This longitudinal study is being conducted by Jacquelynne Eccles and Bonnie Barber. It began in 1982, with a sample of approximately 3,000 sixth graders in 12 different school districts of southeastern Michigan; these districts serve primarily working-class and middle-class small-city communities. The sample is predominantly White but does include about 150 African American adolescents. Approximately 2,000 of these adolescents have been tracked well into their early adulthood years with standard survey questions either designed by Eccles, Barber, and their colleagues or borrowed from other investigators. Emboldened by Spence's advice to create their own measures, they designed all of the scales reported in this chapter. Most have been used in a variety of studies and have well-established reliabilities and good predictive and face validity. The longitudinal sample differs from the original random sample in only a few regards: The adolescents in the longitudinal sample came from slightly wealthier families and were more likely to complete high school and go on to college than the original sample of 3,000. However, the longitudinal sample is still quite diverse and representative of the working/ middle-class populations of southeastern Michigan: Slightly less than 50% have gone on to a 4-year college by the time they were age 20, and only 35% finished a bachelor's degree by the time they were age 25.

ECCLES ET AL.

EXPECTATIONS AND PERSONAL EFFICACY AS MEDIATORS OF ACHIEVEMENT-RELATED CHOICES

Expectations for success, confidence in one's abilities to succeed, and personal efficacy have long been recognized by decision and achievement theorists as important mediators of behavioral choice (e.g., Atkinson, 1964; Lewin, 1938; Weiner, 1974). Numerous studies demonstrate the link between expectations for success and a variety of achievement-related behaviors. For example, Hollinger (1983) has documented the relation between gifted girls' confidence in their math abilities and their aspirations to enter math-related vocations, such as engineering and computer science. Similarly, Terman (1926) has found a positive relation between gifted students' subject matter preferences and their ratings of the ease of the subject for themselves. More recently, Betz and Hackett (1986) demonstrated a link between ratings of personal efficacy in various academic subjects and career choice (see also Betz & Fitzgerald, 1987).

But do the male and female populations differ on measures commonly linked to expectations for success? Even more important, do the female and male populations differ in their expectations for success at various academic subjects and in various occupations in a traditional gender-role-stereotyped manner? In most but not all studies, the answer to both these questions is *yes*. For example, at the general level, Fox (1976) found that highly motivated gifted girls have lower self-confidence than do equally highly motivated gifted boys; similarly, both Terman (1926) and Strauss and Subotnik (1991) found that gifted girls were more likely to underestimate their intellectual skills and their relative class standing whereas gifted boys were more likely to overestimate theirs. But even more important for this chapter, in several studies the pattern of gender differences in young children's and adolescents' confidence in their abilities and expectations for success mirrors traditional gender-role stereotypes. For example, girls rated themselves as having more English and social ability but less athletic and math ability than did their male peers (e.g., Eccles, 1987; Eccles [Parsons], Adler, & Meece,

160

1984; Eccles & Harold, 1991; Eccles et al., 1989; Eccles, Wigfield, Harold, & Blumenfeld, 1993; Wigfield, Eccles, Mac Iver, Reuman, & Midgley, 1991).

In contrast, several studies of gifted youth f-- ¹
ences on measures ~f

..... ~quivalent
......~a. aD111ty (Eccles & Harold, 1992). Fi-
..ally, in the longitudinal study of intellectually capable students, gender differences in expectations for success in future math courses did not mediate the gender differences in math course enrollment, but the perceived value of the math course did (Eccles [Parsons] et al., 1984).

Given this mixed set of results for intellectually able and gifted youth, it is not clear that gifted girls are either less confident than are gifted boys of their intellectual abilities in general or of their mathematical ability in particular. Although the differences, when found, do support this conclusion, these differences are always quite small and are often not found at all. It is also not clear whether this difference, even when found, is the primary mediator of gender differences in the educational and occupational decisions of either intellectually able or gifted youth. Thus, it is also not clear that the gender differences in the selection of careers in math and science among intellectually able youth are primarily due to gender differences in their expectations for success in mathematics. Gender differences in task value may be just as important. These differences are discussed in the next section.

Occupational Ability Self Concepts

Eccles and Barber have extended their work on academic and athletic self concepts by looking at adolescents' competence ratings for skills more directly linked to adult occupational choice. As the MSALT sample moved into and through high school, they were asked a series of questions directly related to future job choices. First, the sample was asked to rate how good they were compared with other students at each of several job-related skills. Second, the sample was asked to rate the probability that they would succeed at each of a series of standard careers. The results from their responses when they were seniors are summarized in Table 1.

On the one hand, the results are quite gender-role stereotyped: The female students were less confident of success than were the male students in science-related professions and in male-typed skilled labor occupations; in contrast, the male students were less confident of their success than were the female students in health-related professions and female-typed skilled labor occupations (Jozefowicz, Barber, & Eccles, 1993). On the other hand, there were no gender differences in these seniors' ratings of either their confidence of success in business and law or their leadership, independence, intellectual, and computer skills. Furthermore, although the male students were more confident of success in physical science and engineering fields, the female students were more confident than were the male students of success in health-related fields that involve extensive scientific training. Clearly, these young women see themselves as quite efficacious in terms of possible future occupational pathways. Which particular pathway they select or end up on likely has as much, if not more, to do with their values as with their sense of efficacy. In the next section, we review findings regarding gender differences in achievement-related values.

Subjective Task Values as Mediators of Achievement-Related Choices

Subjective task value is the second major component of the expectancy-value model of achievement-related choices, as shown in Figure 1: Decisions regarding course enrollments, college majors, and occupational choice are assumed to be influenced by the value individuals attach to the various achievement-related options they believe are available to them. Furthermore, given the probable impact of gender-role socialization on the variables associated with subjective task value, gender differences in the subjective value of various achievement-related op-

Table 1

Gender Differences in Values, Expectations, and Perceived Ability: Multiple Analysis of Variance

~~....~~ ~~.....~~ ...... (female)/human services[b]	4.5 (1.2)	3.3 (1.2)*
5. Business and law[b]	4.6 (1.4)	4.9 (1.4)
6. Artist[a]	3.5 (1.9)	3.3 (1.7)
Self-perception of skills		
1. Working with others[b]	5.5 (0.9)	4.8 (1.0)*
2. Leadership[a]	5.3 (1.1)	5.3 (1.0)
3. Independence[a]	5.2 (1.1)	5.3 (1.0)
4. Intellectual[a]	5.1 (1.2)	5.3 (1.0)
5. Mechanical[a]	2.3 (1.4)	4.2 (1.7)*
6. Computers[a]	4.0 (1.7)	4.2 (1.6)
Lifestyle values		
1. High status/competitive[a]	4.4 (1.4)	4.8 (1.4)*
2. Risk taking[a]	4.7 (1.1)	5.1 (1.0)*
3. Careerism[a]	5.7 (1.0)	5.5 (1.0)
4. Family and friends before work[b]	4.5 (1.0)	4.0 (1.1)*
5. Material wealth[a]	4.7 (1.2)	5.1 (1.1)*
Valued job characteristics		
1. Flexibility to meet family obligations[a]	5.5 (1.1)	5.4 (1.0)
2. People/society oriented[b]	5.7 (1.0)	5.1 (1.1)*
3. Prestige/responsibility[a]	5.4 (1.1)	5.6 (0.9)
4. Creative/educational[a]	5.7 (1.2)	5.8 (1.1)
5. Machinery/manual work[a]	3.0 (1.2)	3.9 (1.6)*
6. Math/computer work[a]	3.9 (1.5)	4.2 (1.5)*

Note. Both multianalyses of variances (MANOVAs) were significant at the $p < .001$ level. Significant relationships reported in the table are based on univariate tests of significance. [a]First MANOVA set. [b]Second MANOVA set. * $p < .001$.

tions are predicted to be important mediators of gender differences in educational and occupational choices in both typical and gifted populations.

Eccles (Parsons) et al.'s (1984) data support this hypothesis. In a longitudinal study of the math course enrollment decisions of intellectually able, college-bound students, gender differences in students' decisions to enroll in advanced mathematics were mediated primarily by gender differences in the value the students' attached to mathematics. More specifically, the girls were less likely than the boys to enroll in advanced mathematics primarily because they felt that math was less important, useful, and enjoyable than did the boys. Eccles and Harold (1992) also found clear evidence of gender differences in the value attached to various school subjects and activities in their study of elementary schoolchildren enrolled in a gifted program. Even though there was no gender difference in expectations for success in mathematics, these girls reported liking math less than the boys did; the girls also rated math as less useful than did the boys. In addition, the boys also attached greater importance to sports than did the girls.

Other studies have yielded similar findings. When asked to name their favorite school subjects, gifted girls rated English, foreign languages, composition, music, and drama higher than did gifted boys; in contrast, the boys rated the physical sciences, physical training, U.S. history, and sometimes mathematics higher than did the girls (Benbow & Stanley, 1982; George & Denham, 1976; Terman, 1926). Similarly, when asked their occupational interests and anticipated college major, gifted girls rated domestic, secretarial, artistic, and biological sciences and both medical and social service occupations and training higher than did the boys, whereas the boys expressed more interest than did the girls in both higher status and business-related occupations in general and the physical sciences, engineering, and the military in particular (Benbow & Stanley, 1982; Fox, Pasternak, & Peiser, 1976; Terman, 1926). Finally, when asked their leisure time activities and hobbies, similar differences in interest patterns emerged. At all ages, gifted girls both liked and reported spending more time than did the boys on reading, writing, and participating in a variety of activities related to arts and crafts, domestic skills, and drama; in contrast, gifted boys spent more time engaged in sports, working with machines and tools, and involved with scientific, math-related, or electronic hobbies (Dauber & Benbow, 1990. Fox 1976. McG: 1976. T

/ (1076) . gifted girls in their study were less likely than gifted boys to take advanced mathematics in part because they liked language-related courses more than they liked mathematics courses. In addition, Benbow and Stanley found weak but consistent positive relations in their gifted samples between the liking of biology, chemistry, and physics and subsequent plans to major in biology, chemistry, and physics, respectively. In addition, students' interest predicted their course taking in high school and college (Benbow & Minor, 1986).

The more fundamental question, however, is whether individual differences in relative perceived value of a variety of occupations mediate individual differences in occupational choice. Eccles and Barber have been studying this question for the last 10 years. Because of their interest in understanding career choice, they extended MSALT to include a series of measures of more general life and occupational values. When the participants were seniors, they were asked to rate how important each of a series of job-related and life-related values and a series of job characteristics were to them (see appendices for sample items). The results are summarized in Table 1. As was true for the job-related skills, they found evidence of both gender-role stereotypic differences and of gender-role transcendence. In keeping with traditional stereotypes, the female students rated family and friends as more important to them than did the male students; the female students also were more likely than the male students to want jobs that were people oriented. In contrast but also consistent with both traditional stereotypes and the work of Spence and Helmreich (1978, 1983), the male students placed a higher value on high-risk and competitive activities and wealth than did the female students; they also were more interested in jobs that allowed for work with machinery, math, or computers. However, counter to traditional stereotypes, there were no gender differences in careerism; the female and male students were equally likely to want jobs that allowed for flexibility to meet family obligations, that entailed prestige and responsibility, and that allowed for creative and intellectual work. As seen in the next section, these values are significant predictors of occupational aspirations.

Evidence from other investigators also provides good support for a key role of perceived task value in achievement-related decisions. For example, using a longitudinal, correlational design, Dunteman, Wisenbaker, and Taylor (1978) studied the link between personal values and selection of one's college major. They identified two sets of values that both predicted students' subsequent choice of major and differentiated the sexes: The first set (labeled *thing orientation*) reflected an interest in manipulating objects and understanding the physical world; the second set (labeled *person orientation*) reflected an interest in understanding human social interaction and a concern for helping people. Students who were high on thing orientation and low on person orientation were more likely than the other students to select a math or science major. Not surprisingly, female students in their study were more likely than male students to be person oriented and to major in something other than math or science; in contrast, the male students were more likely than the female students both to be thing oriented and to major in math and science.

Predicting Achievement-Related Choices Using the Eccles et al. Expectancy-Value Model

The MSALT study has been used to predict achievement-related choices in several domains. The evidence supporting the power of expectancies and values as both direct effects and as mediators of gender differences in behavioral choices is quite strong. In this section, we summarize this evidence in three domains: athletics, course enrollment, and career aspirations. In each set of analyses, Eccles and Wigfield (1995) used their measure of self concept of ability as the expectation-related measure because factor analyses indicate that both ratings of one's current com-petence and expectati~~~ ~

~u~~ Eccles and Harold's (1991) data and national statistics indicate that females participate less than do males in competitive athletics at all ages. Figure 2 illustrates the path analyses they did to assess whether gender differences in expectation-related and value-related self beliefs

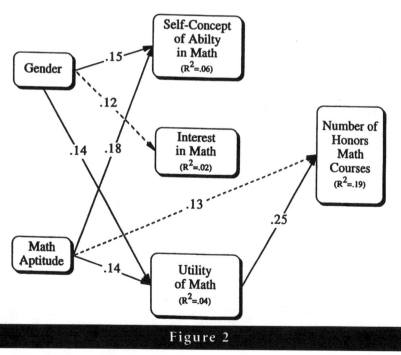

Figure 2

Predicting number of honors math classes.

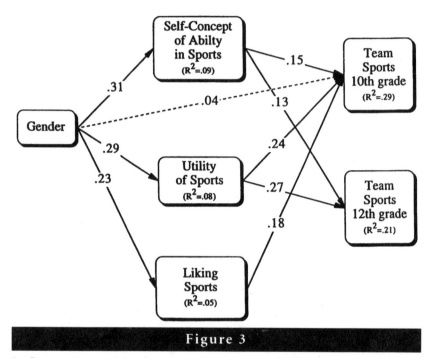

Figure 3

Predicting sport team involvement.

explain this gender difference in participation at both 10th and 12th grades. They entered all three psychological predictors at the same time in these analyses. There was a significant gender difference in participation (assessed in terms of number of competitive sports participated in during the last 12 months) at both grades: Male students were more likely to have participated than were female students (see Figure 3). These differences, however, are totally mediated by the three psychological predictors gathered at 10th grade. The strongest predictor when all three psychological variables were entered into the same model was perceived importance/utility.

Honors Track Math

Figure 4 illustrates the path analyses for the total number of honor's track math courses taken during their high school career by those adolescents who began high school in the honors math track (Updegraff,

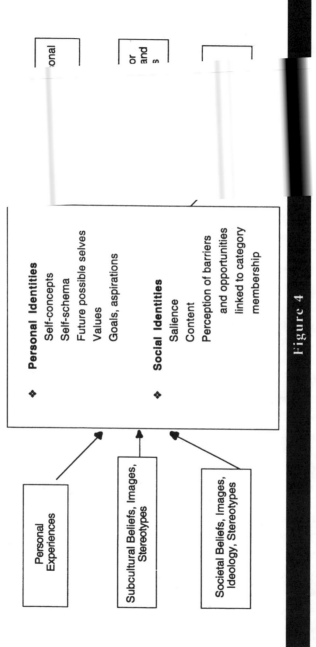

Figure 4

Model of identity influence on behavior.

Eccles, Barber, & O'Brien, 1996). The researchers entered all three psychological predictors at the same time in these analyses. They also entered the students' Differential Aptitude Test (DAT)-quantitative score as a control for ability differences. There was a significant zero-order relation of both gender and DAT to the number of honors track math courses taken in this set of students—the male students took slightly more courses than did the female students and those with higher DAT scores took slightly more courses than did those with lower DAT scores. The gender effect was totally mediated by one of the three psychological predictors: perceived importance/utility. The DAT relationships were also substantially mediated by perceived importance/utility. Neither 10th-grade enjoyment/interest nor self concept of ability predicted the number of courses taken.

So here again we find good support for the Eccles et al. model. Most important is the power of the two subjective value belief constructs in explaining both individual and gender differences in honors students' high school math course enrollment patterns. We are particularly struck by the strength of the importance/utility construct. Recall the example we gave about the two young women deciding whether to take the college math course. We stressed that there was a perceived importance of the course for the young women's future plans. These data support this emphasis. At this point in the students' lives, they must begin to choose between elective courses. These finding suggest that they weigh the utility of the course for their future educational and vocational goals heavily in making these choices.

Career Aspirations

Four sets of values and beliefs were assessed using a 7-item, Likert-scale format. These sets include (a) values regarding work, future success, relationships, and leadership (lifestyle values); (b) specific job characteristics adolescents might desire in their future occupational settings (valued job characteristics); (c) estimates of future success in different categories of occupations (expected efficacy in jobs); and (d) self-ratings of job-relevant skills (self-perception of skills). Each of the four sets of items was factor analyzed. Factors obtained from the analyses were further broken down based on theoretical and conceptual grounds. Scale items, alphas, means, and standard deviations are presented in the Appendices. We already reported on the gender differences in these beliefs (see Table 1).

Occupational aspirations were assessed using the following open-ended probe: "If you could have ~~~ · '

~~~ ,~~~g women aspired to human service jobs, health professions, and female-typed skilled labor more than did their male peers. However, the majority of both the male and female students aspired to business and law occupations (31% and 30%, respectively).

We used discriminant analyses, run separately for male and female participants, to determine which values, job characteristics, skills, and efficacy expectations best discriminated between adolescents who aspired to each of the nine occupational categories. The results of discriminant analyses for the women's and the men's aspirations for both science- and math-related professions and health professions are presented in Table 2. In each of these analyses, the discriminate function generated indicators of the extent to which various expectancy and value-related characteristics distinguished between the female (or male) students who aspired to the targeted occupation and the female (or male) students who did not aspire to this occupation.

We first focus on health careers. Both female and male students who aspired to these careers expected to do well in health-related occupations, and they valued people/society-oriented job characteristics in comparison with those who did not aspire to health careers. For female students, those who chose health-related careers also expected to do well in science-related occupations. For male students, those who chose health-related careers rated their machinery skills low and their working with others skills high in comparison with male students who did not aspire to these careers.

Table 2
Discriminations Between Those Who Do and Those Who Do Not Aspire to Certain Professions

Occupation	Males		Females	
	Discriminating variable	Structure coefficient	Discriminating variable	Structure coefficient
Science related	(N = 90 aspiring/331 not aspiring)		(N = 45 aspiring/536 not aspiring)	
	Efficacy—science related	.51	Efficacy—science related	.61
	Job value—math/composition	.51	Job value—people/society	−.40
	Skills—computers	.32	Efficacy—male typed	.27
	Skills—machinery	.31	Job value—math/composition	.27
	Efficacy—business/law	−.28		
Health related	(N = 20 aspiring/401 not aspiring)		(N = 56 aspiring/525 not aspiring)	
	Efficacy—health related	.65	Efficacy—health related	.81
	Skills—machinery	−.28	Efficacy—science related	.56
	Skills—working with others	.26	Job value—people/society	.29
	Job value—people/society	.25		

Note. Only coefficients correlating with the function at .25 or above are reported here.

With regard to science–math careers, male and female students who aspired to these careers expected to do well in science-related fields and valued math and computer job tasks when compared with other students. Male students who ~~~~~ ~ ~

~~~~~ ~~~~~~. For both male and female students, occupational aspirations are mediated by expectatancy beliefs and values. In addition, both approach- (i.e., "I expect to do well in science, therefore I will choose a science career") and avoidance- (i.e., "I do not value people/society-oriented job tasks, therefore I will aspire to something else") related beliefs predict the occupational choices for both male and female students. The importance of considering all of these factors in explaining occupational choice has been stressed by Eccles and her colleagues (e.g., Eccles, 1987; Eccles [Parsons] et al., 1983).

Second, there are intriguing gender and occupational category differences in the discriminating characteristics. For instance, expecting to do well in science-related occupations discriminates against female students who chose science-related or health careers from those who do not aspire to such careers. This is not true of male students, where only science-related expectancies discriminate between those male students who choose science careers and those who do not. In regard to the female students who chose science-related or health careers, it is important to point out that the value of people–society job characteristics also discriminates between those female students who aspire to health or science–math careers and those who do not. However, it discriminates in opposite directions for these two career options. That is, female students who aspire to health careers place high value on people/society-oriented job characteristics; in contrast, female students who aspire to science-related careers place unusually low value on the people/

173

society-oriented aspects of jobs. Considering that they both expect to do well in science-related careers, it follows that one of the critical components influencing female students' decisions to go into a science-versus health-related field is not a science-related efficacy but the value these students place on having a job associated with people and humanistic concerns. Thus, increased emphasis on the humanistic and people-oriented aspects of science-related careers, not increased emphasis on ability perceptions alone, is important in encouraging more female students to consider science-related occupations.

GENDER ROLES AND GENDER DIFFERENCES IN OCCUPATIONAL CHOICE

This analysis has a number of important implications for understanding how gender can lead to differences in the educational and vocational choices. Because socialization shapes individuals' self-perceptions, identity formation, goals and values, men and women should acquire different self concepts, different patterns of expectations for success across various activities, and different values and goals through the processes associated with gendered socialization. Through the potential impact of the socialization practices linked to various gender roles on both expectations for success and subjective task value, these socialization experiences can affect educational vocational choices in several ways. (Like Spence, 1993, we explicitly use the term *gender roles* instead of gender role because there are many gender roles linked to various aspects of life.)

For one, because gendered socialization experiences influence identity formation, such experiences could lead male and female students to have different hierarchies of core personal values (e.g., their terminal and instrumental values; Rokeach, 1973). Several studies document such differences. For example, among the high school seniors in a longitudinal study of adolescent life transitions (MSALT), female students placed more value than did male students on the importance of making occupational sacrifices for one's family and of having a job that allows one to help others and do something worthwhile for society. In contrast, the male students placed more value on becoming famous, making lots of money, seeking out challenging tasks, and doing work that involves the use of math and computers (Jozefowicz ~+ ~1 ~~~~~ ~~

~~ ~ ~~~~~~~~~, ~~-

~~~~~~, and political values (George & Denham, 1976; McGinn, 1976). Gifted boys and girls, however, typically scored equally high on investigative interests (Fox et al., 1976; George & Denham, 1976; McGinn, 1976). To the extent that these differences exist, tasks embodying various characteristics should have different subjective values for women and men. For example, both boys and girls stereotype mathematicians and scientists as loners who have little time for their families or friends because they work long hours in a laboratory on abstract problems that typically have limited immediate social implications (Boswell, 1979). If the analysis developed in the previous section is correct, such a profession should hold little appeal to someone who rates social values high and thinks it is very important to devote time and energy to one's family.

Gender-role socialization could also lead male and female students to place different values on various long-range goals and adult activities. The essence of gender roles (and of social roles in general) is that they define the activities central to those roles. In other words, they define what one should do with one's life to be successful in those roles one considers central to one's identity. If success in various gender-related roles is a central component of one's identity, then activities that fulfill these roles would have high subjective task value and activities that hamper efforts at successfully fulfilling one's internalized gender roles would have lower subjective task value. Gender roles mandate different primary activities for women and men. Traditionally in the gendered roles of wives and mothers, women are supposed to support their husbands' careers and raise their children; men are supposed to compete successfully in the occupational world to confirm their worth as human beings and support their families. To the extent that a woman has internalized this culture's traditional definition of the female roles, she should rank order the importance of the associated adult activities differently than would her male peers. In particular, she should rate the parenting and the spouse-support roles as more important than a professional career role and be more likely than her male peers to resolve life's decisions in favor of these family roles.

Evidence of these gender differences is found in MSALT. As noted earlier, the women in this study indicated they would be more likely to make sacrifices in their professional life for the needs of their family than did the men (Jozefowicz et al., 1993). They were also more likely to mention both family and career concerns in qualitative descriptions of what they thought a day in their lives would be like when they were age 25. Clearly, their future family roles were much more salient to them than to their male peers. Most interesting, occupational concerns were also quite salient in their day-in-the-life descriptions. Many of these young women were anticipating a life filled with both heavy work and family responsibilities. They were not yet fully aware of the difficulties such a life would entail. Both Sears (1979) and Kerr (1985) provided compelling examples of how such a life influenced the career-related decisions of gifted women—many of whom ended up choosing to limit their career development after they had had their families to fulfill their image of their role as wife and mother. Whether the MSALT generation of young women will make the same choices as they move through adulthood remains to be seen. Certainly, on the one hand, more women today are continuing their careers after they have children. On the other hand, women today are still more likely than men to work part time and to modify their career behavior to accommodate their spouses' career needs (Crosby, 1991).

In contrast, men should find integrating family and career roles easier. In fact, because they can fulfill their family role by having a successful career, men should expect these two sets of gendered roles to be compatible. Consequently, aspiring after a high status, time-consuming career should not pose as much of a conflict for men and such careers should have high subjective value, not only because of the rewards inherent in these occupations but also be~~~~ ~~ ~ ~ ~ male gender-role ~~~ ¹

~~~~~ to

~~~ ~~~ parenting role provides an excellent example of this process. If men define success in the parenting role as an extension of their occupational role, then they would respond to parenthood with increased commitment to their career goals and with an emphasis on encouraging a competitive drive in their children. In contrast, if women define success in the parenting role as high levels of involvement in their children's lives, they would respond to parenthood with decreased commitment to their career goals. Furthermore, if staying home with her children and being psychologically available to them most of the time are central components of a woman's gender-role schema, then involvement in a demanding, high-level career would have reduced subjective value precisely because it conflicts with a more central component of her identity.

Women and men may also differ in the density of their goals and values. Some evidence suggests that men are more likely than women to exhibit a single-minded devotion to one particular goal, especially their occupational goal. In contrast, women seem more likely than men to be involved in, and to value, competence in several activities simultaneously (Maines, 1983). Similar results emerge from studies of gifted children and adults (e.g., McGinn, 1976; Terman & Oden, 1947). For example, in one study the gifted boys evidenced a more unidimensional set of interests than did gifted girls on the Strong Vocational Interest Blank. That is, the boys scored quite high on investigative interests and low on most other interests; in contrast, the girls scored higher than average on several interest clusters (McGinn, 1976). A similar discrepancy emerged when these gifted boys and girls were asked to rate several occupations on the Semantic Differential scales. The boys gave positive ratings only to traditional male scientific and mathematical professions; all of the female professions and the homemaker role were rated negatively. In contrast, the gifted girls gave both male- and female-typed professions, as well as the homemaker role, very positive ratings. A similar pattern emerges from a recent wave of data collection from the Terman (1926) sample (Sears, 1979). These gifted women and men were asked to rate how important each of six goals was to them in making their life plans during early adulthood. The men rated only one area (occupation) as having had higher importance than did the women; in contrast, the women rated four areas as having had higher importance than did the men (family, friends, richness of one's cultural life, and joy in living). These data suggest that these gifted women had desired a more varied, or multi-faceted, type of life than the men had desired at precisely the time in one's life when people make major decisions about their life plans.

One other pattern characterized the responses of these gifted women and men: The men rated family and occupation as of equal importance, whereas the women rated family as more important than occupation, which is consistent with our hypothesis and our findings. Several researchers have suggested that the perceived conflict of traditional female values and roles with the demands of male-typed achievement activities is very salient to women (e.g., Barnett & Baruch, 1978; Baruch, Barnett, & Rivers, 1983; Eccles, 1987; Farmer, 1985). How this conflict affects women's lives is a complex issue. Some studies emphasize its negative consequence. For example, recent interviews with the Terman (1926) sample women suggest that they now have regrets about the sacrifices they made in their professional development for their family's needs (Sears, 1979).

Similar studies with children and adolescents suggest that girls and young women feel caught between their need to be "nice" and their need to achieve. This conflict in gifted girls' lives is well illustrated by a recent ethnographic study of a group of gifted elementary school girls

by Lee Anne Bell (1989). She interviewed a multiethnic group of third to sixth grade gifted girls in an urban elementary school, regarding the barriers they perceived to their achievement in school. Five gender-role related themes emerged with great regularity: (a) conce~~ ~~
someone else's feeling b~~ ~~

~~--~~ing their
~~ ~~ or doing the "caring" thing.
~~S~~imilarly, in his study of the worries of doctoral students in mathematics, Maines (1983) found that men were most concerned about their professional status and about their mentors' estimates of their professional potential. In contrast, women were most concerned about the impact of their graduate training on their families and their other interests; they felt that graduate training was taking too much time and energy away from other activities that they valued just as much. Thus, the women appeared to place high attainment value on several goals and activities; in contrast, the men appeared more likely to focus on one main goal: their professional development. If this were true, then the psychological cost of engaging in their primary goal in terms of time and energy lost for other important goals would certainly be less for these men than for their female colleagues.

Several investigators have pointed out that this conflict results, in part, from the fact that women have multiple roles and multiple goals (e.g., Barnett & Baruch, 1978; Crosby, 1991; Eccles, 1994). These multiple roles, however, provide richness to women's lives as well as stress. There is growing evidence that women with multiple roles are healthier both mentally and physically than are women with fewer roles and than men in general (Barnett & Baruch, 1978; Crosby, 1991).

Finally, as predicted in the model of Figure 1, gender roles could affect the subjective value of various educational and vocational options indirectly through their influence on the behaviors and attitudes of the people to whom individuals are exposed as they grow up. If, for example, parents, friends, teachers, and counselors provide boys and girls with different feedback on their performance in various school subjects, different advice regarding the importance of various school subjects, different information regarding the importance of preparing to support oneself and one's family, different information regarding the occupational opportunities that the student should be considering, and different opportunities to develop various skills, then it is likely that girls and boys will develop different self-perceptions, different patterns of expectations for success, and different estimates of the value of various educational and vocational options. Similarly, if the female and male individuals around the children engage in different educational and vocational activities, then girls and boys should develop different ideas regarding those activities for which they are best suited. Finally, if one's peers reinforce traditional gender-role behaviors and values, female and male individuals will likely engage in different activities as they grow up and thus are likely to acquire different competencies, different patterns of expectations or success, and different values and long-term goals.

CONCLUSION

In this chapter, we suggested that gender roles have their largest impact on life trajectories through their affect on both personal and social identities. As girls and boys grow up, some learn to value those aspects of life and personality that are consistent with their various gender-related roles. They learn to see themselves in terms of these gender roles. Such a socialization process affects their expectations and values, which in turn affect their life choices (see Figure 4). Exactly why some women and men place great importance on such roles and others do not is the subject of extensive theorizing and empirical work. Developmental psychologists have linked it to gendered socialization pressures from parents, peers, and the larger social context and to the child's early need to form stable social categories and personal identities and then to become competent members of the groups they have identified with (e.g., Eccles, 1990; Eccles & Bryan, 1994; Huston, 1983). To the extent that the child grows up in a gendered world with strong pressures toward conformity to that world, the child will attach great importance to behaving in accord with the norms of this ~~gender~~ ' trast. to the ---

---...uun.cation,

---...ung these various theories further is beyond the scope of this chapter. But critical for this chapter is our belief that gender roles affect behavioral choices largely through their influence on identity formation, which in turn shapes expectations for success and values.

REFERENCES

Atkinson, J. W. (1964). *An introduction to motivation.* Princeton, NJ: Van Nostrand.

Barnett, R. C., & Baruch, G. K. (1978). *The competent woman.* New York: Irvington.

Baruch, G., Barnett, R., & Rivers, C. (1983). *Life prints.* New York: McGraw-Hill.

Bell, L. A. (1989). Something's wrong here and it's not me: Challenging the dilemmas that block girls' success. *Journal for the Education of the Gifted, 12,* 118–130.

Benbow, C. P. (1988). Sex differences in mathematical reasoning ability in intellectually talented preadolescents: Their nature, effects, and possible causes. *Behavioral and Brain Sciences, 11,* 169–183.

Benbow, C. P., & Minor, L. L. (1986). Mathematically talented males and females and achievement in the high school sciences. *American Educational Research Journal, 23,* 425–436.

Benbow, C. P., & Stanley, J. C. (1982). Consequences in high school and college of sex differences in mathematical reasoning ability: A longitudinal perspective. *American Educational Research Journal, 19,* 598–622.

Betz, N. E., & Fitzgerald, L. F. (1987). *The career psychology of women.* Orlando, FL: Academic Press.

Betz, N. E., & Hackett, G. (1986). Applications of self-efficacy theory to understanding career choice behavior. *Journal of Social and Clinical Psychology, 4,* 279–289.

Boswell, S. (1979, April). *Nice girls don't study mathematics: The perspective from elementary school.* Paper presented at the annual meeting of the American Educational Research Association, San Francisco, CA.

Crandall, V. C. (1969). Sex differences in expectancy of intellectual and academic reinforcement. In C. P. Smith (Ed.), *Achievement-related behaviors in children* (pp. 11–45). New York: Russell Sage Foundation.

Crosby, F. J. (1991). *Juggling.* New York: Free Press.

Dauber, S. L., & Benbow, C. P. (1990). Aspects of personality and peer relations of extremely talented adolescents. *Gifted Child Quarterly, 34,* 10–15.

Dunteman, G. H., Wisenbaker, J., & Taylor, M. E. (1978). *Race and sex differences in college science program participation.* Research Triangle Park, NC: National Science Foundation.

Eccles, J. S. (1987). Gender roles and women's achievement-related decisions. *Psychology of Women Quarterly, 11,* 135–172.

Eccles, J. S. (1990). Gender-role socialization. In W. G. Graziano & R. M. Baron (Eds.), *Social psychology* (pp. 160–191). New York: Holt, Rinehart, & Winston.

Eccles, J. S. (1994). Understanding women's educational and occupational choices: Applying the Eccles et al. model of achievement-related choices. *Psychology of Women Quarterly, 18,* 585–609.

Eccles (Parsons), J., Adler, T. F., Futterman, R., Goff, S. B., Kaczala, C. M., Meece, J. L., & Midgley, C. (1983). Expectations, values and academic behaviors. In J. T. Spence (Ed.), *Perspective on achievement and achievement motives: Psychological and sociological approaches* (pp. 75–146). San Francisco: Freeman.

Eccles (Parsons), J., Adler, T., & Meece, J. L. (1984). Sex differences in achievement: A test of alternate theories. *Journal of Personality and Social Psychology, 46,* 26–43.

Eccles, J. S., & Bryan, J. (1994). Adolescence and gender-role transcendence. In

M. Stevenson (Eds.), *Gender-roles across the life span* (pp. 111–148). Muncie, IN: Ball State University Press.

Eccles, J. S., & Harold, R. D. (1991). Gender differences in sport involvement: Applying the Eccles' et al. ~~~~~~ The structure of adolescents' achievement values and expectancy-related beliefs. *Personality and Social Psychology Bulletin, 21,* 215–225.

Eccles, J. S., Wigfield, A., Flanagan, C. A., Miller, C., Reuman, D. A., & Yee, D. (1989). Self-concepts, domain values, and self-esteem: Relations and changes at early adolescence. *Journal of Personality, 57,* 283–310.

Eccles, J. S., Wigfield, A., Harold, R. D., & Blumenfeld, P. (1993). Ontogeny of children's self-perceptions and subjective task values across activity domains during the early elementary school years. *Child Development, 64,* 830–847.

Farmer, H. S. (1985). Model of career and achievement motivation for women and men. *Journal of Counseling Psychology, 32,* 363–390.

Fox, L. H. (1976). Sex differences in mathematical precocity: Bridging the gap. In D. P. Keating (Ed.), *Intellectual talent: Research and development* (pp. 183–214). Baltimore: Johns Hopkins University Press.

Fox, L. H., Pasternak, S. R., & Peiser, N. L. (1976). Career-related interests of adolescent boys and girls. In D. P. Keating (Ed.), *Intellectual talent: Research and development* (pp. 242–261). Baltimore: Johns Hopkins University Press.

George, W. C., & Denham, S. A. (1976). Curriculum experimentation for the mathematically talented. In D. P. Keating (Ed.), *Intellectual talent: Research and development* (pp. 103–131). Baltimore: Johns Hopkins University Press.

Goldberg, S. (1973). *The inevitability of patriarchy.* New York: Morrow.

Hollinger, C. L. (1983). Self-perception and the career aspirations of mathematically talented female adolescents. *Journal of Vocational Behavior, 22,* 49–62.

Huston, A. C. (1983). Sex-typing. In P. Mussen & E. M. Hetherington (Eds.), *Handbook of child psychology* (Vol. 4, pp. 387–467). New York: Wiley.

Jozefowicz, D. M., Barber, B. L., & Eccles, J. S. (1993, March). *Adolescent work-related values and beliefs: Gender differences and relation to occupational aspirations.* Paper presented at the biennial meeting of the Society for Research on Child Development, New Orleans, LA.

Kerr, B. A. (1985). *Smart girls, gifted women.* Dayton, OH: Ohio Psychology.

Lewin, K. (1938). *The conceptual representation and the measurement of psychological forces.* Durham, NC: Duke University Press.

Maines, D. R. (1983, April). *A theory of informal barriers for women in mathematics.* Paper presented at the annual meeting of the American Educational Research Association, Montreal, Quebec, Canada.

McGinn, P. V. (1976). Verbally gifted youth: Selection and description. In D. P. Keating (Ed.), *Intellectual talent: Research and development* (pp. 160–182). Baltimore: Johns Hopkins University Press.

Meece, J. L., Eccles (Parsons), J., Kaczala, C. M., Goff, S. B., & Futterman, R. (1982). Sex differences in math achievement: Toward a model of academic choice. *Psychological Bulletin, 91,* 324–348.

National Science Foundation. (1996). *Women, minorities and persons with physical disabilities in science and engineering.* Washington, DC: Author.

Rokeach, M. (1973). *The nature of human values.* New York: Free Press.

Schunk, D. H., & Lilly, M. W. (1982, April). *Attributional and expectancy change in gifted adolescents.* Paper presented at the annual meeting of the American Educational Research Association, New York, NY.

Sears, P. S. (1979). The Terman genetic studies of genius, 1922–1972. In A. H. Passow (Ed.), *The gifted and the talented: Their education and development. The seventy-eighth yearbook of the National Society of the Study of Education* (pp. 75–96). Chicago: University of Chicago Press.

Spence, J. T. (1993). Men, women, and society: Plus ca change, plus c'est la meme chose [The more things change, the more they stay the same]. In S. Oskamp & M. Costanzo (Eds.), *Claremont Symposium on Applied Social*

Psychology, 1992: Gender and social psychology (pp. 3–17). Newbury Park, CA: Sage.

Spence, J. T., & Helmreich, R. L. (1978). *Masculinity and femininity: Their psychological dimensions, correlates, and antecedents.* Austin: University of

versity of New York.

Terman, L. M. (1926). *Genetic studies of genius* (Vol. 1). Stanford, CA: Stanford University Press.

Terman, L. M., & Oden, M. H. (Eds.). (1947). *Genetic studies of genius. Vol. 4: The gifted child grows up.* Stanford, CA: Stanford University Press.

Tomlinson-Keasey, C., & Smith-Winberry, C. (1983). Educational strategies and personality outcomes of gifted and nongifted college students. *Gifted Child Quarterly, 27,* 35–41.

Vetter, B., & Babco, E. (1986). *Professional women and minorities.* Washington, DC: Commission on Professionals in Science and Technology.

Weiner, B. (1974). *Achievement motivation and attribution theory.* Morristown, NJ: General Learning Press.

Wigfield, A., Eccles, J. S., Mac Iver, D., Reuman, D. A., & Midgley, C. M. (1991). Transitions at early adolescence: Changes in children's domain-specific self-perceptions and general self-esteem across the transition to junior high school. *Developmental Psychology, 27,* 552–565.

Updegraff, K. A., Eccles, J. S., Barber, B. L., & O'Brien, K. M. (1996). Course enrollment as self-regulatory behavior: Who takes optional high school math courses. *Learning and Individual Differences, 8,* 239–259.

APPENDIX A

Lifestyle Values

Scale item	α	M	SD
High status/competitive	.76	4.6	1.4
I'd like to accomplish something in life that will be well known.			
I feel that winning is very important.			
I'd like to be famous.			
I would rather be president of a club than just a member.			
When a group I belong to plans an activity, I would rather organize it myself than have someone else organize it and just help out.			
It is important for me to perform better than others on a task.			
Risk taking	.64	4.9	1.1
I more often attempt difficult tasks that I am not sure I can do than easier tasks I believe I can do.			
I like to try things I've never done before.			
I would rather do something at which I feel confident and relaxed than something that is challenging and difficult. (reverse coded)			
I really enjoy working in situations involving skill and competition.			
Careerism	.60	5.6	1.0
Doing my best at the tasks I take on is very important to me.			
I want to do my best in my job even if this sometimes means working overtime.			
I expect my work to be a very central part of my life.			
Family and friends before job	.52	4.3	1.1

Scale item	α	M	SD
I would turn down a promotion in my career if it meant			
	.⌣⌣	⌣.⌣	⌣.⌣
I would give up a secure job for a chance to make big money.			
I would like a lot of expensive possessions.			

Note.   1 = *strongly disagree* to 7 = *strongly agree.*

APPENDIX B

Valued Job Characteristics

Scale item	α	M	SD
Flexibility to meet family needs	.79	5.5	1.1
Has a flexible working schedule you can adjust to meet the needs of your family.			
Leaves a lot of time for other things in your life.			
Does not require you to be away from your family.			
Allows you to be at home when children are out of school (like teaching).			
You have more than 2 weeks vacation.			
Makes it easy to take a lot of time off for family responsibilities.			
People/society oriented	.77	5.4	1.1
Gives you an opportunity to be directly helpful to others.			
Gives you contact with a lot of people.			
Involves working with children.			
Gives you a chance to make friends.			
Is worthwhile to society.			
Prestige/responsibility	.73	5.4	1.0
Has high status and prestige.			
You get a chance to participate in decision making.			
You get a chance to work on difficult and challenging problems.			
You are your own boss most of the time.			
Creative/educational	.70	5.8	1.1
You have the chance to be creative.			
You can learn new things and new skills.			
Machinery/manual work	.60	3.4	1.5
Involves a lot of work with your hands.			
Involves operating heavy machinery.			

Scale item	α	M	SD
Math/computer work	.50	4.0	1.5

APPENDIX C

Expect Efficacy in Jobs

Scale item	α	M	SD
Health related	.87	4.0	1.8
Health paraprofessional (like paramedic, dental hygienist, medical technician, vet's assistant).			
Health professional (like registered nurse, physical therapist, pharmacist).			
Health (like physician, dentist, psychiatrist, veterinarian).			
Skilled labor/protective services (male typed)	.80	3.2	1.4
Transportation (like taxicab, bus, or truck driver).			
Factory (like assembly line worker, welder).			
Protective or military service (like police officer, fire fighter, military duty).			
Skilled worker in electronics or computer repair.			
Other skilled worker (like carpenter or mechanic).			
Professional athlete.			
Science related	.73	3.7	1.9
Science- or math-related field (like engineer, architect, science teacher).			
Science (like scientist or a PhD).			
Business and law	.70	4.7	1.4
Owner of small business (like restaurant owner, shop owner).			
Business manager or administrator, stock broker.			
Lawyer.			
Skilled labor/human services (female typed)	.69	4.0	1.3
Full-time homemaker.			
Child care/day care.			
Personal service (like cosmetologist, masseuse, tailor, chef).			

Clerical or office worker (like typist, receptionist, secretary).

Scale item	α	M	SD

$7 = I$ *would do well).*

APPENDIX D

Self-Perception Skills

Scale item	α	M	SD
Working with others	.77	5.2	1.0
Taking care of children			
Listening to and understanding others			
Teaching and explaining to others			
Helping others solve their problems			
Patience			
Leadership	.75	5.0	1.2
Supervising others			
Being a leader			
Independence	.75	5.3	1.1
Independence			
Self-confidence			
Decisiveness			
Intellectual	.73	5.1	1.2
Logical, analytical thinking			
Intelligence			
Mechanical	na	3.2	1.8
Repairing mechanical equipment			
Computers	na	4.1	1.7
Computer skills			

Note. Participants were given a list of skills and abilities and were asked the following: Compared with others, how good are you at each of the following (7-point Likert scale: *a lot worse than others* to *a lot better than others*).

8

Sexism and Other "Isms":

The questions we address in this chapter can be traced through 2½ decades of work by Janet Taylor Spence and her colleagues. More than any other single researcher, Spence has sought to establish the content of beliefs about women, to determine whether these beliefs are merely descriptions of women or prescriptions for how women ought to be, and to document what has changed and what has remained the same in attitudes toward women across decades of social turmoil in male–female relations. Twenty-five years ago, Spence and Helmreich (1972b) asked, "Who Likes Competent Women?" in an effort to determine whether women who violate gender stereotypes are disliked. This article addresses the issue of whether gender stereotypes are purely descriptive expectations or prescriptions that are enforced through punishment when they are violated. Implicit in the question is the notion that "feminine" women are seen as very likable but as less competent than men. At the same time, Spence and her colleagues developed the first psychometrically sound and, subsequently, most widely used instruments to measure attitudes toward and stereotypes about women: the Attitudes Toward Women Scale (Spence & Helmreich, 1972a) and the Personal Attributes Questionnaire (PAQ; Spence, Helmreich, &

Stapp, 1974). With these tools, Spence continued to examine historical changes in attitudes toward women (e.g., Spence & Hahn, 1997) and the persistence of gender stereotypes from the early 1970s through the late 1990s (Spence & Buckner, in press).

Spence's work raises a number of questions that stereotyping researchers ought to be able to answer. Why do some stereotypes, such as those of women, remain stable over time, whereas others change drastically over the space of a few decades? Why are stereotypes of some cultural minorities (women, again) partially affectionate, albeit in a patronizing way, whereas other groups are stereotyped in a primarily hostile manner? Why are stereotypes of some groups relatively *prescriptive*, specifying what group members ought to be like, whereas other stereotypes are purely *descriptive*, suggesting only what group members are like?

OVERVIEW

Our own prescriptive notion is that social psychologists ought to be able to answer these questions with relatively more ease than they currently can. Although various theorists have laid most of the pieces to this puzzle on the table, not enough work has been done to put them together. To suggest some preliminary answers to the questions just outlined, we try to synthesize a useful framework for addressing these issues. In particular, we suggest that (a) stereotypes typically categorize groups along two dimensions, *competence* (ability to achieve prestigious goals) and *likability* (interpersonal pleasantness); (b) perceived competence is primarily determined by a group's status (with higher status groups stereotyped as more competent), whereas perceived likability is determined by intergroup *competition* (negative interdependence, which leads to negative trait ascriptions) versus *cooperation* (positive interdependence, which leads to more "benevolent" inferences about the interpersonal traits of members of subordinate groups); and (c) stereotypes of subordinate groups become prescriptive and paternalistic when the dominant group is dependent on the subordinate group in a significant way.

STEREOTYPES: OLD AND NEW

To address the issues raised above, we look particularly at a tale of two stereotypes: those of women and of African Americans. In a classic

shows or ignorance to get help).

Hacker's (1951) version of the stereotype of Blacks is as outdated as the term *Negro* and only recognizable today from movies made 40 or more years ago that depict a wide-eyed, deferential, superstitious, happy-go-lucky caricature. Today, stereotypes of Blacks continue to assert that they are less intelligent than Whites, but Blacks are no longer seen as supplicatory, deferential, and content. In addition to traits lost, other traits have been added that portray Blacks as criminal, hostile, loud, and dangerous (Devine & Elliot, 1995). In contrast, the overall stereotype of women has remained remarkably stable, despite sweeping changes in gender relations. Spence and Buckner (1998) found that stereotypes of men and women on the central dimensions of expressivity and instrumentality, as assessed by the PAQ, were virtually the same in a 1996 student sample as they were in 1974. We believe that stereotypes of women still contain significant prescriptive content as well (e.g., that women ought to be nurturant and supportive of others). This is not to say that stereotypes of women have been unresponsive to social change. Changes, such as the movement of women into the paid workforce, are reflected in images of subtypes of women (e.g., career women), which are quite different than the general stereotype of women as a group (Ashmore, Del Boca, & Titus, 1984; the proliferation of these subtypes is addressed in more detail below).

The traits in both old and new stereotypes of Blacks and continuing (general) stereotypes of women seem to cluster on two basic factors, as identified by Spence and Helmreich (1978): expressive or communal

orientation toward others, which is what lies behind women's stereo-
typical likability (Eagly & Mladinic, 1993), and instrumental or agentic
competence in valued (typically masculine) domains (e.g., analytical
skills).[1] In each case, Hacker's (1951) stereotypes suggest a combination
of likability and a lack of task competence (the ability to achieve prestigious goals). The new stereotype of Blacks retains the ascription of
lower competence, but the amiability that previously was attributed to
Blacks has now changed to nastiness. Although the old stereotype was
by no means flattering, it also possessed a certain kind of paternalistic
warmth; it portrayed Blacks as easy to get along with and interpersonally pleasant. It is crucial to note, however, that the "positive" aspects
of these attitudes are also extremely patronizing. Such liking is of the
sort expressed for a pleasant buffoon or a silly child—for Uncle Tom
or little Black Sambo. Still, such feelings on the part of racially biased
Whites who held these stereotypes suggest that some aspects of the
stereotype had a subjectively positive valence, conveying a kind of affection (perhaps similar to the kind people reserve for their pets and
which some men still direct toward some women). It has been precisely
these subjectively positive, even though patronizing, trait ascriptions
that have disappeared from the stereotype, only to be replaced with a
set of purely hostile ones: loudness, nastiness, criminality.

Another important change has occurred in the stereotype of Blacks.
The earlier stereotype, like its female counterpart, seems to have had a
more prescriptive tone to it than does the present stereotype. The old
stereotype suggests that Blacks were just fine as long as they "knew their
place." Blacks were supposed to be deferential and supplicatory, content

---

[1] Readers may wish for greater clarification on what, exactly, we mean by *competence* and *likability*.
We use *competence* as a shorthand for task competence, the skills that are commonly believed
required for success outside the home and typically seen as requiring stereotypically masculine
traits (i.e., agentic traits, e.g., ambition, independence, and competitiveness, or masculine physical
traits, e.g., strength and mechanical ability). We are particularly concerned with competence at
tasks that are accorded high status or prestige in a culture (which is why our focus is often on
cognitive skills, although physical prowess can also bring high status). The *likability* dimension
often involves another kind of competence, interpersonal skills such as social sensitivity. Nevertheless, such competence per se is not what this dimension refers to, as one can imagine a socially
bumbling but sweet person who is deemed quite likable by others. Thus, this dimension accords
well with stereotypically feminine communal traits (e.g., caring).

with their place in society—just as some people still think that women are supposed to be nurturant and supportive toward men and content to be cared for by them. As Fiske and Stevens (1993) noted, however, current stereotypes of Blacks are clearly descriptive rather than pre-

Two Kinds of Out-Groups

On a closer examination, other generic group stereotypes, in addition to those of women and older concepts of Negroes (in their cooperative, subordinate status), fit the likable but incompetent stereotype. So, too, do African Caribbeans and Latinos, who as recent immigrant groups sometimes fill lower status interdependent roles in American society. In their day, the Italians and Irish were seen as bumbling and lovable. Some stereotypes of older people and of people who are physically challenged fit this pattern as well. A preliminary scale developed by McGroarty and Fiske (1997) reveals that blind people are presumed to be socially sensitive (intuitive and friendly) but also evoke pity for their presumed incompetence (helpless, dependent, incapable). In this sense, blind people fill some similar roles to traditional women and Blacks, a grateful burden on the superior party, in this case, sighted people. Thus, one cluster of out-groups appears to be liked but not respected, representing a certain kind of ambivalence.

A contrasting cluster of out-groups is indeed respected but not liked. Lin and Fiske (1997) have validated a scale of attitudes toward Asians and Asian Americans, which also shows ambivalence but in the opposite direction. Asian Americans are currently viewed as a "model" minority, respected as highly competent but disliked for their perceived lack of amiability. Competence items carry a further and significant tinge of envy for Asian Americans' economic success (striving for economic power, overly competitive, acting too smart, working all the

time); these attributes reflect the perceived threat of this out-group to the in-group's status. Sociability items on the Lin and Fiske measure carry disdain (rarely initiates social events, not very "street smart," has less fun). Similarly, Jews have historically been viewed as high achieving but greedy and abrasive. So, too, among stereotypes of Europeans, Germans have been viewed as efficient but cold. Many ethnic minorities view Whites (or at least White men) in a similar manner. This cluster, then, represents a distinct kind of ambivalence, respected but disliked, competent but not likable. It is worth noting that the respect for these groups carries a large element of envy, so it is not in itself a purely positive form of admiration. The respect itself is ambivalent. But the overall cluster is distinctive in being high on perceived competence and low on perceived likability.

In terms of gender relations, women have traditionally been stereotyped as the former type of group—not competent but highly likable. In contrast, men have traditionally been stereotyped as the latter sort of group—ambitious and analytical but insensitive to others (Eagly & Mladinic, 1993). These twin dimensions of gender stereotypes have been recognized before. Spence and Helmreich (1978) have suggested that gender stereotypes are largely encompassed by two dimensions: expressivity and instrumentality.

In keeping with our speculation that these dimensions are not unique to gender relations, other theorists have identified these dimensions as capturing stereotypes of a variety of groups. Allport (1954) noted these twin dimensions, as did Bettleheim and Janowitz (1950). Speaking the language of psychoanalytic projection, they described how some groups represent projections of the stereotyper's id—impulsive, emotional, pleasure seeking, appealing, likable, childish—whereas other groups represent projections of the superego—adherence to standards of achievement and propriety, competent and adult, sober but not exactly warm.

Convergent evidence appears farther afield in other work on person perception and in work on self-perception. Not just stereotyped groups but individual people are generally viewed along two dimensions, as Asch noted as early as 1946. Later, quantitative analyses of descriptions and evaluations of people (Rosenberg, Nelson, & Vivekananthan, 1968) reveal a two-dimensional solution dominated by socially good (honest, amiable, helpful) and socially bad (cold, unhappy, unpopular) traits, on

What is interesting from the perspective of stereotypes is that so many groups have come out high on one dimension but low on the other, representing a practically ubiquitous form of ambivalence on the part of the perceiver.[2] We believe that this is no accident. Stereotype content responds to principles. By *content*, we mean the specific traits contained within a stereotype (e.g., women are sympathetic). Social psychologists have generally focused on stereotype process, without linking it to stereotype content. *Process* refers to the underlying psychological mechanisms that help explain why people form stereotypes (e.g., the use of categorization to simplify information processing). Many process researchers view stereotype content as essentially irrelevant to what they study. For example, that stereotypes serve as a cognitive, labor-saving device holds true, regardless of the specific content of the stereotype or which group the research targets.

Some eminent social psychologists have attempted to understand how historical particulars—specifically, the social roles that groups inhabit—determine the content of stereotypes. Campbell (1967; Levine & Campbell, 1972) argued that stereotypes of rural laborers, for ex-

---

[2]Interpersonal perception research typically shows a positive correlation between perceptions of another's competence and likability (Cooper, 1981). Our observations suggest that in stereotypes about groups these dimensions tend toward a negative correlation. We believe this is because intergroup competition is typically fueled when groups have relatively equal status (Tajfel, 1981). When another group is respected because of their status, competitive drives are heightened, creating hostility that is vented by viewing the group as unlikable. Subordinated groups often may be viewed with paternalistic affection, but because of their low status, they are not respected.

ample, share elements characteristic of how White Americans view Black Americans whereas stereotypes of urban dwellers overlap with stereotypes of Whites. Eagly (1987; Eagly & Steffen, 1984), among others, has argued that stereotypes of women and men follow from the social roles they most typically fill. Because women, more often than men, fill caretaker roles, they are seen as possessing communal traits, whereas because men disproportionately have filled provider roles, they are seen as possessing agentic traits.

Although we agree that historical particulars do matter, we make a different point than do these social-role analyses, namely, that certain dimensions of the structural relationships between men and women, or between any other two groups, predict the content of the stereotypes they develop. To anticipate our argument, we theorize that relative status predicts who will be respected as competent whereas positive (cooperative) or negative (competitive) interdependence predicts who will be stereotyped as likable.[3]

Current Examples

Our theory of ambivalent sexism (Glick & Fiske, 1996) proposes dimensions that reflect the ambivalent view of women as likable but incompetent. That theory, along with the accompanying inventory designed to test its implications, the Ambivalent Sexism Inventory (ASI), identifies three dimensions of relationships between men and women, each with a hostile and a benevolent side. The first, *power dynamics,* entails both protective paternalism and dominant paternalism. The second, *gender differentiation,* entails both complementary and competitive conceptions of women's (as compared with men's) traits and behavior. The third, *heterosexuality,* entails both intimacy seeking and potential hostility. These three dimensions are related to the competence–likability dimensions as follows.

---

[3]We use the terms *positive* and *cooperative* here in the technical sense of indicating a stable kind of interdependence that is accepted by both the dominant and the subordinate group but not to indicate that these are healthy or good relations. As Jackman (1994) pointed out, such cooperation can be the result of long-term coercion of subordinates who accept their low-status role because of the norms and reward systems imposed by the dominant group.

Men's greater social status, which could be viewed as structural power (Guttentag & Secord, 1983), presupposes men's competence. This aspect is tapped by the ASI power dimension (paternalism of the

------, ------, --- ------ ----,.

Thus, the generic female stereotype presupposes conventional women, including subtypes such as housewife and chick (for a review, see Fiske, 1998), who are in a cooperative but low-status relationship with a man. Consequently, she is nice but incompetent, fitting established gender stereotypes, traditional heterosexual needs, and accepting the power relationship. The contrasting subtypes of women describe the nontraditional ones: career woman and feminist–athlete–lesbian, who are seen as competent but not likable. They violate conventional gender expectations, do not meet heterosexual needs, and challenge the societal power relationship. Thus, our theory and the ASI suggest two types of women, who contrast on the two dimensions of stereotyped out-groups, according to conventional or unconventional gender attributes and behavior.

In summary, evidence is emerging for the theoretically extendable prospect of two distinct kinds of out-groups, respected but disliked or liked but disrespected. These two types of groups not only fit with stereotypes of men and women but also seem to hold true for social groups in general. In the next section, we elaborate the structural bases for the competence versus likability dimensions.

STATUS AND INTERDEPENDENCE UNDERLIE STEREOTYPE CONTENT

Whether there are, at both the intergroup and the interpersonal level, two general dimensions of classification—likability and agentic competence—is an empirical question. If this were true, as past research suggests it is likely to be, the next question would be *Why*? If one considers people to be pragmatic thinkers, one would suspect that these two dimensions are seen as particularly informative about people (cf. Fiske, 1992; and Stangor, Lynch, Duan, & Glass, 1992). Considering these dimensions within a social context reveals why these dimensions are so important: They reflect differences in social status and whether members of another group are viewed as helpers or competitors.

Perspectives From Intergroup Research: Unstable Systems

When a person first meets someone, he or she needs to establish his or her own status relative to the other. Relative status profoundly affects social interactions, from the choice of formal or informal modes of address to who controls the degree of intimacy permitted (Goffman, 1956; Henley, 1975). In addition, one seeks to determine whether the other person will be a friend or foe, someone from whom one can expect cooperation or with whom one must compete (Fiske & Ruscher, 1993). Arguably, a crucial reason why people rely so much on group stereotypes is that stereotypes allow individuals quickly to infer another's status and whether others are likely to be friends, as in-group members are often assumed to be, or foes, as out-group members are often treated.

How do status and intergroup competitiveness relate to the dimensions of competence and interpersonal orientation? High-status individuals and groups are typically viewed as high in competence, whereas those with low social status are viewed as incompetent. This fact was recognized by Tajfel (1981), who noted the influence of structural relations among groups, particularly social status, on shared social stereotypes. As a result, both dominant and subordinate groups tend to share stereotypes that cast members of lower status groups as less competent (see Jost & Banaji, 1994).

Likewise, the issue of intergroup competition has long been a staple of stereotyping research, tracing back to Sherif's (1966) classic work and on through realistic conflict theory (Levine & Campbell, 1972) and social identity theory (Tajfel, 1981). Sherif showed how cooperation between groups could be induced by a common goal, leading to liking.

However, the emphasis in intergroup research is that the "natural" state of intergroup interaction is competition. Indeed, people are known to be more competitive in intergroup than interpersonal situations; simply

than the competence dimension. One's perceived enemies are likely to be seen as interpersonally nasty, immoral, self-serving, and manipulative. Hostility due to perceived competition is not likely to come out on the competence dimension because it is important to assess accurately the competence of one's competitors (Ruscher & Fiske, 1990; Ruscher, Fiske, Miki, & Van Manen, 1991). Underestimating a competitor can undermine one's own ability to compete and can be easily disconfirmed by more objective indicators of success (e.g., it is difficult to deny that another group has been more economically successful). In contrast, the interpersonal dimension (as Allport, 1954, recognized) allows one to freely vent one's hostility, may both motivate and justify one's own competitiveness by portraying it as self-defense, and is less subject to disconfirmation because the behavior that is apparently friendly or helpful can always be viewed as merely manipulative (see Rothbart, 1981).

Mary Jackman (1994) has recently argued, however, that the competitive (social identity theory) view of intergroup relations is incomplete. Although in today's world hostile competition between groups is an ubiquitous phenomenon, she suggested that this competitive mode characterizes intergroup relationships only under particular social conditions: when the social system is unstable, allowing for group mobility on the part of lower status groups (who then become more direct competitors with dominant groups) or when groups have relatively equal status (a factor that social identity theorists have already proven to heighten intergroup competition; Tajfel, 1981).

Stable Systems of Interdependent Exploitation

Consider a social context in which differences in group status are large and stable and in which the groups are interdependent in ways that promote daily intergroup contact. In these circumstances, intergroup relations are not likely to be overtly competitive. Rather, these social circumstances promote what might be labeled *exploitative interdependence*. Think of such historical circumstances as European colonialism, slavery in the American Old South, the caste system in India, or the relations between men and women in most societies throughout most of recorded human history. In these cases, there have often been long periods in which severe differences in an in-group's status have been maintained. Such stable systems, as Jost and Banaji (1994) and Jackman (1994) argued, spawn system-justifying ideologies, which to some significant extent are accepted by both the dominant and subordinate groups. Although highly exploitative, these group relations are characterized by a high degree of cooperative interdependence between groups, including dependence of the dominant group on the subordinate group, often for their labor but also in the case of men and women their love.

Tajfel (1981) identified the stability and perceived legitimacy of group status differences as important variables for understanding intergroup relationships. Naomi Ellemers and her colleagues have extended this analysis (e.g., Ellemers, Van Rijswijk, Roefs, & Simons, 1997). These theorists, however, have emphasized how social variables affect the tendency of subordinate group members to develop a minority consciousness and to seek social change through collective action, such as the Civil Rights or feminist movements. Our concern here, however, is to consider how these variables affect the content of stereotypes about groups, particularly subordinate or minority groups. Furthermore, whereas Tajfel and Ellemers et al. concentrated on social change and instability, we wish to devote some attention to stereotypes under conditions of more stable group relations.

Jackman (1994) contended that stable and (according to the perceptions of the society's members) "legitimate" group status differences create very different intergroup attitudes from the competitive, hostile type people are used to thinking about. Rather than overt competition between groups, daily group interactions within stable systems may (at the interpersonal level) be highly cooperative. This cooperation is in-

~~following quotation, cited by Jackman, of the reaction by a Black slave,~~ Lorenza Ezell, who was driven to feelings of revenge on the Yankees for the tragedies they inflicted during the Civil War on the White family that owned her: "I was so mad, I could have kilt [sic] all de [sic] Yankees ... I hated dem [sic] 'cause dey [sic] hurt my white people" (Litwack, 1979, as quoted by Jackman, 1994, p. 85). Or consider the feelings of this upper-middle-class White Virginian who was interviewed in the 1940s:

> I loved my Negro mammy and kissed her as I would my white mother. The social side has nothing to do with the human side. I wouldn't have gone to school with the colored boys, but I was in sports with them, camped out with them, ate and slept with them. (Johnson, 1943, as quoted by Jackman, 1994, p. 16)

By no means are we trying to imply that these were "good" group relations, as such relationships are coercive, exploitative, and paternalistic. Neither are we denying the many atrocities that were inflicted on slaves. Nevertheless, as Jackman pointed out, this kind of situation and its consequences for the social psychological character of intergroup relations has been given little attention by intergroup theorists.

That power differences and intimate affection can coexist, however, comes as no great shock to researchers of heterosexual close relationships, who have long understood this feature of heterosexual relationships. Through recorded human history, male dominance and female submissiveness have not merely coexisted with love between the sexes but form part of the essence of cultural images of romance (the powerful male hero who saves the delicate damsel in distress, sweeps her off her feet, and tames her feisty nature). These ideals are reflected in modern dating scripts, in which the man, not the woman, initiates the date, pays for meals, and makes the first sexual "move." Although these norms (and related phenomena, e.g., men's dominance in a couple's decision making) may not be as strong as they once were, they are still prevalent (Peplau, 1983).

By understanding the paternalistic mixture of domination and affection that pervade (but are not necessarily unique to) heterosexual relations, we can better understand the dynamics of stereotyping, in particular, why and when stereotypes of groups will be negative or positive on the likability and competence dimensions and under what conditions stereotypes will be prescriptive rather than descriptive. A more general understanding of these processes, in turn, can help explain how conceptions of women are affected by changes in contemporary society.

Benevolent and Hostile System-Justifying Ideologies

In a stable system of *interdependent exploitation,* system-justifying beliefs are likely to be widely endorsed, as such ideologies are critical to system maintenance (a basic Marxist as well as Tajfelian principle). Jackman (1994) presented compelling historical evidence that in such stable systems, the justifying ideologies have a paternalistically benevolent, rather than a purely hostile, competitive tone. This does not mean that the processes identified by social identity theory are not at work as well. Dominant groups still stereotype subordinate groups as grossly inferior on competence dimensions, thereby providing rationalizations to justify the higher status of the dominant group. Thus, dominant group members still obtain the boost to their self-image that comes from a sense of relative superiority (Oakes & Turner, 1980). However, when there is a considerable dependence of dominants on subordinates, these hostile attitudes coexist with benevolent rationalizations (e.g., the notion of the "White man's burden") as well as stereotypes of subordinate group members as having favorable interpersonal qualities but of the kind that might help keep members in these groups "in their place." These dual aspects can be seen both in stereotypes about women and the old Southern stereotype of Blacks.

beliefs that the Ngwani were closer to the gods and were direct descendants of the first man and woman. Furthermore, the society was depicted as stable, peaceful, and interdependent (e.g., with both groups working the same fields). Under these conditions, although participants stereotyped the Ngwani as more competent (or agentic) than the Gunada, they also stereotyped the Gunada as more interpersonally pleasant (more communal) than the Ngwani. Thus, at least for participants who read about a society with stable and "legitimate" status differences between interdependent groups, the stereotype our reasoning predicts for the subordinate group—incompetent but likable—did indeed emerge.

Imagine how different responses might have been if Conway et al. (1996) had depicted a society in flux, one in which some of the "inferior" Gunada had begun to question the status differences within the society, reject the legitimizing ideology used to justify the traditional status difference, and demand bigger huts and a bigger slice of the society's resources. How would outside observers stereotype such Gunadan activists? More important, how would the Ngwani be expected to stereotype the Gunadans? In thinking about this situation, it seems clear that one would expect most Ngwani to have a very hostile reaction to the Gunadan activists. Indeed, this seems obvious, but a closer examination as to why such hostility is likely helps to explain another aspect of stereotypes within stable social systems with clear status differentiations between interdependent groups: their prescriptive, rather than purely descriptive, nature.

Prescriptive and Descriptive Stereotypes

As noted already, many theorists have suggested that stable status differences between groups are maintained by, and themselves promote, justificatory ideologies (cf. Fiske, 1993; Jackman, 1994; Jost & Banaji, 1994; and Tajfel, 1969). By their very nature, these ideologies not only offer an explanation as to why society is structured in the manner that it is but also justify this as "the way things ought to be." In psychological terms, these ideologies address two sets of motivations. One is what Tajfel labeled the *search for coherence*—the need for a psychologically satisfying explanation of social circumstances (particularly, for Tajfel, under conditions of social flux). This need can be fulfilled by beliefs that are purely descriptive, such as stereotypes that "explain" that the reason one group has lower status is that "they are not as smart" as other groups. Jost and Banaji suggested that this explanatory need itself might lead agreed-on explanations for group-status differences to become elevated to ideologies about how things ought to be. We think this notion does not hold up. Consider again the change in stereotypes of Black Americans. It is difficult to believe that most White people think that Blacks ought to be criminals. The prescription is quite the opposite—that Blacks should not be criminally inclined, even though "that's the way they are" according to the stereotype. In contrast, stereotypes of conventional women remain highly prescriptive—women are not only expected to be nurturant but are desired to be so.

Why do stereotypes of women remain prescriptive? We suggest that an ought quality is attached to stereotypes under conditions in which a second set of motivations is involved: self or group interests. These motivations lead to prescriptive justificatory ideologies, based on what Jost and Banaji (1994) called *ego* and *group* justification. In our view (for which we are strongly indebted to Jackman, 1994), prescriptive rather than merely descriptive stereotypes come about because of a form of dependency by dominant group members on a lower status group because it is such dependencies that create the strongest motivations to maintain the status quo. These dependencies can occur for a variety of reasons, including economics (e.g., relying on the labor of another group) and role divisions (e.g., men's reliance on women to raise the children). The greater these dependencies, the more stake the dominant group has in maintaining the status quo and, in turn, the more prescriptive the resultant stereotypes are about the traits of sub-

cation (prescription) in the realm of stereotypes about groups. Our view is that the old stereotypes of American Blacks, rooted in the slavery system, and traditional stereotypes of women can be viewed as the products of stable social systems, in which the dominant group is significantly dependent on the subordinate group (not only for their labor, in the case of both Blacks and women, but also for many more reasons when it comes to women).

For these stereotypes, a prescriptive tone can be detected on both dimensions of stereotyping: competence and interpersonal pleasantness. Part of keeping "one's place" for members of both of these subordinate groups involved downplaying their competence (e.g., the "shows of ignorance," as mentioned by Hacker, 1951) and behaving in a friendly, deferential manner when interacting with members of the dominant group. Current stereotypes about Blacks, presumably reflecting social changes that have removed any direct dependency Whites had on Blacks, are now merely descriptive. The old prescriptions are out of date because social structural changes have destroyed the interdependence that once existed (especially in the Old South) between Whites and Blacks. In contrast, prescriptive stereotypes of women remain because even if most work outside the home, men are still dependent on them to fulfill domestic roles as wives and mothers.

The conditions under which stereotypes serve primarily descriptive, rather than both descriptive and prescriptive, functions is crucial to an understanding of what maintains specific stereotypes and how counterstereotypical behavior is evaluated. For example, in current U.S. social circumstances in which Whites' stereotypes about Blacks serve a more descriptive function, a Black person who defies the stereotypic expectation of a lack of competence is likely to be evaluated in an extremely favorable manner (e.g., Linville & Jones, 1980). In contrast, gender stereotypes remain (for many people) both descriptive and prescriptive. This may be less true today on the competence dimension, as women in the United States are often expected to work outside the home (although the job market remains highly segregated with many women's jobs as extensions of domestic tasks, e.g., childcare, that are seen as requiring likability more so than agentic competence; Glick, Wilk, & Perreault, 1995). On the likability dimension, however, prescriptions may remain quite strong as women are still expected to be nurturers at home (see below for further discussion). If this is the case, women who defy the stereotypic expectations of interpersonal pleasantness would be treated especially harshly. Because some forms of agentic competence, such as stereotypically masculine forms of leadership, are not high in amiability, women who take on such styles may be therefore punished (in a way that a man would not) for being unpleasant (see Eagly, Makhijani, & Klonsky's, 1992, meta-analysis of reactions to male and female leaders).

IMPLICATIONS FOR GENDER STEREOTYPES

A sharper focus on gender stereotyping is warranted here because attitudes toward women provide a particularly intriguing case study for understanding the prescriptive versus descriptive functions of stereotypes and how stereotypes respond to social change. Relations between women and men have long been characterized by men's dominance in terms of *structural power* (Guttentag & Secord, 1983), as noted previously, namely, control over economic, legal, social, and religious institutions. Nevertheless, also as noted previously, the biology of sexual reproduction ensures that women have some degree of what Guttentag and Secord termed *dyadic power*: power that accrues to women because of men's dependency on women—as wives, mothers, and romantic partners—in interpersonal relationships.

Ambivalent Sexism

We (Glick & Fiske, 1996) have argued that this combination of men's power over and dependence on women often creates ambivalent attitudes toward women. Male ~~structural~~ ~~~~~~~

~~~~~~~~~~ ~~~~~~ ~~~~~~~~

feelings of protectiveness toward women, the belief that men should provide for women, and the notion that women are men's "better half," without whom men are incomplete. These paternalistic justifications, as we have argued, come about when the dominant group is dependent on the subordinate group. We chose the term benevolent not because we believe that these attitudes reflect the best interests of women but rather to acknowledge the subjectively positive feelings associated with these attitudes. We consider them to be sexist because these beliefs reflect very traditional and controlling presumptions about women, such as "the weaker sex," and thus they are in need of men's protection.

We (Glick & Fiske, 1996) have recently validated the ASI, which contains hostile and benevolent sexism subscales. Using confirmatory factor analytic techniques, we have repeatedly confirmed—in both undergraduate and adult samples—that hostile and benevolent sexism are distinct entities, although the two scales are often positively correlated (which supports our assumption that both are forms of sexism). Nevertheless, these two forms of sexism do predict opposing valences when it comes to men's attitudes toward women; hostile sexism predicts negative attitudes and stereotypes, whereas benevolent sexism predicts positive attitudes and stereotypes (see also Glick, Diebold, Bailey-Werner, & Zhu, 1997).

If we couple the ambivalent sexism framework with our current speculation about the conditions that lead to prescriptive stereotyping of subordinate groups, the explanation as to why stereotypes about women are still prescriptive seems clear: Men are still (and will probably always be) dependent on women. To understand the content of the prescriptions for women, one needs to understand the nature of the dependency. Because the greatest dependencies stem from close, interpersonal relationships, the strongest prescriptions should be related to women's interpersonal traits (i.e., women ought to be supportive, nurturant, and sympathetic) rather than the competence dimension. As a result, at an interpersonal level, sexist men may tend to have stronger prescriptive notions about how women are supposed to behave within romantic relationships than about how women are supposed to behave on the job. Indeed, given the current economy, many men have become dependent on their spouses to be competent at an occupation and bring in income. The increase in egalitarian attitudes documented by Spence and her colleagues with the Attitudes Toward Women Scale (see Spence & Hahn, 1997) may well be, in part, a response to these economic changes. In either case, this change in attitudes also suggests that stereotypes of female incompetence are not as strongly held as before and, certainly, not as strongly prescriptive as they were.

Furthermore, our analysis suggests that men are not directly dependent on women as a group (because men have structural power) but rather on the women, or types of women, with whom they may form close attachments (thus lending these women dyadic power). For sexist men, the women able to fulfill this need for a close relationship have the desired stereotypically feminine interpersonal qualities (e.g., nurturance) and are not particularly interested in reversing traditional power relations between the sexes. Thus, sexist men are likely to make sharp distinctions between conventional women and unconventional women (who take on roles that used to be reserved for men or who actively campaign for gender equality). Increasingly, gender stereotype researchers (e.g., Deaux, Winton, Crowley, & Lewis, 1985; Haddock & Zanna, 1994; Six & Eckes, 1991) have indeed recognized that the "basic" level of stereotyping of women—the one most commonly used in everyday interaction—is at the level of such subtypes (e.g., the "career woman"). The stereotypes applied to different subtypes of women, as well as the attitudes these stereotypes reflect, vary widely; so much so that these subtypes can be said to represent highly polarized attitudes toward women.

To understand stereotypes of and attitudes toward these types of women, one needs to consider again an earlier example based upon

activist and economic changes are likely to go hand-in-hand), we would certainly expect hostile reactions from at least some Ngwani.

In analytical terms, our fictitious society would experience a change from a stable, cooperative, interdependent, and legitimate system of status difference (in which, we have argued, the subordinate group is perceived as incompetent but likable) to an unstable system of competing groups. In other words, this Amazonian society would begin to resemble the modern norm in which group relations are characterized by overt competition for status and resources; this type of group relation fits social identity theory so well. How will stereotypes change in these new circumstances? This depends, in part, on the economic success of the Gunada. If they do indeed become successful, they are no longer likely to be stereotyped as incompetent (as is evident in stereotypes about such successful minorities as Jews and Asian Americans). If, however, they are not yet successful, they will remain stereotyped as incompetent. In either case, we can expect a significant change in the stereotype along the interpersonal dimension. The old stereotype of content, friendly, nurturant Gunada is gone and is replaced by stereotypes of hostile, angry, demanding, ungrateful Gunada. Under unstable, competitive group conditions (in which the old interdependencies and coercive cooperation are a thing of the past), relative status remains the most important determinant of stereotypes about competence, but stereotypes on the interpersonal dimension more purely reflect the hostile competition between the groups.

Let us complicate the situation a bit further by imagining that while this social flux is taking place because some Gunada are becoming activists and some are competing successfully for status, many other Gunada remain in their traditional role with its traditional status. Imagine further that this traditional role is where the Gunada contently (or at least overtly so) perform valuable services for the Ngwani, such as tilling the fields or raising Ngwani children, and that most Ngwani are highly dependent on these "traditional" Gunada. Certainly, we would expect the Ngwani to make a sharp distinction between the traditional and nontraditional Gunada. The former are still likely to be treated with paternalistic benevolence—perhaps even more so now that there are other possible roles for them to enact. Thus, the traditional Gunada are likely to be stereotyped in much the same way that they have always been—as interpersonally pleasant but not competent enough to assume high-status roles. Coupled with the hostility directed at the nontraditional Gunada, this would help to entice at least some Gunada to remain in their traditional role. These processes seem especially germane to men's current attitudes toward different types of women.

Current Subtypes of Women

With respect to women, then, we suggest that social changes have not affected the overall stereotype of women but have been accommodated through the use of substereotypes of women, with a traditional versus nontraditional split being the most important dimension on which these subtypes vary. Ashmore et al. (1984) have already made this essential argument, noting that the most common subtypes of women vary along a traditional–nontraditional dimension, helping people to account for what is changing and what remains constant in gender relations. Nontraditional women (e.g., career women or feminists) may be viewed by traditionally minded men as the types of women on whom they are not dependent and who are merely competitors for status and resources (e.g., jobs). Because such women have made considerable economic gains over the past few decades, we would expect them to be stereotyped as competent. However, because they have now become serious competitors, they are likely to be stereotyped quite negatively on the interpersonal dimension. Research on stereotypes of feminists, in particular, reveals a considerable amount of hostility and

evoke the same old benevolently paternalistic feelings in men who hold traditional attitudes. Because beliefs about the "prototypical" woman still seems to be the traditional type (Armstrong, Gleitman, & Gleitman, 1983), Eagly and Mladinic (1993) found that the overall stereotype of women is more favorable than that of men when it comes to the interpersonal dimension (the "women are wonderful" effect) but that women are still seen as less competent than men. Similarly, Haddock and Zanna (1994) found that men had warm and fuzzy feelings toward housewives in contrast to their hostility toward feminists.

That sexist men have polarized views of different subtypes of women was confirmed by Glick et al. (1997). In one study, male undergraduates generated eight types of women (an arbitrary number chosen to get sufficient variety) that represented their most frequently used classifications of women. Many of the types that the men spontaneously generated reflected the traditional–nontraditional dimension. Additional ratings of men's evaluations of their types revealed that sexist men, as indexed by higher scores on the ASI, had more polarized reactions to the types they generated (i.e., they were more likely to hate some and love others). As expected, negative stereotypes about and feelings toward these female types were predicted by men's hostile sex-

---

[4]By *traditional* we mean women who fulfill conventional roles that are subordinate to men's roles and that serve men's needs. Although homemaker is a relatively recent role historically speaking, it fits the general pattern of being a subordinate role in the service to men; it is in this sense that we label it a traditional role.

ism scores, whereas the benevolent sexism scale predicted more positive feelings and stereotypes about the female types. A second study that focuses on one traditional type (homemaker) and one nontraditional type (career women) reveals that homemakers evoked benevolent sexist feelings, with the benevolent sexism scale predicting positive stereotypes toward this type. In contrast, career women elicited hostile sexism, with the hostile sexism scale predicting negative stereotypes toward this type. An examination of the content of these stereotypes confirms that homemakers were viewed primarily in terms of their pleasant interpersonal traits (e.g., warmth) but were seen as less competent (e.g., not as intelligent) whereas even relatively sexist men viewed career women as competent at accomplishing work tasks, but they also viewed them as quite nasty—aggressive, selfish, and cold. Furthermore, consistent with the notion that sexist men view nontraditional women as competitors, these men mentioned feelings of fear, envy, intimidation, and competition toward career women.

In other words, sexist men split women into (at least) two polarized types: the traditional woman who is likable but incompetent and the nontraditional woman who is competent but not likable. The former remains a type on which traditional men remain dependent for intimate relationships; as a result, the interpersonal traits required for the kind of relationships these men desire—in which the woman is supportive, nurturant, and deferent—continue, we think, to be prescriptive aspects of the stereotype. In contrast, the stereotypes of nontraditional women are simply descriptive. Such women are seen as competent because of the considerable (even if still limited) success they have had in the workplace. That this type of woman is seen as nasty is due to the competitive impulses explained by social identity theory, but this too is not a prescription. Rather, such women may be penalized for not fulfilling the prescriptions that are seen characterizing the prototypic woman. It is when such prescriptions about interpersonal traits "spill over" (Gutek, 1985) into the workplace that someone who fits the stereotype of a career woman but therefore violates the prescriptive stereotype associated with traditional women is told that she is "not feminine enough" (Fiske, Bersoff, Borgida, Deaux, & Heilman, 1991).

216

CONCLUSION

We believe that gender relations do present a unique case, in some respects, because of the degree of dependence that men continue to

unpleasant (due to the competitive drives that the group's success actually heightens). Stereotypes of the greedy, manipulative but smart Jew or the inscrutable, clannish but shrewd Asian are two prominent examples. It is only by understanding the structural relations between groups—their relative status, the stability of group relations, and their degree of interdependence—that researchers will truly be able to understand the content of stereotypes and the degree to which they serve as descriptions or prescriptions for group members' behavior.

REFERENCES

Allport, G. (1954). *The nature of prejudice.* Reading, MA: Addison-Wesley.

Armstrong, S. L., Gleitman, L. R., & Gleitman, H. (1983). What some concepts might not be. *Cognition, 13,* 263–308.

Asch, S. E. (1946). Forming impressions of personality. *Journal of Abnormal and Social Psychology, 41,* 1230–1240.

Ashmore, R. D., Del Boca, F. K., & Titus, D. (1984, August). *Types of women: Yours, mine, and ours.* Paper presented at the 92nd Annual Convention of the American Psychological Association, Toronto, Ontario, Canada.

Bettleheim, B., & Janowitz, M. (1950). *Social change and prejudice.* London: Free Press.

Campbell, D. T. (1967). Stereotypes and the perception of group differences. *American Psychologist, 22,* 817–829.

Conway, M., Pizzamiglio, M. T., & Mount, L. (1996). Status, communality, and agency: Implications for stereotypes of gender and other groups. *Journal of Personality and Social Psychology, 71,* 25–38.

Cooper, W. H. (1981). Ubiquitous halo. *Psychological Bulletin, 90,* 218–224.

Deaux, K., Winton, W., Crowley, M., & Lewis, L. L. (1985). Level of categorization and content of gender stereotypes. *Social Cognition, 3*(2), 145–167.

Devine, P. G., & Elliot, A. J. (1995). Are racial stereotypes really fading? The Princeton trilogy revisited. *Personality and Social Psychology Bulletin, 21,* 1139–1150.

Eagly, A. H. (1987). *Sex differences in social behavior: A social role interpretation.* Hillsdale, NJ: Erlbaum.

Eagly, A. H., Makhijani, M. G., & Klonsky, B. G. (1992). Gender and evaluation of leaders: A meta-analysis. *Psychological Bulletin, 111,* 3–22.

Eagly, A. H., & Mladinic, A. (1993). Are people prejudiced against women? Some answers from research on attitudes, gender stereotypes, and judgments of competence. In W. Stroebe & M. Hewstone (Eds.), *European review of social psychology* (Vol. 5, pp. 1–35). New York: Wiley.

Eagly, A. H., & Steffen, V. J. (1984). Gender stereotypes stem from the distribution of women and men into social roles. *Journal of Personality and Social Psychology, 46,* 735–754.

Ellemers, N., Van Rijswijk, W., Roefs, M., & Simons, C. (1997). Bias in intergroup perceptions: Balancing group identity with social reality. *Personality and Social Psychology Bulletin, 23,* 186–198.

Fiske, S. T. (1992). Thinking is for doing: Portraits of social cognition from daguerreotype to laserphoto. *Journal of Personality and Social Psychology, 63,* 877–889.

Fiske, S. T. (1993). Controlling other people: The impact of power on stereotyping. *American Psychologist, 48,* 621–628.

Fiske, S. T. (1998). Stereotyping, prejudice, and discrimination. In D. T. Gilbert, S. T. Fiske, & G. Lindzey (Eds.), *The handbook of social psychology* (4th ed., pp. 357–411). New York: McGraw-Hill.

Fiske, S. T., Bersoff, D. N., Borgida, E., Deaux, K., & Heilman, M. E. (1991). Social science research on trial: Use of sex stereotyping research in *Price Waterhouse v. Hopkins. American Psychologist, 46,* 1049–1060.

Fiske, S. T., & Ruscher, J. B. (1993). Negative interdependence and prejudice: Whence the affect? In D. M. Mackie & D. L. Hamilton (Eds.), *Affect, cognition, and stereotyping: Interactive processes in group perception* (pp. 239–268). New York: Academic Press.

Fiske, S., & Stevens, L. (1993). What's so special about sex? Gender stereotyping and discrimination. In S. Oskamp & M. Costanzo (Eds.), *Gender issues in social psychology* (pp. 173–196). Newbury Park, CA: Sage.

Goffman, E. (1956). The nature of deference and demeanor. *American Anthropologist, 58,* 473–502.

Gutek, B. A. (1985). *Sex and the workplace.* San Francisco: Jossey-Bass.

Guttentag, M., & Secord, P. (1983). *Too many women?* Beverly Hills, CA: Sage.

Hacker, H. M. (1951). Women as a minority group. *Social Forces, 30,* 60–69.

Haddock, G., & Zanna, M. P. (1994). Preferring "housewives" to "feminists": Categorization and the favorability of attitudes toward women. *Psychology of Women Quarterly, 18,* 25–52.

Henley, N. (1975). Power, sex, and nonverbal communication. In B. Thorne & N. Henley (Eds.), *Language and sex: Difference and dominance* (pp. 184–203). Rowley, MA: Newbury.

Jackman, M. R. (1994). *The velvet glove: Paternalism and conflict in gender, class, and race relations.* Berkeley: University of California Press.

Jost, J. T., & Banaji, M. R. (1994). The role of stereotyping in system-justification and the production of false-consciousness. *British Journal of Social Psychology, 33,* 1–27.

Levine, R. A., & Campbell, D. T. (1972). *Ethnocentrism: Theories of conflict, ethnic attitudes, and group behavior.* New York: Wiley.

Lin, M., & Fiske, S. T. (1997). *Attitudes toward Asian Americans.* Unpublished scale, University of Massachusetts at Amherst.

Linville, P. W., & Jones, E. E. (1980). Polarized appraisals of outgroup members. *Journal of Personality and Social Psychology, 38,* 689–703.

McGroarty, C., & Fiske, S. T. (1997). *Attitudes toward blind people.* Unpublished scale, University of Massachusetts at Amherst.

Oakes, P. J., & Turner, J. C. (1980). Social categorization and intergroup behavior: Does the minimal intergroup discrimination make social identity more positive? *European Journal of Social Psychology, 10,* 295–301.

Peplau, L. A. (1983). Roles and gender. In H. H. Kelley, E. Bersheid, A. Christensen, J. H. Harvey, T. L. Huston, G. Levinger, E. McClintock, L. A. Peplau, & D. R. Peterson (Eds.), *Close relationships* (pp. 220–264). New York: Freeman.

Rosenberg, S., Nelson, C., & Vivekananthan, P. S. (1968). A multidimensional approach to the structure of personality impressions. *Journal of Personality and Social Psychology, 9,* 283–294.

Rothbart, M. (1981). Memory processes and social beliefs. In D. Hamilton (Ed.), *Cognitive processes in stereotyping and intergroup behavior* (pp. 145–182). Hillsdale, NJ: Erlbaum.

Ruscher, J. B., & Fiske, S. T. (1990). Interpersonal competition can cause individuating impression formation. *Journal of Personality and Social Psychology, 58,* 832–842.

Ruscher, J. B., Fiske, S. T., Miki, H., & Van Manen, S. (1991). Individuating processes in competition: Interpersonal versus intergroup. *Personality and Social Psychology Bulletin, 17,* 595–605.

Schopler, J., Insko, C. A., Graetz, K. A., Drigotas, S., Smith, V. A., & Dahl, K. (1993). Individual–group discontinuity: Further evidence for mediation by fear and greed. *Personality and Social Psychology Bulletin, 19,* 419–431.

Sherif, M. (1966). *In common predicament: Social psychology of intergroup conflict and cooperation.* Boston: Houghton Mifflin.

Sidanius, J., Pratto, F., & Bobo, L. (1994). Social dominance orientation and the political psychology of gender: A case of invariance? *Journal of Personality and Social Psychology, 67,* 998–1011.

Six, B., & Eckes, T. (1991). A closer look at the complex structure of gender stereotypes. *Sex Roles, 24,* 57–71.

Spence, J. T., & Buckner, C. E. (in press). Instrumental and expressive traits, trait stereotypes, and sexist attitudes: What do they signify? *Psychology of Women Quarterly.*

Spence, J. T., & Hahn, E. D. (1997). The Attitudes Toward Women Scale and attitude change in college students. *Sex Roles, 21,* 17–34.

Spence, J. T., & Helmreich, R. L. (1972a). The Attitudes Toward Women Scale:

An objective instrument to measure attitudes toward the rights and roles of women in contemporary society. *JSAS Catalog of Selected Documents in Psychology*, 2, 66–67 (Ms. 153).

̃ ̃ ̃ ̃ ̃ ̃ ̃ ̃ ̃ ̃ ̃ women? Com-

Spence, J. T., Helmreich, K. L., & Stapp, J. ̃
Questionnaire: A measure of sex-role stereotypes and masculinity–femininity. *JSAS Catalog of Selected Documents in Psychology*, 4, 43–44 (Ms. 617).

Stangor, C., Lynch, L., Duan, C., & Glass, B. (1992). Categorization of individuals on the basis of multiple social features. *Journal of Personality and Social Psychology*, 62, 207–218.

Tafarodi, R. W., & Swann, W. B., Jr. (1995). Self-liking and self-competence as dimensions of global self-esteem: Initial validation of a measure. *Journal of Personality Assessment*, 65, 322–342.

Tajfel, H. (1969). Cognitive aspects of prejudice. *Journal of Social Issues*, 25, 79–97.

Tajfel, H. (1981). *Human groups and social categories*. Cambridge, England: Cambridge University Press.

9

Gender and Self-Esteem:

O ne of the many questions explored by Janet Taylor Spence and her colleagues concerns the relationships among gender, self-esteem, and so-called "masculine" agentic personality characteristics and "feminine" communal personality characteristics. In what has been considered a surprising finding, Spence's research indicates that the same relationships are typically observed in both men and women: Possession of masculine attributes is substantially and positively correlated with self-esteem, whereas possession of feminine attributes tends to have a minimal relationship with self-esteem (e.g., Spence, Helmreich, & Stapp, 1975). One implication of this finding is that men might be higher than women in global self-esteem by virtue of their superiority in masculine attributes. Yet, despite thousands of articles related to gender and self-esteem that have appeared in the scholarly journals, no one has yet to offer a definitive answer to the seemingly simple question, Are men and women different in global self-esteem?

Global self-esteem is widely regarded by many psychologists as one of the most important determinants of personal well-being and ad-

Preparation of this chapter was supported by National Science Foundation Grant SBR-9596226.

justment. It is also one of the most frequently researched topics in psychology. High self-esteem has been shown to predict mental health (Taylor & Brown, 1988), physical health (Mechanic, 1983), and life satisfaction (Deiner, 1984). Indeed, high self-esteem has been regarded as so critical that in the 1980s, the state of California created a task force to promote self-esteem among its citizens. Given the importance of self-esteem, it is perhaps not surprising that the question of whether women and men differ in their self-esteem has fascinated psychologists for decades.

The purpose of the present chapter is to review the empirical research on gender and global self-esteem. Two influential qualitative reviews of this literature appeared approximately 20 years ago, and their conclusions have held authoritative status in the field for two decades (Maccoby & Jacklin, 1974; Wylie, 1979). Since then, despite the appearance of an enormous number of new articles on this topic, no new comprehensive review of this literature has been undertaken. This is due, in part, to the enormity of the task. The current paper presents a meta-analysis of 10 years of empirical research on gender and global self-esteem.

Meta-analysis statistically integrates the mathematical findings of independent research studies and is considered by many to be superior to the traditional qualitative review (Cooper & Rosenthal, 1980) and vote-counting methods (Hedges & Olkin, 1980) for integrating research results. Meta-analysis also permits systematic analysis of factors that potentially moderate the magnitude and nature of the relationship between gender and self-esteem, a perspective that has been missing in past reviews of this literature. In the current review, we examine age, social class, ethnicity, and the measure used to assess self-esteem, as potential moderators of the gender–self-esteem relationship.

CONCEPTUALIZATION OF SELF-ESTEEM

We restrict our review to the relationship between gender and what has been described as global self-esteem. By *global self-esteem*, we mean a generalized feeling of self-acceptance, goodness, worthiness, and self-

respect (Rosenberg, 1979). Self-esteem can be distinguished from the
⁺ which is a more objective perception of oneself in terms
(Rosenberg, 1979). Global self-esteem
⁺⁰ ⁰ˢ dimension-

Swaiii.,
between gender and seii-c....
ers to distinguish among these different aspeciu -

For example, domain-specific self-evaluations refer to an iiuiviu
ual's attitudes toward and appraisals of particular aspects of self,
such as his or her appearance, intellectual ability, or athletic ability.
People can have a negative evaluation of themselves in a specific ability
domain, such as mechanical ability, yet have a positive global self-
evaluation if that ability is not highly valued by themselves or their
culture or peer group. Likewise, a person can evaluate herself or himself
positively in a specific domain, such as intellectual ability, but still have
a low sense of self-worth. Domain-specific self-evaluations often reflect
gender stereotypes (e.g., Josephs, Markus, & Tafarodi, 1992; Marsh,
Parker, & Barnes, 1985). For example, Spence et al. (1975) demonstrated
that women are more likely to characterize themselves in terms of socially desirable expressive traits, such as nurturing, empathy, and kind-
ness, whereas men are more likely to characterize themselves in terms
of socially desirable instrumental traits, such as having leadership ability, being assertive, and making decisions easily. Gender differences in
domain-specific self conceptions, however, do not necessarily imply the
existence of corresponding gender differences in global self-esteem.

THEORETICAL PERSPECTIVES ON GENDER
AND SELF-ESTEEM

An inspection of the psychological literature reveals two different answers to the question of whether women and men differ in self-esteem.

Most writers of "self-help" psychology books believe the answer to this question is *yes* (e.g., Sanford & Donovan, 1985). Many scholars have arrived at a similar conclusion (e.g., Bardwick, 1971; Harter, 1993). This position is clearly articulated in early psychodynamic perspectives (see Wylie, 1979, for a review). Freud (1927/1964), for example, postulated that a girl experiences unconscious feelings of inferiority to boys and men when she realizes that she lacks a penis and "develops, like a scar, a sense of inferiority" (p. 138). Horney (1967) agreed that the little girl sees herself as comparatively disadvantaged in that she lacks a penis, but, according to Horney, the girl's envy is based on the realistic assessment that she has fewer possibilities for gratification of her goals than does a little boy.

Other psychological and sociological models emphasize the detrimental influence on women's self-esteem of a variety of social and cultural factors that collectively disadvantage, devalue, and disempower women relative to men (e.g., Bardwick, 1971; Bush, Simmons, Hutchinson, & Blyth, 1977; Hacker, 1951). These factors include a societal preference for the male population (McKee & Sherriffs, 1957), a higher valuation of male rather than female attributes (Rosenkrantz, Vogel, Bee, Broverman, & Broverman, 1968), negative stereotypes of women (Broverman, Vogel, Broverman, Clarkson, & Rosenkrantz, 1972; Rosenkrantz et al., 1968; but see Eagly & Mladinic, 1989), minority group status (Hacker, 1951), and interpersonal and institutional barriers that limit women's aspirations, potential for achievement, and economic advancement, and hence relegate women to second class status (Hoiberg, 1982).

A number of different theoretical perspectives on the development of the self suggest that these social and cultural factors produce lower self-esteem among women than men (see Crocker & Major, 1989, for a review). The theory of *reflected appraisals*, for example, proposes that individuals incorporate the evaluations of others, particularly significant others, into their self-image (Cooley, 1956; Mead, 1934). Thus, according to this theory, women who are aware that their gender and many of their gender-related attributes are regarded more negatively than those of men should incorporate those negative attitudes into their self concepts and should, consequently, have lower self-esteem than do men. This perspective was articulated by Bardwick (1971), who contended that girls and women experience a loss in self-esteem after they become

_____ __ _ _ the social hierarchy. The

own self views (Deaux & Major,

perspective that leads to a similar prediction is *efficacy-based self-esteem* (e.g., Gecas & Schwalbe, 1983). According to this perspective, high self-esteem develops as one learns that one can successfully control and manipulate one's environment. Conditions that block the opportunity to interact successfully with the environment may prevent the development of high self-esteem. Thus, social–structural conditions, such as sex segregation at work, glass ceilings, and unequal distributions of household work and child care responsibilities, may limit the possibilities for women to form high self-esteem by limiting their access to resources that are necessary for producing such intended effects.

The prediction that women have lower self-esteem than do men also is consistent with a substantial literature on gender and depression. Reviews of this literature (e.g., Nolen-Hoeksema, 1987) indicate that the prevalence of clinical depression among women is approximately twice that of men, although rates vary with age, ethnicity, and culture. Although low self-esteem is not synonymous with depression, low self-esteem is one of the symptoms of depression, and low self-esteem tends to be associated with depressed affect (Beck, 1967). Furthermore, many of the factors that are hypothesized as associated with higher depression rates among women could also contribute to lower self-esteem among women. Hence, logically, one might expect women to score lower than men on measures of global self-esteem because of its association with depression.

The research of Spence and her colleagues on the association between global self-esteem and gender-linked personality attributes also predicts lower self-esteem among women than men. As noted above, Spence et al. (e.g., 1975) have shown that self-ratings on socially desirable instrumental traits, such as leadership, are more highly correlated with global self-esteem than are self-ratings on socially desirable expressive traits, such as nurturing (see Whitley, 1983, for a review). Because men typically evaluate themselves more highly than women do on traits that are more positively related to self-esteem, one might expect men to score higher than women on measures of global self-esteem.

In summary, a number of theories of the development of self-esteem as well as findings of several related areas of research converge to predict that women will have a lesser sense of self-worth, or lower self-regard, than will men.

An alternative prediction concerning the relationship between gender and self-esteem can be derived from Crocker and Major's (1989) review of research on the relationship between membership in a stigmatized or socially devalued group and global self-esteem. On the basis of their qualitative review of more than 20 years of research, they concluded that little empirical evidence supports the prediction that members of stigmatized groups, including women, have lower self-esteem, on average, than do members of nonstigmatized groups. For example, they reviewed research indicating that despite their stigmatized status and the relative social disadvantage they experience, African Americans have self-esteem that is, on average, equal to or higher than that of European Americans. Likewise, there is little evidence of lower self-esteem among Chicanos, people with mental retardation, those with physically handicaps, gay men, lesbian women, or juvenile delinquents (see Crocker & Major, 1989, for a review). Crocker and Major proposed that the lack of differences in self-esteem between members of stigmatized and nonstigmatized groups may be understood by considering the ways in which membership in a stigmatized group may actually help to protect self-esteem. They discussed three psychological processes in particular that may help to protect self-esteem among the stigmatized.

First, members of stigmatized groups may socially compare their

outcomes with others of their in-group, who are also apt to be relatively disadvantaged, rather than with members of the advantaged out-group. ˙˙˙ˉˉ˙ ˉˉˉˉˉ members may protect their self-
ˉ ˉˉˉ Crocker

personal deserving.
matized groups may selectively devalue, or disidentify,
mensions on which their group fares poorly relative to advantaged out-groups and selectively value, or identify with, those dimensions on which their group fares well relative to the out-group. This process of reducing the psychological centrality to the self concept of domains in which oneself or one's group fares poorly is proposed to protect one's self-esteem from poor outcomes in these domains (e.g., James, 1890/1950).

Returning specifically to gender, Crocker and Major's (1989) analysis suggests that to the extent that women are similar to other types of stigmatized and socially devalued groups, they have access to group-based strategies that enable them to protect their self-esteem from the damaging effects of social devaluation. That is, they compare their situations with other women rather than with men, attribute negative outcomes to sex discrimination rather than to personal deservingness, and selectively value attributes on which women excel and devalue attributes on which men excel. Hence, their analysis predicts no gender differences in overall global self-esteem.

CONCLUSIONS OF PRIOR REVIEWS

At least three qualitative reviews of empirical research on gender and self-esteem have been published (Maccoby & Jacklin, 1974; Skaalvik, 1986; Wylie, 1979). The most influential and widely cited review is Maccoby and Jacklin's. On the basis of their review of 30 studies, they concluded that there were no overall sex differences in self-esteem and that "the similarity of the two sexes in self-esteem is remarkably uniform across age levels through college age" (Maccoby & Jacklin, 1974, p. 153). Wylie (1979) arrived at a similar conclusion on the basis of her review of 47 studies published between 1961 and 1975; she concluded that

> a clear trend emerges from these 47 investigations of the relationship between sex and self-regard: null results prevail. . . . The pattern is the same whether one considers the many studies of children and adolescents or the relatively few studies of college students and adults. (p. 271)

Several limitations to these reviews suggest that their conclusions may warrant a second look. First, Maccoby and Jacklin (1974) combined in their review studies that used a wide variety of measures of self-esteem, including other people's reports about the self-esteem of the individual in question (usually a child). Second, the majority of the studies in both Maccoby and Jacklin's and Wylie's (1979) reviews were of children; thus, it is unclear whether their conclusions generalize to adults. Third, Maccoby and Jacklin's and Wylie's reviews were published approximately 20 years ago. Since then, a significant amount of new data has been accumulated. Indeed, Skaalvik (1986) concluded on the basis of her qualitative review of 29 studies published between 1975 and 1985 that there is a "strong indication that self-esteem measured by context-free instruments is higher for males than for females aged 12 to 18 years" (p. 174).

Several small meta-analyses have also been performed on selected studies examining gender and self-esteem. In meta-analysis, an effect size is calculated for each study, which is based on the difference between the means of the groups being compared divided by the within-groups standard deviation (SD). These statistics are then averaged to obtain a mean effect size (typically d). A mean effect size is statistically significant when its 95% confidence interval (CI) does not include .00.

Hall (1990) meta-analysed results of 10 studies from four journals (*Journal of Personality, Journal of Personality and Social Psychology, Journal of Personality Assessment,* and *Sex Roles*) published between 1975 and 1983. Sex differences on measures of self-esteem or self concept constituted the self-esteem category. She obtained an effect size of .12 (see Feingold, 1994), in the direction favoring men in having higher ̈ ̈ ̈ ̈ ̈ ̈ ̈ ̈ ̈ (̈ ̈ ̈ did not report the CI). Feingold rep-

differences in self-esteem. On the basis of these analyses, ̈ ̈ ̈ ̈ (1994) concluded that "there was no appreciable sex difference in self-esteem" (p. 438).

These meta-analyses have several limitations. First, none was based on a comprehensive search of the literature, and all were based on small samples of studies. Second, with only one exception (Feingold, 1994, as discussed below), the researchers did not code for variables that might potentially moderate the relationship between gender and self-esteem. One advantage of meta-analyses is that it allows for systematic examination of variables that might account for variation among studies in effect sizes. On the basis of our review of relevant theory and research, we selected four variables for consideration as moderators of the relationship between gender and self-esteem: age, ethnicity, socioeconomic status (SES), and the measure used to assess self-esteem.

POTENTIAL MODERATORS OF THE RELATIONSHIP BETWEEN GENDER AND SELF-ESTEEM

Age

Although Maccoby and Jacklin (1974) concluded that age did not affect the relationship between gender and self-esteem, Feingold (1994) arrived at a different conclusion on the basis of his meta-analysis of the studies Maccoby and Jacklin had reviewed qualitatively. He found that girls (mean ages = 2–12 years) tended to have higher self-esteem than boys (weighted $d = -.11$, CI $= -.05$ to $-.17$, $k = 22$), whereas male adolescents and adults (mean ages = 13 years or older) tended to have higher self-esteem than female adolescents and adults (weighted $d = .10$, CI $= .00$ to $.19$, $k = 12$). Feingold noted, however, that these developmental effects were confounded with method effects because the studies of children usually used behavioral measures of traits whereas the studies of adolescents and adults usually used self-report personality scales.

Adolescence has been identified by a number of theorists as an especially difficult period of identity crisis and self-esteem disturbance for girls (e.g., Brown & Gilligan, 1992; Nolen-Hoeksema & Girgus, 1994; Petersen, Sarigiani, & Kennedy, 1991; Simmons & Blyth, 1987). For example, a widely publicized study sponsored by the American Association of University Women (AAUW; 1995) reported that although both boys and girls experienced a significant loss in self-esteem as they went through adolescence, the loss was most dramatic for girls. In particular, authors of this study concluded that whereas girls at ages 8 and 9 felt good about themselves, they emerged from adolescence with a poor self-image, constrained views of their future and their place in society, and much less confidence about themselves and their abilities. Simmons and her colleagues arrived at a similar conclusion on the basis of their research on adolescence (e.g., Simmons & Blyth, 1987). Research on gender differences in depression also is consistent with this hypothesis. Gender differences in rates of depression generally are not observed prior to adolescence, but from adolescence onward, as we noted, women generally have rates of depression twice as high as those of men (e.g., Nolen-Hoeksema, 1987; Nolen-Hoeksema & Girgus, 1994). Thus, this literature suggests that age may be an important moderator of the relationship between gender and self-esteem.

Ethnicity

Ethnicity may also moderate the relationship between gender and self-esteem. There is increasing evidence that self-esteem must be considered within a cultural context and that assessments of personal worth are made with respect to culture-specific standards of appropriateness (e.g.,

National Advisory Mental Health Council Task Force, 1996). Cultural
standards of appropriateness for women and men may vary within
‗ ‗ ‗‗‗‗‗ ‗‗ well as differences in status between women

tween the self-esteem of African American women ‗‗
tween White American women and men, with White women having
the lowest self-esteem of all the groups (e.g., Demo & Parker, 1987;
Richman, Clark, & Brown, 1985; AAUW, 1995). On the basis of this
literature, we expect ethnicity to moderate the relationship between
gender and self-esteem.

Socioeconomic Status

Very little has been written about the relationships among social class,
gender, and self-esteem. Indeed, relatively few articles in psychological
journals mention the social class of participants at all. It is well documented that SES is an important predictor of virtually all major psy-
chosocial risk factors for mental illness (National Advisory Mental
Health Council Task Force, 1996). A few studies have shown a positive
relationship between SES and self-esteem (e.g., Richman et al., 1985),
particularly among adults (Rosenberg & Pearlin, 1978). Like ethnicity,
one's position in the social hierarchy may be an important moderator
of the relationship between gender and self-esteem. Indeed, low SES
may account for many effects commonly attributed to ethnicity. Gender
standards may be more strictly applied and rigidly enforced among
lower SES groups than among higher SES groups (McGrath, Keita,
Strickland, & Russo, 1990). Nolen-Hoeksema and Girgus (1994) suggested that girls who adopt feminine-typed activities may be more likely
to end up in low-status, low-paying jobs, being married early, and having children early—all factors that have been found to be associated

with lower SES and increased risk for depression. Such factors might also be related to lower self-esteem.

Measure of Self-Esteem

Several authors have argued that conflicting findings in the literature on gender and self-esteem may be due to variations in how researchers define and measure self-esteem (e.g., Skaalvik, 1986; Wylie, 1979). It is estimated that there are now over 200 different measures of self-esteem (Blascovich & Tomaka, 1991). Some measures of global self-esteem are derived by summing across a number of self-evaluations in specific domains. This is true, for example, of the Piers–Harris Self-Concept Scale (Piers, 1984) and the Tennessee Self-Concept Scale (Fitts, 1965; Roid & Fitts, 1988). Other measures, such as the Rosenberg Self-Esteem Scale (Rosenberg, 1965) assess a sense of self-worth that is independent of domains or context free. Yet other measures, such as the Texas Social Behavior Inventory (Helmreich & Stapp, 1974; Helmreich, Stapp, & Ervin, 1974), are oriented toward self-esteem that is social in orientation. To determine whether gender differences in self-esteem emerge on some types of measures but not on other types, we examined the self-esteem measure used as a possible moderator of the relationship between gender and self-esteem.

A META-ANALYSIS OF GENDER
AND SELF-ESTEEM

Method

Sample of Studies

Studies used in our sample were obtained primarily through computer searches of *Psychological Abstracts* and *Sociological Abstracts* using the key word *self-esteem* and paired with *gender* or *sex.* In addition, we searched all journals from which six or more studies had been obtained.

Finally, we located additional studies through a backward search of the reference lists of all located articles. Computer searches of the *Psycho-* `· · · ¹ ¹¹·····` databases resulted in the re-

The obtained sample was then evaluated following criteria: (a) The study used one or more measures of global personal self-esteem, as opposed to measures of specific aspects of the self concept (e.g., self-ratings of ability), evaluations of specific self-domains (e.g., body satisfaction), or self-confidence; (b) both male and female participants were tested on the self-esteem measure(s); and (c) the study was published in English. Studies were omitted from the sample if only unique populations such as clinically abnormal or institutionalized populations were tested. Studies were also excluded from the sample if the sample sizes for the male and female participants were not reported or if any comparison of males' and females' self-esteem, or any way of determining this, was not reported. The resulting sample for our meta-analysis included 226 samples (effect sizes) contained in 185 articles and chapters published between January 1982 and January 1992 measuring global self-esteem of male and female participants. A complete listing of all of the studies included in the meta-analysis can be obtained from Brenda Major.

Variables Coded From Each Study

In addition to coding variables necessary to compute an overall effect size (e.g., number of female and male participants, direction of any discrepancy between males' and females' self-esteem scores), the following variables were selected for coding on the basis of theoretical reasons outline above: (a) age of participants, (b) ethnicity of participants, (c)

SES of participants, and (d) self-esteem measure.[1] Coding was performed by two people, typically Brenda Major and Leslie Barr. Reliability was 85%, and all discrepancies were resolved by a discussion.

Age was coded as one of four age subgroups: 5–10 years, 11–13 years, 14–18 years, and 19 years and older. These age groupings corresponded to the age groupings most commonly used in the literature from which these data were obtained. In addition, these age groups correspond to developmental transition periods that research suggests affect the self concept and self-esteem. If the article did not report age but described the population in terms of level in school (e.g., elementary school students, junior high school students, high school or secondary students, university students), the average age corresponding to that school level was assigned (e.g., 14–18 years for high school). An unspecified category code was assigned to those samples where it was impossible to discern age.

Most of the published research was conducted in the United States or Canada, which we combined into a North American category. Ethnicity was coded as North American–White, North American–Black, North American–other ethnicity (e.g., Asian, Hispanic, Native American),[2] North American–unspecified, and non-North American. This last category included all countries other than the United States or Canada.

SES was coded on the basis of the description of the sample provided by the authors when it was provided. SES was initially coded as lower class, working class, middle class, upper class, professional, or unspecified. Because of the small number of studies in the lower- and working-class categories, these two were combined into one category. Likewise, upper class and professional were combined into one category to increase sample size.

---

[1]We also coded the description of participant population as (a) elementary school students, (b) junior high school students, (c) high school or secondary students, (d) university students, (e) miscellaneous–adults, (f) miscellaneous–children, and (g) a combination of adults and children. This grouping was used primarily to separate the effect sizes obtained from university students from those obtained from adult, nonstudent participants. Because we used sample description to assign age when it was not provided, however, this coding category correlated .95 with age and yielded redundant information. Thus, this code is not discussed further.
[2]These were combined into one category because too few studies were conducted on other ethnicities to provide a meaningful grouping.

More than 50 different self-esteem measures were represented in our sample. The most commonly used measures were the Rosenberg ⌐⌐¹⌐ ⁺ʰ⌐ Coopersmith Self-Esteem Inventory (Cooper-

separately.[3]

Computation and Analysis of Effect Sizes

The effect size index used in our study was Cohen's d, defined as the difference between the means for female and male populations divided by the pooled within-sex SD. The effect sizes were computed using DSTAT (Johnson, 1989), statistical software designed for meta-analysis. Positive values for d signify higher self-esteem among female participants than male participants and negative values signify higher self-esteem among male participants. A complete listing of the effect sizes for all studies is available from the Brenda Major. Most of the effect sizes were estimated from a t or F formula and, less frequently, an r formula or percentages. However, studies that reported no significant gender differences rarely reported an inferential test statistic. In these cases, if the study reported means for male and female participants and a SD, then the effect size was computed using this information. If a study simply reported that there were no significant gender differences and provided no other statistical information, the effect size was coded as zero. This is considered a conservative estimate (Rosenthal, 1984).

After the mean weighted effect size was tested for significance (as indicated by a 95% CI not including zero), the homogeneity of the effect sizes was tested by Q_w, which has an approximate chi-square distribution with $k - 1$ degrees of freedom where k is the number of

---

[3]The 32-item and 16-item versions of the Texas Social Behavior Inventory were combined into one category.

effect sizes. A significant Q_w means that the set of effect sizes tested is heterogeneous. Heterogeneity indicates that the variability of the effect sizes is not due to sampling error alone (Hedges & Olkin, 1980).

If the summary analysis of the effect sizes indicated heterogeneity, we conducted tests of categorical moderator variables. These tests were achieved by dividing the effect sizes into categories on the basis of the characteristics coded from the studies and then comparing their mean effect sizes. This comparison was done by computing Q_b, which has an approximate chi-square distribution with $p - 1$ degrees of freedom where p is the number of categories within each moderator variable (Hedges & Olkin, 1980). We then computed contrasts between pairs of mean effect sizes to determine which categories differed significantly from one another. Finally, when possible, we examined interactions among the categorial moderator variables.

Results

Summary Analysis: Overall Gender Differences in Global Self-Esteem

A total of 82,569 participants in 226 samples yielded an average sample size of approximately 365 for male and female participants combined. The overall analysis of the study level effect sizes yielded a mean weighted effect size of $-.14$, with a 95% CI of $-.15$ to $-.13$. This negative effect size indicates that summarizing across studies, male participants reported significantly higher global self-esteem than did female participants. Of the 226 studies included in the analysis, 140 (62%) of the effect sizes were negative reflecting higher global self-esteem for male participants, 49 (22%) were positive reflecting higher global self-esteem for female participants, and 37 (16%) were exactly zero. To address the issue of sampling bias in our literature search, we calculated a fail-safe N (Orwin, 1983; Rosenthal, 1979). The fail-safe N is an estimate of the number of studies with null results that would need to be added to the meta-analysis to reduce the obtained effect size to a smaller criterion effect size. The fail-safe N analysis indicated that 405 studies with null results would need to be added to our sample to reduce our effect size from $-.14$ to $-.05$.

Although the summary analyses allowed us to determine whether, collapsed across samples, male or female participants reported greater ~~·····~~ homogeneity analyses indicated that the set of effect

the remaining analyses were based on all 226 samples.

Categorical Model Tests: The Impact of Moderator Variables

We next examined whether age, ethnicity, SES, and measure accounted for some of the variability in effect sizes by testing them in categorical models. Table 1 displays the results of these tests. Because all of our categorical models contained more than two classes, contrasts between the mean weighted effect sizes were computed to allow interpretation of any significant between-classes effects obtained (e.g., Hedges & Olkin, 1980).[4] Results of contrasts with the unspecified or miscellaneous categories are not discussed because of the difficulty of meaningfully interpreting findings involving this categorization.

Age Group

As expected, the analysis of age group produced a significant between-classes effect, indicating that age moderated the observed relationship between gender and global self-esteem ($Q_b = 26.79$, $p < .0001$). As can be seen in Table 1, the effect sizes were negative (favoring male participants) for all age groups. However, the effect size among the youngest age group (5- to 10-year-olds) was almost .00 ($d = -.01$) and did not differ from .00. Thus, there is no reliable relationship between gender and self-esteem among preadolescent boys and girls. Among all of the older age groups, in contrast, all of the effect sizes were significantly

---

[4]Contrasts were computed using Z^2. All contrasts were post hoc unless a priori was indicated. Contrasts not described were not significant.

Table 1

Tests of Categorical Moderators of Effect Size

Variable and class	Between-classes effect (Q_b)	k	Mean weighted effect size (d^+)	95% CI for d^+ Lower	Upper	Homogeneity within each class (Q_w)
Age (in years)	26.79****					
5–10		24	−.01	−.07	+.05	37.19*
11–13		34	−.12	−.16	−.07	119.49****
14–18		65	−.16	−.19	−.15	265.21****
19+		97	−.13	−.16	−.11	156.03***
Combined–unspecified		6	−.12	−.17	−.06	11.06
Ethnicity	61.11****					
North American–White		37	−.20	−.23	−.17	68.59**
North American–Black		4	+.03	−.03	+.08	11.47*
North American–other		6	−.10	−.22	+.02	8.18
Non-North American		39	−.14	−.17	−.11	186.06****
North American–unspecified		140	−.13	−.15	−.11	280.36****

		k	d^+	
Socioeconomic status	16.83***			
Lower–working class		13	−.22	6.21
Middle class		31	−.21	6.32****
Upper–professional		21	−.11	6.63****
Combined–unspecified		161	−.13	39.78****
Measure	19.76***			
Coopersmith's (1967) Self-Esteem Inventory		46	−.09	83.19***
Piers–Harris Self-Concept Scale		13	−.10	17.73
Rosenberg's (1965) Self-Esteem Scale		78	−.16	49.47****
Tennessee Self-Concept Scale		9	−.00	16.56
Texas Social Behavior Inventory		14	−.15	33.08**
Other		66	−.13	195.99****

Note. k = number of effect sizes; d^+ = mean weighted effect size; CI = confidence interval.
*p < .05. **p < .01. ***p < .001. ****p < .0001.

different from .00, with the effect sizes of male participants higher than that of female participants. Contrasts indicated that the effect size for the 5- to 10-year-old group was marginally smaller than the effect size for the 11- to 13-year-old group ($p < .10$) and was significantly smaller than the effect size for both the 14- to 18-year-old group and the 19-year-old + group ($ps < .01$). The 11- to 13-year-old, 14- to 18-year-old, and 19-year-old + groups did not differ from each other ($ps > .40$).

Ethnicity

Ethnicity also was a significant moderator of the overall effect size ($Q_b = 61.11$, $p < .00001$). Among White–North Americans, a significant effect size of $-.20$ was observed, in the direction of White male participants having higher self-esteem than did White female participants. A smaller but still significant effect size ($d = -.13$) was observed among the large category of race-unspecified North Americans, who, given the racial composition of the United States and Canada, were likely to be predominately but not exclusively White. A similar effect size was observed among non-North Americans ($d = -.14$), a broad category that included England and Australia as well as all other non-North American countries. In contrast, among African Americans and other North American minority groups (e.g., Hispanic, Asian, Native American), the effect size was nonsignificant. Indeed, among African Americans, the effect size ($d = .03$) was close to zero and positive in direction. Contrasts revealed that the effect size for Black–North Americans differed significantly from the effect sizes found for White–North Americans and non-North Americans ($ps < .0001$). No other groups differed significantly from each other.

Socioeconomic Status

The model for SES also revealed a significant between-classes effect ($Q_b = 16.83$, $p < .001$). As can be seen in Table 1, all four of the effect sizes were negative and differed significantly from .00, indicating that male participants were significantly higher than female participants among all SES groups. However, the effect size was larger among participants described as lower–working class ($d = -.22$) and as middle class ($d =$

−.21) than it was among participants described as upper class or professional ($d = -.11$). Contrasts indicated that the effect size for the upper-class/professional category was marginally smaller than that for

~~l~~ ~~i~~ ~~l~~ ~~r~~ ~~10)~~ ~~and~~ ~~was~~ significantly smaller

significantly different from .00. Contrasts indicated that the Rosenberg Self-Esteem Scale SES ($d = -.16$) yielded marginally larger effect sizes than the Coopersmith Self-Esteem Inventory ($d = -.09$) and the Tennessee Self-Concept Scale ($d = -.002$, $ps < .10$). No other contrasts were significant.

Interactions Among Moderator Variables

We also examined theoretically meaningful interactions among the moderator variables. Our analyses were hampered, however, by the relative infrequency with which some moderator variables, most notably race and SES, were mentioned by researchers. This created many cell sizes of 0 or 1 when moderator variables were examined simultaneously. The covariation of moderator variables across studies was nonetheless revealing.

An examination of the Ethnicity × SES interaction, for example, revealed that of the 10 studies that were based on African American or other North American minority group participants, five (50%) did not mention the SES of the sample, four described the sample as low SES, and one described it as middle class. None of these samples was described as high SES. The absence of any studies of African American or other North American minority group participants in the high SES category indicates that the nonsignificant gender effects observed among these ethnic categories and the smaller gender effect observed among high SES participants are independent of each other. The only ethnic group for which meaningful SES comparisons could be made was White–North Americans. These comparisons revealed a significant effect size in the direction favoring male participants among low SES ($d = -.24$) and middle SES ($d = -.22$) participants but not among higher SES participants ($d = -.06$). This pattern paralleled the pattern observed for the sample as a whole.

The covariation of age and ethnicity across studies also was revealing. None of the studies of children (5–10 years of age) were based on African American or other North American minority group participants. Hence, the finding of a nonsignificant gender difference in self-esteem among African American and other North American minority groups cannot be attributed to disproportionately high numbers of children of these ethnic groups studied; neither can the finding of a nonsignificant gender difference in self-esteem among children be attributed to a disproportionately high number of African American or other minority group children studied.

CONCLUSIONS

Do women and men differ in global self-esteem? The answer to this question differs depending on whether one chooses to emphasize the significance or the magnitude of the overall effect size. Focusing on the significance of the overall effect size leads to the conclusion that, on average, the male population has higher self-esteem than does the female population. Such a conclusion is consistent with a substantial literature illustrating that women are socially devalued and disadvantaged relative to men and with theories of self-esteem development that posit that social devaluation results in lower self-esteem among its targets. This conclusion is inconsistent, however, with theories, such as Crocker and Major's (1989), that posit that women's self-esteem is protected from social devaluation by group-level processes, such as in-group social comparisons, attributions to prejudice, selective valuing of domains in which the in-group excels or is advantaged, and devaluing of domains in which the in-group is disadvantaged.

Focusing on the magnitude of the overall effect size, in contrast, leads to a different conclusion. According to Cohen (1977), effect sizes

of .20, .50, and .80 indicate small, medium, and large effects, respectively. Thus, by these criteria, the overall effect size of .14 that we obtained could be considered so small as to be of little meaning or prac-
~ ----- if it did attain statistical significance. Indeed,

sion also is --
the relationship between stigmatized status and self-esteem.

We believe that an unqualified endorsement of either of these positions would be overly simplistic and would mischaracterize the nature of the relationship between gender and self-esteem. Our meta-analysis of 10 years of research and more than 200 samples examining the self-esteem of women and men indicates that the magnitude and direction of gender effects differs depending on age, social class, and ethnicity of participants as well as the method of assessing self-esteem. Focusing on overall differences between the male and female populations without considering these moderators ignores important effects associated with one's position within the larger social structure. The pattern of findings observed indicates that self-esteem must be considered within a larger cultural context and suggests that men and women may measure themselves against culture-specific as well as age-specific standards of what is appropriate (e.g., Josephs et al., 1992).

Our meta-analysis indicated that age is a significant moderator of the relationship between gender and global self-esteem. The pattern observed is consistent with that observed with respect to depression (e.g., Nolen-Hoeksema & Girgus, 1994). Namely, prior to adolescence, there are no reliable differences between boys and girls in global self-esteem, but beginning in early adolescence (ages 11–13), reliable gender differences emerge in the direction of boys having higher self-esteem than girls. A number of explanations have been offered for this potential drop in self-esteem among adolescent girls. One is the gender intensification hypothesis (Hill & Lynch, 1983). According to this hypothesis, early adolescence is a time of intensification of traditional gender-role expectations. Thus, it is in adolescence that girls become aware of and most keenly experience the limitations that accompany their gender and may be held most strictly to gender-specific standards of appropriateness. Other authors have pointed to the effects of pubertal changes, particularly increasing body dissatisfaction among girls (Brooks-Gunn, 1992), the greater stresses encountered by adolescent girls relative to adolescent boys (Petersen et al., 1991), the simultaneous experience for many girls of pubertal changes with major adolescent transitions (Petersen et al., 1991; Simmons & Blyth, 1987), and the greater prevalence among girls of cognitive styles that make them vulnerable when faced with the greater stresses of adolescence (Nolen-Hoeksema & Girgus, 1994). All of these factors point to the importance of considering the social context of girls and women's lives in attempting to understand their feelings of self-worth.

The findings for ethnicity particularly illustrate the importance of considering social context. Across studies, women and men who were members of North American ethnic minority groups, especially African Americans, did not reliably differ in self-esteem ($d = .03$). White women, in contrast, had reliably lower self-esteem than did White men ($d = -.20$). How can we explain this pattern of findings? One possible explanation for this pattern is that White women, unlike women who are members of ethnic minority groups, do not fit the psychological profile of a stigmatized group and hence do not benefit from the self-protective properties that the stigmatized group status may afford.

The question of whether White women are similar to other types of stigmatized or minority groups was considered by Hacker (1951) more than 40 years ago. Hacker (1951) argued that although (White) women fit the definition of a minority group objectively, they "fail to present in full force the subjective attributes commonly associated with minority groups. That is, they lack a sense of group identification and do not harbor feelings of being treated unfairly because of their sex membership" (p. 62). She suggested that several factors, such as the interdependence and intimacy of intergroup relationships between

women and men, contribute to this tendency. Similar arguments have
ᵇᵉᵉⁿ made more recently (e.g., Gurin, 1985; Gurin & Townsend, 1986;

ᵖˡᵉ Gurin (1985; Gurin & Townsend, 1986)

other disadvantaged

fair and legitimate
this). Consequently, White women tend
outcomes, even when they are aware that those outcomes are
than men's. Major and her colleagues have found that only when White
women are explicitly led to suspect unfairness in the distribution of
rewards between women and men do they compare their outcomes
with men, make attributions to prejudice, and believe their treatment
is unfair (e.g., Bylsma, Major, & Cozzarelli, 1995; Crocker, Voelkl, Testa,
& Major, 1991).

At least three processes may help to protect the self-esteem of ethnic
minority women, relative to White women, from social devaluation due
to gender. One possibility is that ethnic minority women judge their
self-worth against different cultural standards and values than do White
women. For example, perceived physical attractiveness and weight have
been found to be more strongly related to the self-esteem of White
women than they are to the self-esteem of Black women (Wade,
Thompson, Tashakkori, & Valente, 1989), and White women in general
have been shown to be less satisfied with their appearance and weight
than are Black women (Stevens, Kumanyika, & Keil, 1994). A second
possibility is that status differences between African American women
and men are less pronounced than they are between White women and
men (Kane, 1992). Thus, comparisons with same-race men may be less
detrimental to Black women's self-esteem than to White women's self-
esteem. Yet a third possibility is that Black women are more likely than
White women to be critical of the status quo in gender relations (Kane,
1992) and to have a highly developed sense of group consciousness

(Gurin, 1985), both of which may enable them to be more likely than White women to attribute their lower status to discrimination rather than to personal deservingness (Major, 1994).

A similar analysis may also be applied to social class. Gender differences in self-esteem were found to be larger among lower SES and middle-class SES men and women than among upper-class or professional men and women. Because none of the studies included in the high SES category were based on participants described as members of North American ethnic minority groups, this pattern may apply particularly to White women. SES may have a different meaning and consequences for White women than it does for women in a culturally disadvantaged ethnic minority group. For the former, SES may be construed as an achieved status, whereas for the latter, SES may be construed as an ascribed status. Gender standards may also be more strictly applied and rigidly enforced among lower SES than higher SES White women (Nolen-Hoeksema & Girgus, 1994). Education may help White women to see the injustice of their situation and to label it as unfair.

In summary, our analysis suggested that part of the reason for the lack of a definitive answer to the question of which gender, on average, has higher self-esteem is that the self-esteem of particular women and men is moderated by important personality, social, and cultural factors. These factors are often obscured when the focus of attention is on aggregate group differences between women and men.

REFERENCES

American Association of University Women. (1995). *How schools shortchange girls.* New York: Marlowe.

Bardwick, J. M. (1971). *Psychology of women: A study of bio-cultural conflicts.* New York: Harper & Row.

Beck, A. T. (1967). *Depression: Clinical, experimental, and theoretical perspectives.* New York: Harper & Row.

Blascovich, J., & Tomaka, J. (1991). Measures of self-esteem. In J. P. Robinson, P. R. Shaver, & L. S. Wrightsman (Eds.), *Measures of personality and social psychological attitudes* (Vol. 1, pp. 115–160). San Diego, CA: Academic Press.

Brooks-Gunn, J. (1992). Growing up female: Stressful events and the transition to adolescence. In T. M. Field, P. M. McCabe, & N. Schneiderman (Eds.), *Stress and coping in infancy and childhood* (pp. 119–145). Hillsdale, NJ:

perception of sex-roles ... _
459–474.

Bylsma, W. H., Major, B., & Cozzarelli, C. (1995). The influence of legitimacy appraisals on the determinants of entitlement beliefs. *Basic & Applied Social Psychology, 17,* 223–237.

Cohen, J. (1977). *Statistical power analysis for the behavioral sciences* (rev. ed.). New York: Academic Press.

Cooley, C. H. (1956). *Human nature and the social order.* New York: Free Press.

Cooper, H. M., & Rosenthal, R. (1980). Statistical versus traditional procedures for summarizing research findings. *Psychological Bulletin, 87,* 442–449.

Coopersmith, S. A. (1967). *The antecedents of self-esteem.* San Francisco: Freeman.

Crocker, J., & Major, B. (1989). Social stigma and self-esteem: The self-protective properties of stigma. *Psychological Review, 96,* 608–630.

Crocker, J., Voelkl, K., Testa, M., & Major, B. (1991). Social stigma: The affective consequences of attributional ambiguity. *Journal of Personality and Social Psychology, 60,* 218–228.

Deaux, K., & Major, B. (1987). Putting gender into context: An interactive model of gender-related behavior. *Psychological Review, 94,* 369–389.

Diener, E. (1984). Subjective well-being. *Psychological Bulletin, 95,* 542–575.

Demo, D. H., & Parker, K. D. (1987). Academic achievement and self-esteem among Black and White college students. *Journal of Social Psychology, 127,* 345–355.

Eagly, A. H., & Mladinic, A. (1989). Gender stereotypes and attitudes toward women and men. *Personality and Social Psychology Bulletin, 15,* 543–558.

Feingold, A. (1994). Gender differences in personality: A meta-analysis. *Psychological Bulletin, 116,* 429–456.

Fitts, W. H. (1965). *Manual: Tennessee Self-Concept Scale.* Nashville, TN: Counselor Recordings & Tests.

Freud, S. (1927). The future of an illusion. New York: Doubleday. (Reprinted in 1964)

Gecas, V., & Schwalbe, M. L. (1983). Beyond the looking-glass self: Social structure and efficacy-based self-esteem. *Social Psychology Quarterly, 46,* 77–88.

Geis, F. L. (1993). Self-fulfilling prophecies: A social psychological view of gender. In A. E. Beall & R. J. Sternberg (Eds.), *The psychology of gender* (pp. 9–54). New York: Guilford Press.

Gurin, P. (1985). Women's gender consciousness. *Public Opinion Quarterly, 49,* 143–163.

Gurin, P., & Townsend, A. (1986). Properties of gender identity and their implications for gender consciousness. *British Journal of Social Psychology, 25,* 139–148.

Hacker, H. M. (1951). Women as a minority group. *Social Forces, 30,* 60–69.

Hall, J. A. (1990). *Nonverbal sex differences: Accuracy of communication and expressive style.* Baltimore: Johns Hopkins University Press.

Harter, S. (1993). Causes and consequences of low self-esteem in children and adolescents. In R. F. Baumeister (Ed.), *Self-esteem: The puzzle of low self-regard* (pp. 87–116). New York: Plenum Press.

Hedges, L. V., & Olkin, I. (1980). Vote-counting methods in research synthesis. *Psychological Bulletin, 88,* 359–369.

Helmreich, R., & Stapp, J. (1974). Short forms of the Texas Social Behavior Inventory (TSBI): An objective measure of self-esteem. *Bulletin of the Psychonomic Society, 4,* 473–475.

Helmreich, R., Stapp, J., & Ervin, C. (1974). The Texas Social Behavior Inventory (TSBI): An objective measure of self-esteem or social competence. *JSAS Catalog of Selected Documents in Psychology, 4,* 79 (Ms. 681).

Hill, J. P., & Lynch, M. E. (1983). The intensification of gender-related role expectations during early adolescence. In J. Brooks-Gunn & A. C. Peterson

(Eds.), *Girls at puberty: Biological and psychological perspectives* (pp. 201–228). New York: Plenum Press.

Hoiberg, A. (1982). *Women and the world of work*. New York: Plenum Press.

~~ ᵃˡᵒᵍʸ~~ New York: Norton.

Kane, E. W. (1992). ~~Race,~~ ~~g~~

Social Psychology Quarterly, 55, 311–320.

Kleugal, J. R., & Smith, E. R. (1986). *Beliefs about inequality: Americans' views of what is and what ought to be.* Hawthorne, NJ: Aldine de Gruyter.

Maccoby, E. E., & Jacklin, C. N. (1974). *The psychology of sex differences.* Stanford, CA: Stanford University Press.

Major, B. (1994). From social inequality to personal entitlement: The role of social comparisons, legitimacy appraisals and group membership. In M. Zanna (Ed.), *Advances in experimental social psychology* (Vol. 26, pp. 293–355). San Diego, CA: Academic Press.

Marsh, H. (1986). Global self-esteem: Its relation to specific facets of self-concept and their importance. *Journal of Personality and Social Psychology, 51*, 1224–1236.

Marsh, H. W., Parker, J., & Barnes, J. (1985). Multidimensional adolescent self-concepts: Their relationship to age, sex, and academic measures. *American Educational Research Journal, 22*, 422–444.

Martinez, R., & Dukes, R. L. (1991). Ethnic and gender differences in self-esteem. *Youth and Society, 22*, 318–338.

McGrath, E., Keita, G. P., Strickland, B. R., & Russo, N. F. (Eds.). (1990). *Women and depression: Risk factors and treatment issues.* Washington, DC: American Psychological Association.

McKee, J. P., & Sherriffs, A. C. (1957). The differential evaluation of males and females. *Journal of Personality, 25*, 356–371.

Mead, G. H. (1934). *Mind, self, and society.* Chicago: University of Chicago Press.

Mechanic, D. (1983). Adolescent health and illness behavior: Review of the literature and a new hypothesis for the study of stress. *Journal of Human Stress, 9,* 4–13.

Merton, R. K. (1948). The self-fulfilling prophecy. *Antioch Review, 8,* 193–210.

National Advisory Mental Health Council Task Force. (1996). Basic behavioral science research for mental health: Sociocultural and environmental processes. *American Psychologist, 51,* 722–731.

Nolen-Hoeksema, S. (1987). Sex differences in unipolar depression: Evidence and theory. *Psychological Bulletin, 101,* 259–282.

Nolen-Hoeksema, S., & Girgus, J. S. (1994). The emergence of gender differences in depression during adolescence. *Psychological Bulletin, 115,* 424–443.

Orwin, R. G. (1983). A fail-safe *N* for effect size in meta-analysis. *Journal of Educational Statistics, 8*(2), 157–159.

Petersen, A. C., Sarigiani, P. A., & Kennedy, R. E. (1991). Adolescent depression: Why more girls? *Journal of Youth and Adolescence, 20,* 247–271.

Piers, E. V. (1984). *Piers–Harris Self-Concept Scale (the way I feel about myself).* Los Angeles, CA: Western Psychological Services.

Richman, C. L., Clark, M. L., & Brown, K. P. (1985). General and specific self-esteem in late adolescent students: Race × Gender × SES effects. *Adolescence, 20,* 555–566.

Roid, G. H., & Fitts, W. H. (1988). *Tennessee Self-Concept Scale* (rev. manual). Los Angeles, CA: Western Psychological Services.

Rosenberg, M. (1965). *Society and the adolescent self-image.* Princeton, NJ: Princeton University Press.

Rosenberg, M. (1979). *Conceiving the self.* New York: Basic Books.

Rosenberg, M., & Pearlin, L. I. (1978). Social class and self-esteem among children and adults. *American Journal of Sociology, 84,* 53–77.

Rosenkrantz, P., Vogel, S., Bee, H., Broverman, I., & Broverman, D. M. (1968). Sex role stereotypes and self-concepts in college students. *Consulting and Clinical Psychology, 32,* 287–295.

Rosenthal, R. (1979). The "file drawer problem" and tolerance for null results. *Psychological Bulletin, 85,* 638–641.

Rosenthal, R. (1984). *Meta-analytic procedures for social research.* Beverly Hills, CA: Sage.

Sanford, L. T., & Donovan, M. E. (1985). *Women & self-esteem: Understanding and improving the way we think and feel about ourselves.* New York: Penguin Books.

~~~ *~~ ~~~ ~~~~ adolescence.* New York:

32, 29–39.

Stevens, J., Kumanyika, S. K., & Keil, J. E. (1994). Attitudes toward body size and dieting: Differences between elderly Black and White women. *American Journal of Public Health, 84,* 1322–1325.

Tafarodi, R. W., & Swann, W. B., Jr. (1995). Self-liking and self-competence as dimensions of global self-esteem: Initial validation of a measure. *Journal of Personality Assessment, 65,* 322–342.

Taylor, S., & Brown, J. (1988). Illusion and well-being: Some social psychological contributions to a theory of mental health. *Psychological Bulletin, 103,* 193–210.

Wade, R. J., Thompson, V., Tashakkori, A., & Valente, E. (1989). A longitudinal analysis of sex by race differences in predictors of adolescent self-esteem. *Personality and Individual Differences, 10,* 717–729.

Whitley, B. E. (1983). Sex role orientation and self-esteem: A critical meta-analytic review. *Journal of Personality and Social Psychology, 44,* 765–778.

Wylie, R. C. (1979). *The self concept* (Vol. 2). Lincoln: University of Nebraska Press.

10

Thirty Years of Gender
¹ Chronicle

Psychology, it was said some time ago, has a short history but a long past. Currently, this remark has lost its pungency for psychology as a whole but is apropos to the study of gender. Although the psychologies of men and women have been the subject of speculation even before the days of Sigmund Freud, gender has become a major topic of social psychological research only in the last 30–35 years. Its relatively recent emergence can be attributed, not to new scientific insights within the field, but to political and ideological changes in society at large that sought to remedy the inequities to which women and members of ethnic minorities had historically been subject. Within psychology, these events have had two interrelated effects. First, affirmative action and other efforts to stamp out discrimination against women resulted in more women obtaining academic positions in which they were able to conduct research. Second, these political actions encouraged a number of women (and a lesser number of men)—some, like

I have been fortunate over the years to work with a number of stimulating colleagues and graduate students both "before gender" and "after gender." My thanks and appreciation go to all of them and, most of all, to Kenneth W. Spence, who taught me what it was to be a psychologist. The names of many of them appear in the list of publications that appears at the end of this volume (in the Appendix), the most prominent (after gender) of which is Robert Helmreich.

myself, already in midcareer—to start investigating gender phenomena. Previously, we may have often thought about the subject or harbored rebellious, feminist ideas, but these were largely kept private (at least at the office) and were certainly not manifested in our research. Over the past 3 decades, the volume of psychological research concerned with gender has swelled. The topic has generally gained acceptance as a legitimate subject of inquiry by serious scholars, although remnants of early suspicions about its worthiness remain.

Considering both the event that occasioned this volume and my status as one who was there "at the beginning"—and well before it— it seems appropriate to cast these remarks in a less formal and more personal vein than is found in the usual chapter. My plan is to devote the bulk of my remarks to an account of some of the initial studies conducted by my colleagues and myself, studies that were designed to test widely accepted beliefs about the fundamental differences between men and women whose validity was seldom questioned. The success of these early investigations led us to pursue various lines of research that our findings suggested would be profitable; these sometimes separated and then converged in unanticipated ways, and sometimes took us far from our starting point. As space restrictions do not allow me to chronicle these later inquiries, I instead give only short, selective updates on these various research themes. Because the authors of the other chapters in this volume are leading contributors to contemporary gender research, I make special (but, in most instances, lamentably brief) reference to their work and ideas.

But first I provide a bit of personal history. It is readily apparent that my research career can roughly be divided into two parts: before gender and after gender. Aside from the obvious switch in subject matter, the disjunction was marked by a change in methodology and conceptual background. At one level, however, there was continuity: my abiding interest in individual differences in motives and beliefs and their implications for behavior. There was also a disjunction at another sort: a shift from problems associated simply with being a woman in a male-dominated profession to a formal concern with the problems faced by women in general.

BEFORE GENDER: THE FIRST 20 YEARS IN BRIEF

My doctoral dissertation, completed at the University of Iowa in the ~~~~~ of 1949 and supervised by Kenneth W. Spence (later my hus-
~~~~~ ~~~~~ ~~~~~ ~~~~~ condi-

·turned out to be my penchant ιυι ~~~~~
would allow me to investigate the topic at hand. (Ironically, the measures themselves, even though often developed to forward the purposes of the studies, have continued to be useful, even when the original studies have been lost in the dust bin of history.)

Although gender as a research interest was far in my future, the influence of gender on my career was not, as was true for almost all women. In the fall of 1949, I joined the faculty of Northwestern University, the first woman in the Department of Psychology; I was hired, I later learned, as an experiment, which some believed would come to no good end. (Fortunately for me, even the doubters proved to be supportive and the experiment was ultimately pronounced successful.) There I continued to investigate and extend my studies of the motivational components of trait anxiety. That phase of my career ended when I married and returned to Iowa City, where I encountered the barriers imposed by the nepotism rules common to most universities. A position as research psychologist was found for me at the Iowa City Veterans Administration Hospital; based on the population that was available, the direction of my research turned from anxiety in college students to the study of motivational processes in schizophrenic patients.

Several years later, there was another change when Kenneth accepted a position in the expanding Department of Psychology at the University of Texas at Austin. There I was tucked into a position at the local state school for the mentally retarded, a position created with funds from the Hogg Foundation for Mental Health in the hope that an on-going, self-sustaining research program could be established. While at the state school, I initiated a series of studies with children, normal and retarded, that were directed at questions that were then of interest to developmental psychologists. Although these questions were not quite the same as those with which I had earlier been concerned, they were at least within the general conceptual ballpark.

As the hope of establishing a research program at the state school became futile, a faculty position was found for me in the University of Texas at Austin Department of Educational Psychology in the School of Education. Because one of my assignments was to teach a graduate course in child development, it seemed prudent to continue my research with children.

It was not until the 1980s and 1990s that the nepotism rules that had shaped the careers of so many married women began to disappear. In my own case, alas, these issues resolved themselves with the death of my husband in 1967. After a short period with a joint appointment, I moved full time to the Department of Psychology as its chair. (Women were beginning to be discovered.)

It was not the easiest of times. The country was in turmoil over Vietnam and the radical changes set off by the Civil Rights Movement and the rise of feminism. Academic psychology was changing as the "cognitive revolution" took hold and learning theories lost their previous ascendancy. My personal circumstances were changing— and I was running out of research ideas I wanted to pursue. It was time for still another change in direction; what that would be I did not know, but I was confident that eventually some inspiration would strike.

AFTER GENDER: THE NEXT (ALMOST) 30 YEARS

How It Began

Seemingly small, chance events can have unexpectedly profound consequences. Sometime in 1969, Robert Helmreich and I had a casual conversation about an experiment he had conducted with our colleague, Elliot Aronson, and one of our graduate students, James Le Fann

(Helmreich, Aronson, & Le Fann, 1970). Using a 2×2 factorial design much beloved by experimental social psychologists of that era, they demonstrated that a male target figure portrayed in a tape as competent ~~~ ~~~ ~~~ ~~~ concluded an interview with a pratfall than

~~~ ~~~ ~~~ ~~~

women? As a lark (while waiting for inspiration to strike about a new research direction), I suggested to Bob that we do a little experiment to find out. However, the "little experiment" grew to be a very elaborate one. It occurred to us, for example, that peoples' attitudes about women's roles, vis-à-vis those of men, would also contribute to our participants' reactions. In the absence of a suitable instrument, we developed one of our own, which we called the Attitudes Toward Women Scale (AWS).

The study, subsequently published under the title (naturally), "Who Likes Competent Women" (Spence & Helmreich, 1972a), had two long-term effects of some significance. First, the outcomes were so intriguing that I became—and have remained ever since—hooked on gender research. Second, the AWS proved to be promising enough to present in separate publication (Spence & Helmreich, 1972b) and to use in my subsequent investigations. The measure, as is well known, has gone on to a long, independent life of its own. (I return later to the subject of the AWS and other attitude measures.)

How It Was Then

Had I read the Helmreich et al. (1970) study several years earlier, I probably would not have found anything remarkable in its design. Prior to the late 1960s, there was a strong (typically unexplained) bias toward the use of only male participants (Holmes & Jorgensen, 1971). Even in studies with both genders, separate analyses of the data from the men and women were rarely undertaken. In general, gender phenomena simply held no interest.

The exception to this prefeminist indifference to gender can be found in the child development literature. The processes by which boys and girls acquire the behaviors and values expected of their gender were the subject of several influential theories in which identification concepts were prominent and generated a substantial amount of empirical research (e.g., Hetherington, 1965; Kagan, 1964; Kohlberg, 1966). Underlying these inquiries into the development of gender-related behaviors was tacit acceptance of the status quo. Thus, one of the accepted goals of childhood socialization was to train boys and girls to adopt beliefs and behaviors that would lead them to become proper men and women, as defined by their culture. Once children were suitably indoctrinated and could manage on their own, it would seem, gender phenomena were of little concern, except in individuals considered abnormal, that is, homosexuals and those who conspicuously deviated in other ways from societal expectations.

But, of course, all this had begun to change by the late 1960s. The rise of the Women's Movement was beginning to have an impact on psychology and other social sciences, and articles devoted to gender were beginning to appear in psychology's prime data journals (Crawford & Marecek, 1989). By the time I learned about the Helmreich et al. (1970) study, I had become sensitized to these challenges, along with many others, and asked an "obvious" question that might not have been obvious to me before. It also seemed reasonable to investigate such questions and even to expect to publish them in psychology's hither-to gender-oblivious journals.

AWS and Other Measures of Sexism: A Contemporary Look

I return at this point to the subject of the AWS, a measure whose development was inspired by the attention that was beginning to be paid to the status of women and was designed to assess gender-role attitudes current at the time.

When societal beliefs and practices are in a state of flux, attitudes related to them cannot themselves be expected to remain stable. Since Helmreich and I first developed the AWS (or, more accurately, the short

~~...... ~ .... ~. ~~ ~~..... ~ ~~~.~.. 1079) ..... ~ University of Texas at

of both genders have systematically shifted in this direction. Although the distributions are showing signs of a ceiling effect and have also become noticeably skewed, the tails are long so that considerable variability remains, even among women. These data are significant in and of themselves but raise questions about the utility of the AWS in current research. As is demonstrated in some of the illustrative data cited below, however, it continues to be more useful and informative than might have been anticipated.

The AWS was one of the first modern measures of gender-role attitudes developed and remains the most popular (Beere, 1990). As an inspection of its content makes readily apparent, the AWS assesses only a limited set of beliefs about the rights and roles of women and men in general. Other facets of sexist attitudes have subsequently been explored, with results that add other insights about both contemporary beliefs and historical trends. For example, the Male–Female Relations Questionnaire (MFRQ; Spence, Helmreich, & Sawin, 1980), which contains separate forms for men and women, asks about the personal role preferences of students or unmarried young adults and their tendency to self-consciously change their behavior in social interactions to correspond to gender expectations. Although cohort changes have taken place in responses to the MFRQ, students tested in the 1990s were more likely to be conservative in their own preferences and in their willingness to play by the old gender rules than their responses to the AWS would suggest (Sherman & Spence, 1997). Furthermore, I regret to say, on several MFRQ items that the two forms have in common, the responses of women were at least as traditional as those of men (e.g., preference for a male over a female boss at work).

Two more recently developed measures, the Ambivalent Sexism Inventory (ASI) devised by Glick and Fiske (1996) and the Modern Sexism Scale devised by Swim, Aikin, Hall, and Hunter (1995), provide novel perspectives on sexist attitudes. Glick and Fiske (1996; chapter 8, this volume) have noted that although men continue to have greater structural power than do women, they are simultaneously dependent on women for satisfaction of their heterosexual and affectional needs. This interdependence, they propose, results in ambivalence. On the one hand, women are often regarded as less competent but more likable than men (a distinction reminiscent of the well-established stereotypes about gender differences in instrumental and expressive characteristics with which my colleagues and I have been concerned). This leads to benevolent beliefs about women: Women have greater purity than men and need to be protected by men; at the same time, men are dependent on women for heterosexual intimacy. On the other hand, women simultaneously elicit hostile beliefs: Women are overdemanding and out to control and dominate men. Results from the ASI, containing separate Benevolent and Hostile Sexism scales, provide impressive confirmation of the authors' predictions: Scores on the two scales were found to be significantly positively correlated in both sexes in most of the student and nonstudent samples Glick and Fiske tested.[1]

Glick and Fiske (chapter 8, this volume) suggest that congruent with stereotypes of subcategories of women, housewives and others who

---

[1]In both their theoretical discussion and their empirical work on the ASI, Glick and Fiske focused on sexist beliefs about women (particularly but not exclusively on the part of men). This is particularly obvious in their Hostile Sexism scale. However, people (especially, perhaps, women) are also likely to hold ambivalent sexist beliefs about men. Studies of trait stereotypes, for example, indicate that men are perceived as more arrogant, domineering, and aggressive than are women (Spence, Helmreich, & Holahan, 1979). Based on such data, it should be relatively simple to develop a scale specifically aimed at hostile beliefs about men in their treatment and beliefs about women. Although the Glick–Fiske Benevolent Sexism scale could be regarded as unisexual in character and as such, to define the benevolent half of ambivalence about men, it would be interesting to determine whether a novel benevolence scale aimed at men could be developed: men as little boys who never grew up, as endearing bumblers, helpless in matters of everyday living, and in need of a woman's care.

accept men's superior status are more likely to elicit benevolent attitudes whereas career women and others who threaten men's status are more ·· · ı ·ıı ·ı·,ı-- These subcategories are relevant pri-

ıccuoıı aııu uccpccc · · · .

their sexual lures or as holding secret powers not available to men.

The ASI has been devised so recently that it cannot be determined whether these two sets of opposing beliefs and their relationships with each other have weakened in intensity since the advent of the Women's Movement. It does seem apparent, however, that the kinds of ambivalent beliefs tapped by the Glick and Fiske inventory have been in existence for a very long time, transcending time and place.

As reflected in its title, this is not true in the case of the Modern Sexism Scale recently developed by Swim et al. (1995), in which they have contrasted modern sexism with its old-fashioned form. The latter, they stated, is characterized by beliefs in traditional gender roles, endorsement of stereotypes about women's lesser competence, and so forth. However, modern sexism is characterized by opposition to feminist demands and by the belief that women are no longer discriminated against and affirmative action is unneeded.

Affirmative action and other programs intended to reduce discrimination against women and other stigmatized groups are not only of relatively recent origin but also, as illustrated by recent decisions of federal courts and actions of state legislatures, are currently undergoing attack. Thus, one suspects that whereas some aspects of sexism have diminished in recent decades the kinds of attitudes tapped by the Modern Sexism Scale may now be headed in the opposite direction. This possibility, too, can be checked only by continuing to monitor changes across time, thus adding to psychologists' understanding of gender phenomena in an era of societal instability.

Relationships of the AWS With Other Attitude Measures

Data from the AWS suggest that modern sexism tends to supplement rather than replace the more blatant, old-fashioned variety. Thus, scores on the AWS, and from the MFRQ as well, are significantly correlated with the Swim et al. Modern Sexism Scale items (Spence & Buckner, in press; Yoder & McDonald, 1997). The AWS has also been reported to be substantially correlated with the scales on the ASI, particularly the Benevolent scale, as well as with other questionnaires measuring other facets of sexism (e.g., Spence, Losoff, & Robbins, 1991). As a predictor of other attitudes and gender-related behaviors, the AWS neither has exhausted its usefulness because it is outdated—as some critics have suggested—nor at the other extreme, does it have the all-purpose virtues that its popularity might suggest.

Whether the kinds of gender-role attitudes assessed by the AWS lie close to some central core of sexism is not known. However, it is apparent that sexism is a multifaceted phenomenon with a number of interrelated aspects. Across time, changes in various components may vary in their rate or even their direction; the magnitude and direction of differences in the sexist beliefs of men and women, as well as subgroups within the genders, may also vary, depending on which facet is assessed. Neither are the various measures necessarily related to the same degree to each other or to other criterion variables. Each different kind of measure adds to the understanding of gender beliefs.

The Personal Attributes Questionnaire

My next major foray into the topic of gender came with the development of the Personal Attributes Questionnaire (PAQ; Spence, Helmreich, & Stapp, 1974, 1975). Unlike the AWS, which was initially put together for a limited purpose, the PAQ was devised with more serious theoretical and programmatic intent.

Theoretical Background

Traditional theories of gender propose that some core essence of masculinity and femininity, often assumed to be biologically rooted, distin-

guished the psychologies of men and women. Along with the belief that women were intellectually inferior to men, these fundamental distinc-
·· ⸺f⸺·· ⸻directly or indirectly linked to two sets of personality

wives. As suggested by the use of the same terms to label gender-related traits and roles, these presumably inborn differences in the personal qualities of men and women have been assumed to explain and to justify the existence of traditional gender-role systems.

Instrumentality and expressiveness were also widely held to be incompatible; possession of one tended to preclude the other. This presumption was intertwined with several others that continued to dominate traditional thinking about gender throughout much of the 20th century. First, not merely instrumental and expressive traits but all gender-related attributes, attitudes, and behaviors contributed to a single bipolar factor, so that the presence or absence of a given masculine characteristic or a given feminine characteristic was predictive of the presence or absence of other masculine and feminine characteristics. The glue that held these gender-related qualities and behaviors together was masculinity and femininity—endpoints of a hypothetical bipolar continuum. Finally, men and women who displayed attributes associated with the other gender or did not accept the roles that society assigned to them were believed to be sexually deviant or to suffer from some other form of psychopathology.

Description

The PAQ was developed in several stages (Spence & Helmreich, 1978; Spence et al., 1974, 1975). Briefly, after collecting extensive data from college students on descriptive trait stereotypes, Helmreich, Stapp, and I (Spence et al., 1974, 1975) winnowed our items down to a set of 55 that produced significant differences in ratings of the typical man and woman by both male and female students. Most items, as it turned out, described instrumental and expressive traits.

Spence et al. (1974) next administered these items to new samples for which we obtained both stereotype and self-ratings, along with responses to several other scales including a measure of global self-esteem and social competence. On the basis of previously collected prescriptive and descriptive stereotype data, we divided the self-report items (dubbed the PAQ) into two major scales: items that were socially desirable to some degree for both sexes but in one case were more characteristic of men than women and in the other were more characteristic of women than men.

Because of the theoretical significance assigned to these two sets of characteristics (as well as for convenience), Helmreich and I (Spence & Helmreich, 1978) soon shortened the PAQ to two unifactorial, 8-item scales that included only instrumental and expressive personality traits. On both the original long form and the now official short form of the PAQ, men's and women's self-reports differ significantly on the instrumental and expressiveness scales, thus providing some verification of the descriptive gender stereotypes and justifying the treatment of the questionnaire as a measure of two sets of gender-related attributes, one masculine and one feminine.

Correlations Between the Scales

The finding, considered at the time to be a dramatic revelation, was that rather than being negatively correlated, as had been presumed, scores on the two scales failed to be significantly related for either men or women. The two dimensions were independent. The exciting implication of this outcome was that at least with respect to their self-images, people could be, and some actually were, *androgynous*, that is, both "masculine" and "feminine." These PAQ outcomes, as it turned out, were not restricted to mostly U.S. middle-class, White college students but were also found in other age and ethnic groups in the United States and in men and women from other countries (e.g., Diaz-Loving, Diaz-

Guerrero, Helmreich, & Spence, 1981; Runge, Frey, Gollwitzer, Helmreich, & Spence, 1981; Spence & Helmreich, 1978).

~~~ ~ ~ ~~~~ ~~ ~~~ ~~~ DAO ~~~ ~~~~ Bam's (1074)

limited sets of desirable personality traits but of such global concepts as masculinity and femininity and gender-role identification. But an account of this disagreement and where it has led is getting ahead of the story.

Recent Trends in Self-Report and Stereotype Scores

Although the significant gender differences consistently found on the PAQ and BSRI scales confirm traditional biologically based beliefs, many contemporary theorists have embraced a social constructionist position, attributing such differences to the differential treatment of males and females and the influence of gender-role-related expectations. This view suggests that the well-documented changes in gender-role attitudes and behaviors that have taken place over the past 3 decades might have had the effect of bringing together men's and women's self-perceptions of their personality characteristics. In a recent study testing this possibility, Twenge (1997) searched the literature for investigations reporting means for men and women on the two PAQ and the two BSRI scales. To detect the presence of temporal trends, she then essentially determined the correlation between the means and the year in which the study was published. No significant changes over time ap-

---

[2]Similar results were obtained by Sandra Bem (1974, 1977) with the BSRI. Although the content of the BSRI, particularly the items on the Feminine scale, is more mixed than the PAQ, the BSRI is predominantly a measure of desirable instrumental and expressive traits and generally produces outcomes that parallel those obtained with the PAQ. However, as described later, the theories in which Bem and my colleagues and I have embedded the two instruments differ quite radically.

peared for the means of the PAQ Expressiveness scale or for the parallel scale on the BSRI. However, significant temporal effects were found for the two masculine scales: The mean scores of women approached those of men.

In a more detailed effort to investigate cohort changes, Camille Buckner and I (Spence & Buckner, in press) recently collected self-report data for the 16 items making up the PAQ from two large samples of introductory students tested at the same university as tested in Helmreich and my early studies; Buckner and I also included the socially desirable instrumental and expressive items from the BSRI. A comparison of the means revealed that in both samples, men scored significantly lower than did women on each of the expressive items. Men, it would appear, have not changed in response to recent messages encouraging them to develop their softer side.

However, as Buckner and I (Spence & Buckner, in press) had suspected and Twenge's (1997) results imply, changes have occurred on the instrumental items since the tests were first developed. Thus, on only 9 of 22 instrumental items (5 out of 8 PAQ items and 6 out of 17 BSRI items) did significant gender differences emerge in both samples. These results suggest that the more egalitarian treatment experienced by contemporary college women has allowed them to develop more instrumental, self-assertive qualities than had their peers tested in earlier decades but not at the expense of their expressive, interpersonally oriented qualities. Most of these students, it should be acknowledged, were White and from middle-class families; women from these backgrounds have benefited the most from the liberalization of gender roles. Whether these increases in instrumental characteristics over time would also be found in women from other ethnic and socioeconomic backgrounds is as yet unknown.

The students in Buckner and my (Spence & Buckner, in press) samples were also asked to rate the typical male and female college student on the same set of items. The same factors that led to women becoming more similar to men in their self-report scores on the instrumental items might also have led to a diminution of students' stereotypes about these same traits. However, in both men and women, significant stereotypes uniformly emerged for all the PAQ items, both instrumental and expressive, and for all but two items from the BSRI.

~ ~ · ~ · · · £~~~ +h~ PAO were com-

types, they have proposed, ~~~ ~~~·· · ~
information is supplied about particular persons. Data based on the shifting standard model presented by Biernat and Kobrynowicz in their chapter (this volume) suggest, instead, that stereotypes of the sort Buckner and I (Spence & Buckner, in press) have investigated can have subtle but powerful effects. Stereotypes, as Biernat and Kobrynowicz aptly characterize them, are "stealthy," their effects often hidden from view. Thus, attempts to understand their persistence are of considerable importance.

The PAQ, Gender, and Self-Esteem

Conventional wisdom had it that self-esteem and other measures of mental health were associated with the presence of gender-congruent traits and the relative absence of gender-incongruent ones. Still another of the PAQ initial findings (Spence et al., 1974) considered remarkable at the time was disconfirmation of this proposition. Scores on the instrumentality scale were substantially related to the self-esteem measure, not only in men but also in women, a result that has consistently been replicated with other measures of self-esteem and psychological adjustment (e.g., Whitley, 1983). Similar results have also been obtained with

---

[3]On the BSRI, one feminine item, loyal, was significant only in women and one masculine item, analytic, failed to reach significance in either gender. In a study by Ruble published in 1983, stereotypes continued to be found on all of the 55 items originally identified by Spence et al. (1974), with the exception of intellectual—an item excluded from the current PAQ because it does not refer to an instrumental or expressive trait. The outcomes for these two items, analytic and intellectual, suggest that with respect to general (as opposed to more specialized) cognitive competencies, gender stereotypes about women's inferiority are weakening, at least among college students.

children (e.g., Spence & Hall, 1996). To the extent that they tap social self-confidence and ease in interpersonal relationships, measures of self-esteem and mental health have also been found to be positively correlated with expressive characteristics in both genders (e.g., Lubinski, Tellegen, & Butcher, 1983; Spence & Helmreich, 1978).

Although the correlation between masculine instrumental characteristics and global self-esteem is substantial in women, not just men, the results for women have to be qualified to some extent. For example, adolescent girls who were not only high in these characteristics but also conspicuously exhibited interests and behaviors that were considered masculine have been shown to be less popular and to have lower self-esteem, presumably because of negative reactions from their peers (Lobel, Slone, & Winch, 1997). The manner in which instrumentality is expressed, then, may qualify its relationship with feelings of self-worth.

Men's continued although dwindling advantage in instrumental attributes might suggest that they are higher in global self-esteem than are women, a proposition that others have endorsed although not necessarily on these grounds. Although data collected by my colleagues and myself do not reveal any systematic gender differences in the samples we have tested, the whole question of gender differences remains a controversial one both empirically and theoretically. As the meta-analyses performed by Brenda Major et al. (as reported in chapter 9, this volume) reveal, there is a small overall trend in favor of men; at the same time, their findings indicate that gender interacts with a multitude of variables to influence global self-esteem. In fact, the variability within each gender with respect to these diverse factors (as illustrated by the personality data of my colleagues and myself from groups that are relatively homogeneous in other respects) may make the significance of a small difference in the self-esteem of men and women as a whole difficult to interpret.

Major et al. (chapter 9, this volume) also note that gender differences in the level of self-esteem aside, it has been suggested that men and women differ in the sources of their self-esteem (e.g., Josephs, Markus, & Tafarodi, 1992). To the extent that these hypotheses implicate differences in personality characteristics such as those measured by the PAQ, our data complicate the issue. If men and women, as groups, do

Achievement

Purported gender differences in intrinsic achievement motives also engaged my interest early on. Due to the emphasis that Americans put on occupational success, and academic success as a contributor to it, achievement and its motivational underpinnings have long been one of the standard topics in psychological research.

Gender and Expectancy-Value Theory

Throughout the 1940s and 1950s, the most influential theory of achievement and achievement motivation was the expectancy-value theory of Atkinson and McClelland (e.g., Atkinson & Feather, 1966; McClelland, Atkinson, Clark, & Lowell, 1953), in which the major outcome variable is task choice. The theory, often tested in laboratory settings, works reasonably well for men but is typically unsuccessful with women. If they develop any at all, women's achievement motivations, some have concluded, are qualitatively different from men's. The most tangible result was that investigators working in this tradition began to use only men as participants.

In 1968, when interest in gender was beginning to become visible, Horner proposed a new concept, *fear of success*: a stable personality variable unique to women that when added to the concepts of expectancy-value theory, was expected to remedy the theory's inability to predict women's behavior. The notion gained a good deal of immediate attention, but the research it generated suggested that to the extent that fear of success was more often found in women than men, it reflected women's concern that others might react negatively to their doing well in masculine domains. These concerns were not without foundation (Spence, 1974).

A far more successful version of expectancy-value theory has subsequently been developed in a series of impressive studies by Eccles and her colleagues (e.g., Eccles, 1994; Eccles et al., chapter 7, this volume). In place of the sparse set of abstract quantitative formulations found in the original theory, Eccles went directly to naturally occurring settings to identify the expectations of parents, teachers, and others in girls' social environment that influence their decision to enter or to avoid activities associated with the other sex.

Intrinsic Motivation and the Work and Family Orientation Questionnaire

Although Helmreich and I (Spence & Helmreich, 1978) were influenced by the expectancy-value theory extant at the time, we adopted a somewhat different conceptual framework and elected to investigate a specific hypothesis that had been advanced for women's failure to achieve at the same level as men. According to this hypothesis, women not only fail to develop the requisite intrinsic motivation but also that in school and jobs, they do their work conscientiously to please those in authority—parents, teachers, or employers. For women who work outside the home, a major source of job satisfaction comes from fulfillment of their interpersonal needs: helping others or simply being with their coworkers. These notions have obvious links to instrumentality (characteristics presumably necessary to develop and maintain intrinsic motivation) and expressiveness, the two dimensions that have always been assumed such great importance in discussions of gender and gender differences.

On the basis in part of our findings with the PAQ, Helmreich and I suspected that any gender differences in intrinsic achievement motivation are of degree, not kind. As others (e.g., Eccles, 1994) have subsequently demonstrated by their research, we proposed instead that internal and external barriers related to gender-role expectations restrict women's access to certain occupations and training programs; further-

more, we suggested, many women with high levels of achievement motivation voluntarily or involuntarily channel its expression solely into
sanctioned activities, such as homemaking, child care, and volunteer

The WOFO contains three modestly correlated scales, each of which
has the same unifactorial structure within each gender. The scales tap
three different facets of intrinsic motivation: *Work Motivation* (the desire to work hard and conscientiously), *Mastery Motivation* (the desire
to master a challenging task and to maintain high performance standards), and *Interpersonal Competitiveness* (the desire to win over others
and be "number one").

From the point of view of gender, the most significant aspect of
these findings is that qualitatively similar results were obtained from
men and women. That is, in Helmreich and my psychometric analyses,
the same three factors emerged for men and women, thus disconfirming
hypotheses about qualitative differences in the nature of their intrinsic
motives. There were quantitative differences, however, between unselected groups of men and women but not in the same direction:
Women tended to score somewhat lower than men on the Mastery and
Competitiveness scales but somewhat higher on the Work scale. Once
again, however, these outcomes have to be qualified to some extent
when other variables are taken into account. In groups engaged in
highly demanding activities (e.g., varsity athletes, college faculty in several disciplines), women continue to score higher on Work and lower
on Interpersonal Competitiveness than do their male peers, but women
score at least as high as men do on Mastery (e.g., Spence & Helmreich,
1978, 1983). Not surprisingly, the highly achieving groups Helmreich
and I tested also scored higher on the PAQ instrumental scale than
unselected groups of same-sex peers but did not differ from them on

the Expressiveness scale. These outcomes held equally for men and for women.

Achievement Motives and Performance

Subsequent studies suggest that instrumentality and expressiveness, constellations of achievement motives, and—as proposed by Eccles et al.'s (this volume, chapter 7) model—a complex set of factors related to gender-related expectations are related to academic and occupational choices. As an example, consider the following: Women nursery school teachers have been shown to be much higher than their female peers in expressiveness as well as to be less competitive and less instrumental (Runge et al., 1981). Some men also exhibit this same personality profile but almost none of them elect to become nursery school teachers—an occupation that is still considered the exclusive province of women.

The major efforts of my colleagues and myself to investigate the implications of achievement motives, however, have not been focused on task choice, as has been the case with those working within the expectancy-value tradition, but rather primarily on task performance. Our studies of both students and adults show that in both genders, scores on the WOFO Work and Mastery scales are positively related to school and job performance but that especially when combined with high degrees of Work and Mastery, Competitiveness may actually impede performance (Spence & Helmreich, 1983). The latter result suggests that women's lower competitiveness is not necessarily a handicap.

Simultaneously, of course, these data indicate the usefulness of the WOFO in predicting achievement-related behaviors in naturally occurring settings. These findings stimulated my interest in pursuing still further the influence of various kinds of achievement-related motives on academic and occupational performance and led to a further series of inquiries (and psychometric instruments) in which the focus shifted from gender to achievement per se (e.g., Spence, Helmreich, & Pred, 1987; Helmreich et al., 1980; Spence & Robbins, 1992). For the purposes of this chapter, the most crucial aspect of all these investigations is that similar results were found in both men and women. The results thus provide still further disconfirmation of the hypotheses attributing women's lesser accomplishments in demanding activities, often dominated by men, to deficiencies in intrinsic achievement.

the change in the ideological climate, some of these findings—such as the demonstration that rather than being incompatible, the desirable instrumental and expressive characteristics measured by the PAQ and BSRI are essentially uncorrelated—have gained instant and enthusiastic acceptance.

However, the efforts of my colleagues and myself to challenge another time-honored set of tacit assumptions about gender phenomena has, at least until quite recently, met with some resistance. I refer here to what I have called the single-factor approach to gender phenomena and a related set of ideas about the nature of masculinity and femininity (Spence, 1984). Typically, the meaning of the terms *masculinity* and *femininity* remains unspecified. Seemingly, each refers to a fundamental psychological quality that along with physical characteristics is at the core of being a man or a woman.

The Early Version of the Bipolar Theory

As illustrated by conventional masculinity–femininity tests (Constantinople, 1973), it was often presumed that masculinity and femininity constituted the endpoints of a hypothetical bipolar continuum, along which individual men and women could be placed; this position could be diagnosed by the degree to which the person exhibited gender congruent qualities and failed to exhibit gender-incongruent ones. Reflecting the view that all gender-related phenomena contribute to the same underlying bipolar factor, the primary rationale for item inclusion on these masculinity–femininity tests is the item's capacity to differentiate the responses of men and women; the specific content is of little importance. Just as masculinity and femininity are psychological opposites, the scores of most men and women are expected to fall toward the gender-appropriate pole. The manner in which items were selected almost guaranteed that this would occur.

Bem's Revised Bipolar Theory

The postfeminist version of this bipolar theory, originally proposed by Sandra Bem (1974, 1977), contends that rather than being negatively correlated, masculine attributes and feminine attributes constitute two independent dimensions. Data from the BSRI and PAQ, of course, convincingly confirm this proposition in the case of the specific clusters of personality traits measured by these inventories. Nonetheless, the revised theory retains the notion of a single bipolar masculinity–femininity dimension. Thus, the theory basically calls for men's and women's scores on the two scales of the BSRI to be combined to form a single distribution. The then-radical departure from the traditional approach comes in the interpretation of what the scores in the middle of the distribution purportedly represent. Empirically, these are men and women who have approximately equal scores on the masculine and feminine scales, regardless of the scores' level. (In descriptive terms, these men and women are usually identified as androgynous individuals, those relatively high on both scales, and undifferentiated individuals, those relatively low on both [Bem, 1977; Spence et al., 1975].) Theoretically, those falling at the middle of the distribution are variously identified as nonsex typed, as having a low degree of gender-role identification, or as gender aschematic; these men and women reject conventional gender ideology and do not view themselves or the world though the lens of gender (Bem, 1981, 1994). Conversely, those with unbalanced scores in the stereotypic direction, masculine men and feminine women, are assumed to be gender schematic and to have gendered personalities. It should be noted parenthetically that in contrast to masculinity–femininity tests with omnibus content, the distributions of scores of men and women on each of the BSRI and PAQ scales approach normality and show considerable overlap. When the two scale scores are combined on these particular instruments, a substantial number of men and women are therefore classified as nonsex typed or aschematic.

questionnaires such as the PAQ and BSRI measure only, whose contents indicate, primarily, certain desirable instrumental and expressive traits; more broadly, I postulated, the diverse classes of phenomena that distinguish between males and females of a given age contribute to a number of different statistically identifiable factors whose relationships to one another are variable and complex. Furthermore, no single dimension or set of dimensions provides the key to masculinity or femininity (e.g., Spence, 1985).

In at least tacit recognition of this multifactorial position, attention has begun to be paid to the obvious fact that males and females differ along many observable dimensions. Huston (1983) and Ashmore (1990), for example, have developed taxonomies of these dimensions. Classification of categories within major dimensions has also been undertaken, such as that proposed by Deaux and Lewis (1984) in their work on the structure of gender stereotypes. Investigators, working with both children and older populations, have also devised measures tapping a number of specific gender-related categories (e.g., Ashmore, 1990; Deaux & Lewis, 1984; Orlofsky, 1981; Spence, 1993; Spence & Buckner, 1995; Spence & Hall, 1996; Yekel, Bigler, & Liben, 1991). As the meta-analysis reported by Signorella (chapter 5, this volume) reflects, the data indicate that the correlations among the various measures, including the PAQ and BSRI, do not exhibit any simple pattern and, in fact, frequently fail to be significantly related at all. These findings add confirmation to my contention that gender phenomena are not merely multidimensional—it is perfectly apparent that they are— but also *multifactorial.* Although male and female groups of a given age may differ significantly in each dimension, the specific constellations of gender-related behaviors, attributes, and beliefs that particular individuals display (and fail to display) are highly variable within each gender, have various etiologies, and are sustained by different sets of contemporary influence.

The claim that gender phenomena contribute to multiple factors does not, of course, imply that the various factors are necessarily orthogonal. For example, sets of unifactorial measures that assess facets of the same general class of phenomena may be expected to exhibit some degree of relationship. Data from the several sexism questionnaires I reviewed above provide one such illustration. The identification of these factors and sets of factors and exploration of the manner in which they are jointly related to other variables are matters of empirical investigation. Similarly, while rejecting the notion of a single overarching gender schema, as opposed to multiple relatively independent gender schemas, the multifactorial position does not deny the usefulness of general models of the processes that determine the development and govern the operation of these schemas. Their utility is amply demonstrated by the research on the cognitive model of Carol Martin and her colleagues (described in chapter 3, this volume) and by the shifting standard perspective on gender stereotypes described by Biernat and Kobrynowicz (chapter 2, this volume).

Masculinity, Femininity, and Gender Identity

Despite the growing acceptance of the multifactorial position and the mounting evidence in its favor, a good many investigators continue to embrace unifactorial approaches and, more particularly, to regard the BSRI and the PAQ as measures of the global masculinity–femininity, gender schematization constructs. In part, investigators may be reluctant to give up a quite parsimonious set of propositions with strong ideological appeal in favor of a more complicated position with less straightforward policy implications. A second factor may be people's intuitive beliefs in the reality of a core essence within themselves that defines them as a man or woman—ineffable qualities that people typically label masculinity and femininity. The latter belief is one I also embrace. However, I strongly doubt that these core essences can be tracked down and uniformly measured by limited sets of observable qualities or larger collections of qualities that empirically differentiate

(Spence, 1985). Briefly, ...
at any early age a firm sense of gender identity as a central feature in their self concept. At various times and stages in life, people may feel threatened or begin to doubt their adequacy as a male or female—their masculinity or femininity in this sense—but, once established, gender identity itself is stable. Very young children may adopt the conspicuous badges of their sex, playing with the right kinds of toys or wearing the right kind of clothes, in an attempt to verify their gender identity. But other forces that vary from child to child are also at work, determining the particular constellations of gender-congruent characteristics—and gender incongruent characteristics—that a given child comes to display or fails to display. Some of these influences are related to gender and others are not, some are biologically based and others are not, some are affected primarily by experiences within the family and others by experiences with the world outside. Quite soon, the driving function that gender identity may have had early on in producing gender-appropriate behaviors and attributes is taken over by other sets of variables whose specifics vary from one individual to the next. I have further proposed (e.g., Spence, 1985) that as the role of gender identity in producing gender-congruent behaviors diminishes, the relationship between the latter and gender identity reverses: The gender-appropriate characteristics that for whatever reason people happen to possess at a given stage of life serve to verify and maintain their sense of gender identity, their existential sense of masculinity or femininity. People's failure to possess other gender-congruent characteristics or their possession of gender-incongruent ones are dismissed as irrelevant to their

279

gender identity. Their fundamental sense of masculinity or femininity is thereby preserved and protected.

Although at the time it was first proposed the theory was designed to fit the available evidence, the developmental aspect of gender identity theory was both speculative and sketchy in its details. As the evidence accumulates, however, it confirms the implications of the theory, as illustrated by the meta-analytic data reported by Signorella in her chapter (this volume). As outlined in chapter 3 (this volume), the data collected by Martin and her colleagues are also supportive of the theory.

It should be noted, however, that my conception of gender identity differs somewhat from that of Martin and her colleagues (see, e.g., chapter 3, this volume). I have proposed a narrower definition (e.g, Spence, 1985), one which corresponds to the usage found in the psychiatric literature in which gender identity is conceived as one of the earliest and crucial features of the self concept to develop and antedates even gender constancy (e.g., Green, 1974). Gender identify theory was designed to reconcile two observations. First, throughout the life span, individuals within each gender are highly diverse with respect to the patterns of gender-linked characteristics they display—a diversity whose etiology cannot be explained by appeal to any simple construct or set of constructs. Yet at the same time, the vast majority of people believe in their own basic masculinity or femininity, even though they cannot articulate what it is, and are willing to concede these qualities to others as long as they exhibit a suitable number or kind of gender-congruent attributes (Spence & Sawin, 1985). The theory of gender identity I have proposed provides unity in the face of diversity.

THREE DECADES OF RESEARCH: DEAUX'S FOUR THEMES

It seems appropriate to conclude by returning to the four themes presented by Kay Deaux in her overview (chapter 1, this volume).

Women and Men Are Different, Aren't They?

A good deal of the social psychological work done in the late 1960s was devoted to testing ideas inherited from earlier theories, theories postulating that inborn differences in men's and women's cognitive and temperamental qualities made it inevitable that women should be sub-ordinate to men and their sphere of responsibility should be restricted

old essentialist theories remain. For example, some contend that females' poorer performance on standardized measures of quantitative ability and their lesser attainments in math and science are in part genetically determined. New biologically based theories such as those proposed by evolutionary psychologists (e.g., Buss, 1995) have also appeared. Confirmation or disconfirmation of such essentialist notions will not come easily, and controversies are likely to endure for many years.

Whatever the source of observable differences between the male and female populations, the research conducted over the last 3 decades should have taught psychologists one important lesson. More often than not, there is not only considerable variability within each gender but also considerable overlap between the distributions of male and female groups. Mean differences, then, are often small relative to the overall variability, and gendered attributes and behaviors per se are often better predictors of other attributes and behaviors than is gender. Psychologists cannot afford to ignore the significance of mean differences between male and female groups simply because they are small in some absolute sense. At the same time, they cannot afford to overlook the implications of individual differences within each gender.

People Think Men and Women Are Different, Don't They?

In recent years, impressive work has been done on stereotypes, much of it related to people's beliefs about differences between men and women and between mainstream Whites and members of various ethnic minorities. Theoretical models of the acquisition and operation of gender stereotypes have been developed, often drawing on other areas of psychology (particularly cognitive); these models, in turn, often have broad implications for other stigmatized groups or for stereotyping in general.

Stereotypes, however, do not exist in isolation. I only mention here several nagging questions about their relationships with other phenomena. People who are more stereotyped in their beliefs about the differences between men and women in their personal and intellectual qualities are more likely to believe in traditional gender-role distinctions and to exhibit other kinds of sexist attitudes. What is the causal direction underlying this correlation? Does endorsement of stereotypes about the different attributes of men and women serve primarily as a rationalization of role-related beliefs? Or is it the other way around? That is, do beliefs about men's and women's capacities lead to beliefs about how societal privileges and responsibilities ought to be allocated? No doubt there is no simple answer, and the causal direction may go both ways. How is it that gender-role attitudes and actual role-related behaviors have changed quite substantially in recent years but at least certain gender stereotypes (e.g., those concerned with instrumental and expressive traits) have not? The dynamic relationships between stereotypes and attitudes is still another of the significant questions that still need to be explored.

Maybe This Is All More Complicated Than We Thought

The research conducted over the past 3 decades has, alas, extinguished all hope that a simple set of principles will suffice to explain all major gender phenomena. The more psychologists (myself included) learn, the more they realize how complicated it all is. However, to put a more positive twist on what has been accomplished, this research has allowed them to abandon old monolithic ideas and to give them the freedom to develop new theories that will advance the understanding. Collectively, they have made a good start.

Psychologists Are Not Alone

In proposing this theme, Deaux (chapter 1, this volume) is calling attention to the importance of social context and the contribution to

society: the rejection by many of a societal system that denied equal rights to women, as well as to members of ethnic minorities, in both public and private spheres. At least tacitly, the purpose of most of us who engaged in gender research back then was to develop the psychological knowledge that could lead to a more egalitarian society. This goal was demonstrated most overtly in the intervention programs initiated in the 1970s and beyond that were designed to reduce sexist attitudes and behaviors.

As Bigler describes in her chapter (this volume), these interventions were often notable for their lack of success. As she suggests, their failures may largely be due to conceptual and empirical limitations in these programs, limitations that the studies she and her colleagues have conducted with children were designed to overcome. She suggests, more specifically, that the most appropriate intervention targets are those that the larger society will tolerate.

The point is a critical one. To survive and operate effectively, every society must be conservative yet flexible enough to accommodate changes in its circumstances. Seemingly sudden and revolutionary challenges to ruling ideologies are usually the consequence of economic and political events that make old social arrangements less functional and more difficult to sustain than they once were. Such challenges succeed to the extent that they bring about changes in value systems and practices in line with current realities. Efforts to go beyond what the majority of people are able to accommodate or accept are likely to fail. Whether, as psychologists, our underlying goal is quite simply to understand gender phenomena as dispassionate observers or to change them in directions compatible with our personal ideologies, we ignore at our peril what is going on our society as a whole, our history, and the nature of our political, economic, and cultural institutions. As Deaux (1997) so pithily put it, "a strictly psychological approach is—well—too psychological."

REFERENCES

Ashmore, R. D. (1990). Sex, gender, and the individual. In L. A. Pervin (Ed.), *Handbook of personality: Theory and research* (pp. 486–526). New York: Guilford.

Atkinson, J. W., & Feather, N. T. (Eds.). (1966). *A theory of achievement motivation.* New York: Wiley.

Beere, C. A. (1990). *Gender roles: A handbook of tests and measures.* Westport, CT: Greenwood Press.

Bem, S. L. (1974). The measurement of psychological androgyny. *Journal of Consulting and Clinical Psychology, 42,* 155–162.

Bem, S. L. (1977). On the utility of alternative procedures for assessing psychological androgyny. *Journal of Consulting and Clinical Psychology, 45,* 196–205.

Bem, S. L. (1981). Gender schema theory: A cognitive account of sex typing. *Psychological Review, 88,* 354–364.

Bem, S. L. (1994). *The lenses of gender.* New Haven, CT: Yale University Press.

Buss, D. M. (1995). Psychological sex differences: Origins through sexual selection. *American Psychologist, 50,* 164–168.

Constantinople, A. (1973). Masculinity–femininity: An exception to the famous dictum? *Psychological Bulletin, 80,* 389–407.

Crawford, M. E., & Marecek, J. (1989). Psychology reconstructs the female: 1969–1988. *Psychology of Women Quarterly, 13,* 147–165.

Deaux, K. (1997, April). *Overview of research on gender and gender roles.* Paper presented at Models of Gender and Gender Differences: Then and Now (a festschrift in honor of Janet Taylor Spence, Austin, TX).

Deaux, K., & Lewis, L. L. (1984). Structure of gender stereotypes: Interrelationships among components and gender label. *Journal of Personality and Social Psychology, 46,* 991–1004.

Diaz-Loving, R., Diaz-Guerrero, R., Helmreich, R. L., & Spence, J. T. (1981). Comparacion transcultural y analysis psicometrico de una medida de rasgos masculinos (instrumentales), y femeninos (expresivos) [Cross-cultural

ating hostile and benevolent sexism. *Journal of Personality and Social Psychology, 70*, 491–512.

Green, R. (1974). *Sexual identity conflict in children and adults.* New York: Basic Books.

Helmreich, R., Aronson, E., & Le Fann, J. (1970). To err is humanizing— Sometimes: Effects of self-esteem, competence, and a pratfall on interpersonal attraction. *Journal of Personality and Social Psychology, 16,* 259–264.

Helmreich, R. L., & Spence, J. T. (1978). The Work and Family Orientation Questionnaire: An objective instrument to assess components of achievement motivation and attitudes toward family and career. *JSAS Catalog of Selected Documents in Psychology, 8,* 35 (Ms. 1677).

Helmreich, R. L., Spence, J. T., Beane, W. E., Lucker, G. W., & Matthews, K. A. (1980). Making it in academic psychology: Demographic and personality correlates of attainment. *Journal of Personality and Social Psychology, 39,* 896–908.

Helmreich, R. L., Spence, J. T., & Gibson, R. H. (1982). Sex-role attitudes: 1972–1980. *Personality and Social Psychology Bulletin, 8,* 656–663.

Hetherington, E. M. (1965). A developmental study of the effects of sex of the dominant parent on sex-role preference, identification, and imitation in children. *Journal of Personality and Social Psychology, 2,* 188–194.

Holmes, D. S., & Jorgensen, B. W. (1971). Do personality and social psychologists study men more than women? *Representative Research in Social Psychology, 2,* 71–76.

Horner, M. (1968). *Sex differences in achievement motivation and performance in competitive and non-competitive situations.* Unpublished doctoral dissertation, University of Michigan.

Huston, A. (1983). Sex-typing. In E. M Hetherington (Ed.), *Handbook of child psychology. Vol. 4: Socialization, personality, and child development* (pp. 388–467). New York: Wiley.

Josephs, R. A., Markus, H. R., & Tafarodi, R. W. (1992). Gender and self-esteem. *Journal of Personality and Social Psychology, 63,* 391–402.

Kagan, J. (1964). Acquisition and significance of sex typing and sex role identity. In M. L. Hoffman & L. W. Hoffman (Eds.), *Review of child development research* (Vol. 2, pp. 137–168). New York: Russell Sage Foundation.

Kohlberg, L. A. (1966). Cognitive-developmental analysis of children's sex-role concepts and attitudes. In E. E. Maccoby (Ed.), *The development of sex differences* (pp. 82–173). Stanford, CA: Stanford University Press.

Lobel, T. E., Slone, M., & Winch, G. (1997). Masculinity, popularity, and self-esteem among adolescent girls. *Sex Roles, 36,* 395–408.

Lubinski, D., Tellegen, A., & Butcher, J. N. (1983). Masculinity, femininity, and androgyny viewed and assessed as distinct concepts. *Journal of Personality and Social Psychology, 44,* 428–439.

McClelland, D. C., Atkinson, J. W., Clark, R. A., & Lowell, E. L. (1953). *The achievement motive.* New York: Appleton-Century-Crofts.

Orlofsky, J. L. (1981). Relationship between sex-role attitudes and personality traits and the Sex Role Behavior Scale—1. A new measure of masculine and feminine role behaviors and interests. *Journal of Personality and Social Psychology, 40,* 927–940.

Parsons, T., & Bales, R. F. (1955). *Family socialization and interaction process.* Glencoe, IL: Free Press.

Ruble, T. L. (1983). Sex stereotypes: Issues of change in the 1970's. *Sex Roles, 9,* 397–402.

Runge, T. E., Frey, D., Gollwitzer, P. M., Helmreich, R. L., & Spence, J. T. (1981). Masculine (instrumental) and feminine (expressive) traits: A comparison between students in the United States and West Germany. *Journal of Cross-Cultural Psychology, 12,* 142–162.

Sherman, P., & Spence, J. T. (1997). A comparison of two cohorts of college students in responses to the Male–Female Relations Questionnaire. *Psychology of Women Quarterly, 21,* 265–278.

Spence, J. T. (1974). The Thematic Apperception Test and attitudes toward achievement in women: A new look at the motive to avoid success and a new method of measurement. Journal of Consulting and Clinical Psy-

deregger (Vol. Ed.), *Nebraska Symposium* ... . *Vol. 32: Psychology and gender* (pp. 59–95). Lincoln: University of Nebraska Press.

Spence, J. T. (1993). Gender-related traits and gender ideology: Evidence for a multifactorial theory. *Journal of Personality and Social Psychology, 64*, 624–635.

Spence, J. T., & Buckner, C. E. (1995). Masculinity and femininity: Defining the undefinable. In P. Kalbfleisch & M. Cody (Eds.), *Gender, power and communication in interpersonal relationships* (pp. 105–138). Hillsdale NJ: Erlbaum.

Spence, J. T., & Buckner, C. E. (in press). Instrumental and expressive traits, trait stereotypes, and sexist attitudes: What do they signify? *Psychology of Women Quarterly.*

Spence, J. T., & Hahn, E. D. (1997). The Attitudes Toward Women Scale and attitude change in college students. *Sex Roles, 21*, 17–34.

Spence, J. T., & Hall, S. K. (1996). Children's gender-related self-perceptions, activity preferences, and occupational stereotypes: A test of three models of gender constructs. *Sex Roles, 35*, 659–692.

Spence, J. T., & Helmreich, R. (1972a). The Attitudes Toward Women Scale: An objective instrument to measure attitudes toward the rights and roles of women in contemporary society. *JSAS Catalog of Selected Documents in Psychology, 2*, 66–67 (Ms. 153).

Spence, J. T., & Helmreich, R. (1972b). Who likes competent women? Competence, sex-role congruence of interest, and subjects' attitudes toward women as determinants of interpersonal attraction. *Journal of Applied Social Psychology, 2*, 197–213.

Spence, J. T., & Helmreich, R. L. (1978). *Masculinity and femininity: Their psychological dimensions, correlates, and antecedents.* Austin: University of Texas Press.

Spence, J. T., & Helmreich, R. L. (1983). Achievement-related motives and behavior. In J. T. Spence (Ed.), *Achievement and achievement motives: Psychological and sociological approaches* (pp. 10–74). San Francisco: Freeman.

Spence, J. T., Helmreich, R. L., & Holahan, C. K. (1979). Negative and positive components of psychological masculinity and femininity and their relationships to self-reports of neurotic and acting out behavior. *Journal of Personality and Social Psychology, 37,* 1673–1682.

Spence, J. T., Helmreich, R. L., & Pred, R. S. (1987). Impatience versus achievement strivings in the Type A pattern: Differential effects on students' health and academic achievement. *Journal of Applied Psychology, 72,* 522–528.

Spence, J. T., Helmreich, R. L., & Sawin, L. L. (1980). The Male–Female Relations Questionnaire: A self-report inventory of sex-role behaviors and preferences and their relationships to masculine and feminine personality traits, sex-role attitudes, and other measures. *JSAS Catalog of Selected Documents in Psychology, 10,* 87 (Ms. 916).

Spence, J. T., Helmreich, R. L., & Stapp, J. (1974). The Personal Attributes Questionnaire: A measure of sex-role stereotypes and masculinity–femininity. *JSAS Catalog of Selected Documents in Psychology, 4,* 43–44 (Ms. 617).

Spence, J. T., Helmreich, R. L., & Stapp, J. (1975). Ratings of self and peers on sex-role attributes and their relations to self-esteem and conceptions of masculinity and femininity. *Journal of Personality and Social Psychology, 32,* 29–39.

Spence, J. T., Losoff, M., & Robbins, A. S. (1991). Sexually aggressive tactics in dating relationships. *Journal of Social and Clinical Psychology, 3,* 289–304.

Spence, J. T., & Robbins, A. S. (1992). Workaholism: Definition, measurement, and preliminary results. *Journal of Personality Assessment, 58,* 160–178.

Spence, J. T., & Sawin, L. L. (1985). Images of masculinity and femininity. A reconceptualization. In V. O'Leary, R. Unger, & B. Wallston (Eds.), *Women, gender and social psychology* (pp. 35–66). Hillsdale, NJ: Erlbaum.

Swim, J. K., Aikin, K. J., Hall, W. S., & Hunter, B. A. (1995). Sexism and racism:

Old-fashioned and modern prejudices. *Journal of Personality and Social Psychology, 68,* 199–214.

Taylor, J. A. (1951). The relationship of anxiety to the conditioned eyelid re-

Whitley, B. E., Jr. (1983). Sex-role orientation and self-esteem: A critical meta-analytic review. *Journal of Personality and Social Psychology, 44,* 765–778.

Yekel, C. A., Bigler, R. S., & Liben, L. S. (1991, April). *Children's gender schemata: Occupation, activity, and trait attributions for self and others.* Paper presented at the biennial meeting of the Society for Research in Children Development, Seattle, WA.

Yoder, J. D., & McDonald, T. W. (1997). The generalizability and construct validity of the Modern Sexism Scale: Some cautionary notes. *Sex Roles, 36,* 655–663.

Appendix:

BOOKS AND EDITED VOLUMES

Spence, K. W., & Spence, J. T. (Eds.). (1967). *The psychology of learning and motivation* (Vol. 1). New York: Academic Press.

Spence, K. W., & Spence, J. T. (Eds.). (1968). *The psychology of learning and motivation* (Vol. 2). New York: Academic Press.

Bower, G., & Spence, J. T. (Eds.). (1969). *The psychology of learning and motivation* (Vol. 3). New York: Academic Press.

Kendler, H. H., & Spence, J. T. (Eds.). (1971). *Essays in neobehaviorism.* New York: Appleton-Century-Crofts.

Spence, J. T., Carson, R. C., & Thibaut, J. W. (Eds.). (1976). *Behavioral approaches to therapy.* Morristown, NJ: General Learning Press.

Thibaut, J. W., Spence, J. T., & Carson, R. C. (Eds.). (1976). *Contemporary topics in social psychology.* Morristown, NJ: General Learning Press.

Spence, J. T., & Helmreich, R. L. (1978). *Masculinity and femininity: Their psychological dimensions, correlates, and antecedents.* Austin: University of Texas Press.

Spence, J. T. (Ed). (1983). *Achievement and achievement motives: Psychological and sociological approaches.* San Francisco: Freeman.

Spence, J. T., & Izard, C. E. (Eds.). (1986). *Motivation, emotion, and personality. Vol. 11: Proceedings of the XXIII International Congress of Psychology.* Amsterdam: North Holland.

Spence, J. T. (1990). *Workbook to accompany* Elementary statistics, *fifth edition.* Englewood Cliffs, NJ: Prentice-Hall.

Spence, J. T., Cotton, J. W., Underwood, B. J., & Duncan, C. P. (1990). *Elementary statistics* (5th ed.). Englewood Cliffs, NJ: Prentice-Hall.

BOOK CHAPTERS

Spence, J. T. (1963). Learning theory and personality. In J. M. Wepman & R. W. Heine (Eds.), *Concepts of personality* (pp. 3–30). Chicago: Aldine Press.

Spence, J. T. (1970). Comments on paper by Logan. In W. A. Hunt (Ed.), *Learning mechanisms in smoking* (pp. 38–40). Chicago: Aldine.

Kendler, H. H., & Spence, J. T. (1971). Tenets of neobehavorism. In H. H. Kendler & J. T. Spence (Eds.), *Essays in neobehaviorism* (pp. 11–40). New York: Appleton-Century-Crofts.

Helmreich, R., & Spence, J. T. (1977). Sex roles and achievement. In D. M. Landers & R. W. Christina (Eds.), *Psychology of motor behavior and sport* (pp. 33–46). Champaign, IL: Human Kinetics.

Spence, J. T. (1979). Traits, roles, and concept of androgyny. In J. E. Gullahorn (Ed.), *Psychology and women: In transition* (pp. 167–187). New York: Wiley.

Spence, J. T. (1983). Women, men, and society: Plus ca change, plus c'est la meme chose [The more things change, the more they stay the same]. In S. Oskamp & M. Costanzo (Eds.), *Claremont Symposium on Applied Social Psychology, 1992: Gender and social psychology* (pp. 3–17). Newbury Park, CA: Sage.

Spence, J. T., & Helmreich, R. L. (1983). Achievement-related motives and behavior. In J. T. Spence (Ed.), *Achievement and achievement motives: Psychological and sociological approaches* (pp. 10–74). San Francisco: Freeman.

Spence, J. T. (1984). Masculinity, femininity, and gender-related traits: A conceptual analysis and critique of current research. In B. A. Maher & W. B. Maher (Eds.), *Progress in expertimental personality research* (pp. 2–97). New York: Academic Press.

Spence, J. T., & Sawin, L. L. (1984). Images of masculinity and femininity: A reconceptualization. In V. O'Leary, R. Unger, & B. Wallston (Eds.), *Sex, gender, and social psychology* (pp. 35–66). Hillsdale, NJ: Erlbaum.

Spence, J. T. (1985). Gender identity and its implications for the concepts of masculinity and femininity. In R. A. Dienstbier (Series Ed.) & T. B. Sonderegger (Vol. Ed.), *Nebraska Symposium on Motivation and Achieve-*

ment. Vol. 32: Psychology and gender (pp. 59–95). Lincoln: University of Nebraska Press.

Spence, J. T., Deaux, K., & Helmreich, R. L. (1985). Sex roles in contemporary

 ⟨⟩ *Handbook of social*

sonality. Vol. 11. Proceedings of ....

chology (pp. 65–75). Amsterdam: North Holland.

Spence, J. T. (1991a). Men, women, and achievement: Past, present, and future. In P. McAllister (Ed.), *Women and the American economy: A national and global context* (pp. 11–26). Cincinnati, OH: University of Cincinnati, the Center for Women's Studies.

Spence, J. T. (1991b). Where's the action? In J. H. Cantor (Ed.), *Psychology at Iowa: Centennial essays* (pp. 141–149). Hillsdale, NJ: Erlbaum.

Spence, J. T. (1993). Men, women, and society: Plus c'est change, plus c'est la meme chose [The more things change, the more they stay the same]. In S. Oskamp & M. Costanzo (Eds.), *Claremont Symposium on Applied Social Psychology, 1992: Gender and social psychology* (pp. 3–17). Newbury Park, CA: Sage.

Spence, J. T., & Buckner, C. E. (1995). Masculinity and femininity: Defining the undefinable. In P. Kalbfleisch & M. Cody (Eds.), *Gender, power and communication in interpersonal relationships* (pp. 105–138). Hillsdale, NJ: Erlbaum.

Spence, J. T., & Spence, K. W. (1996). The motivational components of manifest anxiety: Drive and drive stimuli. In C. Spielberger (Ed.), *Anxiety and behavior* (pp. 291–326). New York: Academic Press.

ARTICLES

Spence, K. W., & Taylor, J. A. (1951). Anxiety and strength of the UCS as determiners of the amount of eyelid conditioning. *Journal of Experimental Psychology, 42,* 183–188.

Taylor, J. A. (1951). The relationship of anxiety to the conditioned eyelid response. *Journal of Experimental Psychology, 41,* 81–92.

Taylor, J. A., & Spence, K. W. (1952). The relationship of anxiety level to performance in serial learning. *Journal of Experimental Psychology, 45,* 265–272.

Taylor, J. A. (1953). A personality scale of manifest anxiety. *Journal of Abnormal and Social Psychology, 48,* 285–290.

Taylor, J. A., & Spence, K. W. (1954). Conditioning level in the behavior disorders. *Journal of Abnormal and Social Psychology, 49,* 497–502.

Lewis, M. A., & Taylor, J. A. (1955). Anxiety and extreme response preferences. *Educational and Psychological Measurement, 15,* 111–116.

Taylor, J. A. (1955). The Taylor Manifest Anxiety Scale and intelligence. *Journal of Abnormal and Social Psychology, 51,* 347.

Taylor, J. A., & Chapman, J. P. (1955). Anxiety and learning of paired associates. *American Journal of Psychology, 68,* 671.

Taylor, J. A. (1956a). Drive theory and manifest anxiety. *Psychological Bulletin, 53,* 303–320.

Taylor, J. A. (1956b). Effect of set for associated words on duration threshold. *Perpetual and Motor Skills, 6,* 131–134.

Taylor, J. A. (1956c). Level of conditioning and intensity of the adaptation stimulus. *Journal of Experimental Psychology, 51,* 127–130.

Taylor, J. A. (1956d). Physiological need, set, and visual duration threshold. *Journal of Abnormal and Social Psychology, 53,* 303–320.

Chapman, L. J., & Taylor, J. A. (1957). Breadth of deviate concepts used by schizophrenics. *Journal of Abnormal and Social Psychology, 54,* 118–123.

Taylor, J. A. (1958a). The effects of anxiety level and psychological stress on verbal learning. *Journal of Abnormal and Social Psychology, 57,* 55–60.

Taylor, J. A. (1958b). Meaning, frequency and visual duration thresholds. *Journal of Experimental Social Psychology, 55,* 329–334.

Taylor, J. A., & Maher, B. A. (1959). Escape and displacement experience as variables in the recovery from approach-evidence conflict. *Journal of Comparative and Physiological Psychology, 52,* 586–590.

Taylor, J. A., & Rechtschaffen, A. (1959). Manifest anxiety and reversed alphabet printing. *Journal of Abnormal and Social Psychology, 58,* 221−224.

Taylor, J. A., & Rennie, B. (1961). Recovery from approach-evidence conflict

parative and Physiological Psychology, 55, 247 − 251.

Spence, J. T., & Maher, B. A. (1962b). Handling and noxious stimulation of the albino rat. II. Effects on subsequent performance in a learning situation. *Journal of Comparative and Physiological Psychology, 55,* 252−255.

Tutko, T. A., & Spence, J. T. (1962). The performance of process and reactive schizophrenics and brain-injured subjects on a conceptual task. *Journal of Abnormal and Social Psychology, 65,* 387−394.

D'Allessio, G. R., & Spence, J. T. (1963). Schizophrenic deficit and its relation to social motivation. *Journal of Abnormal and Social Psychology, 66,* 390−393.

Spence, J. T. (1963a). Associative interference on paired-associative lists from extraexperimental learning. *Journal of Verbal Learning and Verbal Behavior, 2,* 329−338.

Spence, J. T. (1963b). Contribution of response bias to recognition thresholds. *Journal of Abnormal and Social Psychology, 66,* 339−344.

Spence, J. T. (1963c). Further comments on "Performance on a motor learning task as related to MAS scores." *Perceptual and Motor Skills, 17,* 564.

Spence, J. T. (1963d). Patterns of performance on WAIS similarities in schizophrenic, brain-damaged and normal subjects. *Psychological Reports, 13,* 431−436.

Spence, J. T., Lair, C. V., & Goodstein, L. D. (1963). Effects of different feedback conditions on verbal discrimination learning in schizophrenic and non-psychiatric subjects. *Journal of Verbal Learning and Verbal Behavior, 2,* 339−345.

Spence, J. T. (1964a). Performance on a four-alternative task under different reinforcement combinations. *Psychonomic Science, 1,* 241–242.

Spence, J. T. (1964b). Verbal discrimination performance under different verbal reinforcement combinations. *Journal of Experimental Psychology, 67,* 195–197.

Spence, J. T., & Lair, C. V. (1964). Associative interference in the verbal learning performance of schizophrenics and normals. *Journal of Abnormal and Social Psychology, 68,* 204–209.

Spence, K. W., & Spence, J. T. (1964). Relation of eyelid conditioning to manifest anxiety, extraversion and rigidity. *Journal of Abnormal and Social Psychology, 68,* 144–149.

Walker, R. E., & Spence, J. T. (1964). Relationship between digit span and anxiety. *Journal of Consulting Psychology, 28,* 220–223.

Spence, J. T., Goodstein, L. D., & Lair, C. V. (1965). Rote learning in schizophrenic and normal subjects under positive and negative reinforcement conditions. *Journal of Abnormal Psychology, 40,* 251–261.

Spence, J. T., & Lair, C. V. (1965a). Associative interference in the paired-associate learning of remitted and nonremitted schizophrenics. *Journal of Abnormal Psychology, 70,* 119–122.

Spence, J. T., & Lair, C. V. (1965b). The effect of different verbal reinforcement combinations on the verbal discrimination performance of schizophrenics. *Journal of Personality and Social Psychology, 1,* 245–249.

Spence, J. T., & Schulz, R. W. (1965). Negative transfer in paired-associate learning as a function of first-list trials. *Journal of Verbal Learning and Verbal Behavior, 4,* 397–400.

Spence, J. T. (1966a). The effects of verbal reinforcement combination and instructional condition on the performance of a problem-solving task. *Journal of Personality and Social Psychology, 3,* 163–170.

Spence, J. T. (1966b). Verbal-discrimination performance as a function of instructions and verbal-reinforcement combination in normal and retarded children. *Child Development, 37,* 269–281.

Spence, K. W., & Spence, J. T. (1966). Sex and anxiety differences in eyelid conditioning. *Psychological Bulletin, 65,* 137–142.

Spence, J. T., & Dunton, M. C. (1967). The influence of verbal and non-verbal reinforcement combinations in the discrimination learning of middle-class and lower-class children. *Child Development, 38,* 1177–1186.

~~~~~ J. T. & Segner. L. L. (1967). Verbal versus nonverbal reinforcement

velopment, 41, 103–111.

Spence, J. T. (1970b). Verbal reinforcement combinations and concept-identification learning: The role of nonreinforcement. *Journal of Experimental Psychology, 85,* 321–329.

Spence, J. T. (1971a). Do material rewards enhance the performance of lower-class children? *Child Development, 42,* 1461–1470.

Spence, J. T. (1971b). What can you say about a twenty-year-old theory that won't die? *Journal of Motor Behavior, 3,* 193–203.

Spence, J. T. (1972a). The effects of blank versus non-informative feedback and "right" and "wrong" on response repetition in paired-associate learning: A reanalysis and reinterpretation. *Journal of Experimental Psychology, 94,* 1246–1248.

Spence, J. T. (1972b). Verbal and nonverbal rewards and punishments in the discrimination learning of children of varying socio-economic status. *Developmental Psychology, 6,* 381–384.

Spence, J. T., & Helmreich, R. (1972a). The Attitudes Toward Women Scale: An objective instrument to measure attitudes toward the rights and roles of women in contemporary society. *JSAS Catalog of Selected Documents in Psychology, 2,* 66–67 (Ms. 153).

Spence, J. T., & Helmreich, R. (1972b). Who likes competent women? Competence, sex-role congruence of interest, and subjects' attitudes toward women as determinants of interpersonal attraction. *Journal of Applied Social Psychology, 2,* 197–213.

Spence, J. T. (1973). Factors contributing to the effectiveness of social and nonsocial reinforcers in the discrimination learning of children from two socioeconomic groups. *Journal of Experimental Child Psychology*, *15*, 367–380.

Spence, J. T., Helmreich, R., & Stapp, J. (1973). A short version of the Attitudes Toward Women Scale (AWS). *Bulletin of the Psychonomic Society*, *2*, 219–220.

Spence, J. T. (1974). The Thematic Apperception Test and attitudes toward achievement in women: A new look at the motive to avoid success and a new method of measurement. *Journal of Consulting and Clinical Psychology*, *42*, 427–437.

Spence, J. T., Helmreich, R. L., & Stapp, J. (1974). The Personal Attributes Questionnaire: A measure of sex-role stereotypes and masculinity–femininity. *JSAS Catalog of Selected Documents in Psychology*, *4*, 43–44 (Ms. 617).

Kristal, J., Sanders, D., Spence, J. T., & Helmreich, R. (1975). Inferences about the femininity of competent women and their implications for likability. *Journal of Sex Role Research*, *1*, 33–40.

Spence, J. T., Helmreich, R. L., & Stapp, J. (1975a). Likability, sex-role congruence of interest, and competence: It all depends on how you ask. *Journal of Applied Social Psychology*, *5*, 93–109.

Spence, J. T., Helmreich, R. L., & Stapp, J. (1975b). Ratings of self and peers on sex-role attributes and their relations to self-esteem and conceptions of masculinity and femininity. *Journal of Personality and Social Psychology*, *32*, 29–39.

Helmreich, R. L., & Spence, J. T. (1977, December). The secret of success. *Discovery: Research and Scholarship at the University of Texas at Austin*, 4–7.

Helmreich, R. L., Beane, W. E., Lucker, G. W., & Spence, J. T. (1978). Achievement motivation and scientific attainment. *Personality and Social Psychology Bulletin*, *4*, 222–226.

Helmreich, R. L., & Spence, J. T. (1978). The Work and Family Orientation Questionnaire: An objective instrument to assess components of achievement motivation and attitudes toward family and career. *JSAS Catalog of Selected Documents in Psychology*, *8*, 35 (Ms. 1677).

Spence, J. T., & Helmreich, R. L. (1978, Apirl). Masculinity and femininity as personality dimensions. *Society for the Advancement of Social Psychology Newsletter, 4,* 2–3.

Foushee, H. C., Helmreich, R. L., & Spence, J. T. (1979). Implicit theories

Spence, J. T., & Helmreich, R. L. (1979b). Comparison of masculine and feminine personality attributes and sex-role attitudes across age groups. *Developmental Psychology, 15,* 583–584.

Spence, J. T., & Helmreich, R. L. (1979c). The many faces of androgyny: A reply to Locksley and Colten. *Journal of Personality and Social Psychology, 37,* 1032–1046.

Spence, J. T., Helmreich, R. L., & Holahan, C. K. (1979). Negative and positive components of psychological masculinity and femininity and their relationships to self-reports of neurotic and acting out behavior. *Journal of Personality and Social Psychology, 37,* 1673–1682.

Bernstein, W. M., Spence, J. T., Helmreich, R. L., Foushee, H. C., & Snell, W. E., Jr. (1980). Egotism and the agentic personality. *Representative Research in Psychology, 11,* 115–121.

Helmreich, R. L., Spence, J. T., Beane, W. E., Lucker, G. W., & Matthews, K. A. (1980). Making it in academic psychology: Demographic and personality correlates of attainment. *Journal of Personality and Social Psychology, 39,* 896–908.

Holahan, C. K., & Spence, J. T. (1980). Desirable and undesirable masculine and feminine traits in counseling clients and unselected students. *Journal of Consulting and Clinical Psychology, 48,* 300–302.

Spence, J. T. (1980). The psychological dimensions of masculinity and femininity and acheivement motivation. *Psychology: The Leading Edge, 340,* 88–101.

Spence, J. T., & Helmreich, R. L. (1980). Masculine instrumentality and feminine expressiveness: Their relationships with sex role attitudes and behaviors. *Psychology Women Quarterly, 5,* 147–163.

Spence, J. T., Helmreich, R. L., & Sawin, L. L. (1980). The Male–Female Relations Questionnaire: A self-report inventory of sex-role behaviors and preferences and their relationships to masculine and feminine personality traits, sex-role attitudes, and other measures. *JSAS Catalog of Selected Documents in Psychology, 10,* 87 (Ms. 916).

Diaz-Loving, R., Diaz-Guerrero, R., Helmreich, R. L., & Spence, J. T. (1981). Comparacion transcultural y analysis psicometrico de una medida de rasgos masculinos (instrumentales), y femeninos (expresivos) [Cross-cultural comparison and psychometric analysis of a measure of masculine (instrumental) and feminine (expressive) traits]. *Revista de la Asociacion Latinoamericana de Psicologia Social, 1,* 3–37.

Helmreich, R. L., Spence, J. T., & Thorbecke, W. L. (1981). On the stability of productivity and recognition. *Personality and Social Psychology Bulletin, 7,* 516–522.

Runge, T. E., Frey, D., Gollwitzer, P. M., Helmreich, R. L., & Spence, J. T. (1981). Masculine (instrumental) and feminine (expressive) traits: A comparison between students in the United States and West Germany. *Journal of Cross-Cultural Psychology, 12,* 142–162.

Spence, J. T. (1981a). Achievement and achievement motivation. *Texas Psychologist, 33,* 7–10.

Spence, J. T. (1981b). Changing conceptions of men and women: A psychologist's perspective. *Soundings: An Interdisciplinary Journal, 4,* 466–484.

Spence, J. T. (1981c). Roger's "models of Adam": A sidelight. *Personality and Social Psychology Bulletin, 7,* 404–405.

Spence, J. T., & Helmreich, R. L. (1981). Androgyny vs. gender: A comment on Bem's gender schema theory. *Psychological Review, 88,* 365–368.

Helmreich, R. L., & Spence, J. T. (1982). Gender differences in productivity and impact. *American Psychologist, 37,* 1142.

Helmreich, R. L., Spence, J. T., & Gibson, R. H. (1982). Sex-role attitudes: 1972–1980. *Personality and Social Psychology Bulletin, 8,* 656–663.

Helmreich, R. L., Spence, J. T., & Wilhelm, J. A. (1982). A psychometric analysis of the Personal Attributes Questionnaire. *Sex Roles, 7,* 1097–1108.

~ ~~~-'- "Are androgynous individ-

"Masculinity, remmmm; ~-- concepts." *Journal of Personality and Social Psychology, 44,* 440–446.

Spence, J. T. (1983b). Psychology and the role of values: Musings of working psychologists. *Psi Chi Newsletter, 9*(1), 4–7.

Spence, J. T., & Helmreich, R. L. (1983). Beyond face-validity: A comment on Nicholls, Licht, and Pearl. *Psychological Bulletin, 94,* 181–184.

Nyquist, L., Silvkin, K., Spence, J. T., & Helmreich, R. L. (1985). Division of household tasks as related to the personality characteristics of husbands and wives. *Sex Roles, 12,* 15–34.

Spence, J. T. (1985). Achievement American style: The rewards and costs of individualism. *American Psychologist, 40,* 1285–1295.

Nyquist, L., & Spence, J. T. (1986). Effects of dispositional dominance and sex-role expectations on leadership behaviors. *Journal of Personality and Social Psychology, 50,* 87–93.

Pred, R. S., Spence, J. T., & Helmreich, R. L. (1986). The development of new scales for the Jenkins Activity Survey Measure of the Type A construct. *Social and Behavior Sciences Documents, 16,* 51–52 (Ms. 2769).

Siem, F. M., & Spence, J. T. (1986). Gender-related traits and helping behaviors. *Journal of Personality and Social Pyschology, 51,* 615–621.

Beauvois, C., & Spence, J. T. (1987). Gender, prejudice, and categorization. *Sex Roles, 16,* 89–100.

Edwards, V. J., & Spence, J. T. (1987). Gender-related traits, stereotypes, and schemata. *Journal of Personality and Social Psychology, 53,* 146–154.

Spence, J. T. (1987). Centrifugal versus centripetal tendencies in psychology: Will the center hold? *American Psychologist, 42,* 1052–1054.

Spence, J. T., Helmreich, R. L., & Pred, R. S. (1987). Impatience versus achievement strivings in the Type A pattern: Differential effects on students' health and academic achievement. *Journal of Applied Psychology, 72,* 522–528.

Helmreich, R. L., Spence, J. T., & Pred, R. S. (1989). Making it without losing it: Type A, achievement motivation, and scientific attainment revisited. *Personality and Social Psychology Bulletin, 14,* 495–504.

Spence, J. T. (1989). American individualism: Challenges for the 21st century. *International Social Science Review, 64,* 147–152.

Spence, J. T., Pred, R. S., & Helmreich, R. L. (1989). Achievement strivings, scholastic aptitude, and academic performance: A follow-up to "Impatience versus achievement strivings in the Type A pattern." *Journal of Applied Psychology, 74,* 176–178.

Robbins, A. S., Spence, J. T., & Clark, H. (1991). Psychological determinants of health and performance: The tangled web of desirable and undesirable characteristics. *Journal of Personality and Social Psychology, 61,* 755–765.

Spence, J. T. (1991). Do the BSRI and PAQ measure the same or different concepts? *Psychology of Women Quarterly, 15,* 141–166.

Spence, J. T., Losoff, M., & Robbins, A. S. (1991). Sexually aggressive tactics in dating relationships. *Journal of Social and Clinical Psychology, 3,* 289–304.

Spence, J. T., & Robbins, A. S. (1992). Workaholism: Definition, measurement, and preliminary results. *Journal of Personality Assessment, 58,* 160–178.

Spence, J. T. (1993a). Gender-related traits and gender ideology: Evidence for a multifactorial theory. *Journal of Personality and Social Psychology, 64,* 624–635.

Spence, J. T. (1993b). The second sex. Citation classic. *Current Contents, 15*(10), 20.

Spence, J. T., & Hall, S. (1996). Children's gender-related self-perceptions, activity preferences, and occupational stereotypes: A test of three models of gender constructs. *Sex Roles, 35,* 659–692.

Sherman, P., & Spence, J. T. (1997). A comparison of two cohorts of college students in responses to the Male–Female Relations Questionnaire. *Psychology of Women Quarterly, 21,* 265–278.

~~-- 1 ~ ~ /1007\~~ The Attitudes Toward Women Scale

~~tran ~~~~~,1~~ .

of Women Quarterly.

Author Index

312

Subject Index

Fear of success, 271–272
Femininity
children's gender-based inferences,
55–57

development knowledge–attitudes
in children, 111–113
gender identity, 113–114
identification of gender schematics,

achievement motivation, 271–272
on attitudes, 18–20
conceptual development, 13, 256
historical context of, 255–256
impact on professional psychology,
24–26
interdisciplinary, 24, 283
methodological trends, 22–23,
259–260
multidimensional–multifactorial
model, 20–23, 45–46
objectivity–subjectivity in, 12–13
sex differences concepts, 13–18
social impact, 26–27, 283–284
Spence's, 3–5, 27–28, 38–40, 75,
193
validity in, 12–13
Gender roles, 3
achievement-related choices and,
159, 175–177, 179–180, 181
attitudes assessment, 18, 39
perception of success, 177
self-esteem and, 270–271
social pressures to conform, 180–
181
stereotypes and, 200
traditional, 175–176
Gender schemata, 46, 58
assumptions in intervention to
counter sexism, 141–142
components of, 109–111, 113

theory development, 107
Gender-typed toy play, 47–50
Gifted students, 161, 175, 177–178

Handbook of Social Psychology, 12, 23,
25, 46
Height–weight stereotypes, 77, 84–85

Identity
gender
development, 47, 279–280
schemata development, 113–114,
121–122
gendered, 22
hierarchy of core values, 174–175
sex recognition in children, 59–60
Spence's conceptualization, 113–
114, 121–122
Individual differences, 21
Infants, gender recognition by, 60–61
Instrumentality and expressiveness,
198–199, 265
achievement motivation and, 272,
274
assessment, 265–266
measured trends, 267–269
self-esteem and, 270
Intergroup processes
competency–likability stereotyping,
202–203
competition, 202–203

About the Editors

... .,

from the National Science Foundation and Research Scientist Development Awards from the National Institute of Mental Health. His research focuses on social cognition and the interplay between beliefs about others and the self in interpersonal relationships. He has authored numerous articles on these topics and a book entitled *Self-Traps: The Elusive Quest for Higher Self-Esteem.*

Judith H. Langlois is the Charles and Sarah Seay Regents Professor of developmental psychology at the University of Texas at Austin. She received all three of her degrees (BA, MA, PhD) from Louisiana State University, Baton Rouge, in developmental psychology. She has published numerous articles in APA journals, including *Developmental Psychology,* as well as in *Child Development* and *Psychological Science.* Currently, she is working on the development of social stereotypes, especially those associated with facial appearance.

Lucia Albino Gilbert is a professor of educational psychology and the director of the Center for Women's Studies at the University of Texas at Austin. She earned her PhD in counseling psychology from the University of Texas at Austin, where she studied with Janet Taylor Spence. She is a fellow of the American Psychological Association and the American Psychological Society, associate editor of *Psychology of Women Quarterly,* and a recipient of the John Holland and Carolyn Wood Sherif Research Awards. Her research focuses on understanding gender processes in dual-career families and in psychotherapeutic treatment. Her recent books include *Two Careers, One Family: The Promise of Gender Equality* and *Gender and Sex in Counseling and Psychotherapy.*